A Journ

Farzana Versey writes regular columns
gender, culture, society, and the media. She has written for *The Asian Age*, *The Illustrated Weekly of India*, *Times of India*, *The Sunday Observer*, *Gentleman*, *Deccan Chronicle*, *The Friday Times* (Pakistan), *CounterPunch* (USA) and several other print and online publications. Her poetry and short stories have also been published. *A Journey Interrupted* is her first book. She is presently working on a biography of the former Indian prime minister, V.P. Singh.

A Journey Interrupted
Being Indian in Pakistan

FARZANA VERSEY

HarperCollins *Publishers* India
a joint venture with

New Delhi

First published in India in 2008 by
HarperCollins *Publishers* India
a joint venture with
The India Today Group
©Farzana Versey 2008

1 3 5 7 9 8 6 4 2

ISBN: 978-81-7223-755-4

Farzana Versey asserts the moral right to be identified
as the author of this book.

Every effort has been made to trace or contact all copyright holders.
The publishers will be pleased to make good any omissions or rectify
any mistakes brought to their attention at the earliest opportunity.

All rights reserved. No part of this publication may be reproduced,
stored in a retrieval system, or transmitted, in any form or by any
means, electronic, mechanical, photocopying, recording or otherwise,
without the prior permission of the publishers.

HarperCollins *Publishers*
A-53, Sector 57, NOIDA, Uttar Pradesh - 201301, India
77-85 Fulham Palace Road, London W6 8JB, United Kingdom
Hazelton Lanes, 55 Avenue Road, Suite 2900, Toronto, Ontario M5R 3L2
and 1995 Markham Road, Scarborough, Ontario M1B 5M8, Canada
25 Ryde Road, Pymble, Sydney, NSW 2073, Australia
31 View Road, Glenfield, Auckland 10, New Zealand
10 East 53rd Street, New York NY 10022, USA

Typeset in 11/14 Gentium
Jojy Philip New Delhi - 15

Printed and bound at
Thomson Press (India) Ltd.

For

Nanima, who showed me the road
My mother, who taught me to walk without holding
on to anything

Manzil wohi hoti hai
Jahaan hum khadey reh jaate hai
Raahguzar tau bheed mein kho jaate hai
Hum ne reit ko kaarwaan bana diya
Aur saraab mein aaina dekh liya
Tashnagi ka raasta jab chuna hi hai
Tau zameen nahin, aasman ki zaroorat hai

Contents

Acknowledgements ix

Prologue xi

The Indian Question – A Beginning xiii

Section A: Cities, Ruins, Resurrection 1

    1. Vestiges of Valhalla   3

    2. Where Phantoms Walk   33

    3. The Haunted, the Hunted   63

    4. The First Frontier   99

Section B: Inside Outside   129

    5. The Kafir Mussalman and the Confused Muslim   131

    6. The Marginals   147

    7. Changing Faces, Static Masks   160

    8. Dissent and Defence   175

    9. Birth of a Nationalist Mullah   183

10. Soliloquists in a Swarm   194

11. Falcons in the Desert   232

Section C: The Pakistani Question   243

12. Jinnah to Jihad   245

13. Requiem   264

Epilogue   275

Acknowledgements

The trips to Pakistan – except the last – were not intended with a book in mind. If I thank the people I met, it is not only for their quotes. They shared their lives, their secrets, their fears, their hopes; they made me discover unknown crannies in thoughts. Some I have named, a few I have not. I especially single out the anonymous 'nationalist mullah' because, in hindsight, I do believe his job and his reputation could have been at stake for opening up to me the way he did. In the enthusiasm for putting down our conversation with utmost honesty, I may have appeared harsh. Then, there are several people who are not featured but who added to my observation of the mindset, the lifestyle, the minutiae that truly constitute social mores.

Thanks to Saugata Mukherjee, the senior commissioning editor at HarperCollins, India, who took to my idea when it was little more than a seed and watched it not only grow but often branch out into regular 'updates' that he had to put up with. For a person who can only write in confinement, his 'reader' feedback made me realise I wasn't on an island.

Thanks to the readers of my columns and articles for

constantly enquiring about the progress of the book. It made it possible for me to know that someone will read it.

I will not thank my mother but she has been my sounding board and a source of strength throughout. Without her, this would have remained an idea.

Finally, I thank those moments I lost. It is only an empty space that can be filled.

Prologue

'You need to be deported,' he said.

He had the mean look of someone who was hungry for a fight. I was in a desperate situation, sitting at the travel desk of Hotel Pearl Continental in Karachi, a few minutes after I had checked in for three nights.

I had barely entered my room when there was a call from the reception. A curt voice said, 'You will have to leave tomorrow. Your visa is not valid.'

My visa had been issued for one month and due to my hectic travels in different cities, I had lost count of the days. I was asked to go down to the travel desk immediately and arrange a ticket.

The person attending to me looked like an Elvis Presley clone with sideburns and hair puffed in front.

'Can anything be done to extend the visa?' I asked.

He was candid: 'You are from the wrong country and the wrong profession.'

He seemed genuinely apologetic, but it gave the man who was sitting with him and watching me with hawk-eyes the opportunity to probe.

'Which country?' he asked archly.

When he heard the word India, he smiled sourly. The travel agent introduced us. He was a retired army general. I was hoping to make polite, even interesting, conversation with him. He cut me short. 'You need to be deported.'

I managed a nervous laugh. When it registered that he was not joking, I told him I had every intention of returning home and only hoped to stay for another three days.

'Now what do you want from us? We gave you an opportunity in 1947, what is the need to be here at this time? Your family should have come then.'

The agent requested him to stop. I urged him to get my tickets immediately and ran towards the lift, tears streaming down my cheeks. The liftman knew which floor I was on. He was supposed to keep tabs on Indians, but I could sense that he empathised with my hurt. A hurt I had myself not been able to understand.

My last day in Pakistan on my first visit was the beginning of several such journeys – physical, emotional, intellectual – interrupted.

The Indian Question
– A Beginning

Pakistan had to remain a secret: just visiting it made me feel like a traitor. And since August 2001 when I first went there to my last trip in May 2007, I tried to keep much of it under wraps. Now as I peel away the layers of my inhibitions, the adhesive that refuses to let go is the Indian Muslim insecurity, made all the more palpable by the sheer fact of it being noticed and commented on several times across the border too.

Unless I get being the Other out of the way, my reminiscences about the journey through that country will not reveal the undercurrents. For most Indian Muslims Pakistan is like a cave in the forest – you are afraid to enter it due to the fear of bats or of unknown darkness engulfing you.

I did not go to Pakistan for weddings or to visit relatives because of this fear: if there were a war, would I be able to return? And I want to live here. India is home. Pakistan is only a stretch of land spawned by an imagined ideal.

When my aunt moved to Karachi a few years after her marriage, my grandma's tears were filled with remorse. She felt cheated that her youngest child had been taken away.

We became two families, two entities, two nationalities and, in some ways, two cultures.

My cousin and I were born in the same nursing home. She celebrated her first birthday here in India, like I had a few years earlier. Both of us had been trussed up in soft churidar-kurta and velvet waistcoat with zari trimmings – living up to the *Anarkali* hangover of our mothers. But our demeanour was different, our mannerisms were different. My being older was not the only factor. The alienation was deeper.

I recall trips my aunt made after getting desperate telegrams saying that Nanima (my maternal grandmother) was ill – her visa depended to a large extent on such lies. She would bring us chilgozas (pine nuts), sohan halwa, a sweet so sticky it coated your teeth and made your breath smell of burning ghee, and yards of flat crêpe, a soft satiny clothing material. She and my mother would settle down to talking of a shared past, about things they had in common all their childhood and growing years.

With my cousin it was different. She felt no link with India; the maternity ward where her first cries were heard held no sentimental value. And as she grew older, she would talk about Karachi's clean streets. She only saw filth in what was then still called Bombay.

They shifted residence several times, and all those unknown places were just scrawled addresses in our diaries. When they visited us, I remember people descending on our home to send packages to their relatives. Some merely carried letters; letters that would reach on time without being opened, they revealed no state secrets, just a slice of life they wanted to keep private.

My aunt had mastered the art of getting through Pakistani customs – she would carry Indian film magazines and give them away. It worked unfailingly, she said. While my mother and she retained their memories, my cousin and I had none. She also insisted on speaking in Urdu. We were fascinated by the language, but it only emphasised our differences.

It hit us most sharply when we went to watch the film *Gandhi* at Regal cinema. During the interval, she pronounced, 'Yeh Jinnah ko kya samajh ke aise dikhaya hai?' (Why has Jinnah been shown in such a negative light?) I told her it was about Gandhi, Jinnah was not the hero of the film. We had both raised our voices; neither of us understood then what we were trying to defend. Two characters in our old textbooks, photographs on currency notes?

The idea of borders, though, had not yet been formed in our minds. It was best represented by my mother's innocent query to a relative who mentioned Kashmir, 'You have Murree, so why do you want Kashmir?' For her it was about snow and beautiful trees and a wonderful climate. Some of us subsequently realised that life is not so simple.

My mother was not even 10 when Partition took place. As a Bombay family, the tremors were not earth-shaking. My grandmother would take a pencil and occasionally sketch. If the face turned out to be obnoxious-looking, and she was asked who it was, she would say, 'Valbho'. That was her derisive reference to Sardar Vallabhai Patel, who was perceived as being anti-Muslim. When Mahatma Gandhi was assassinated, they were asked to stay indoors; it was assumed the culprit was a Muslim and there would be a backlash.

My mother knew another country was created somewhere. Whose country was it? At school, she heard the taunts, but she took it as part of ragging in a new class. There would be the occasional riot, and the women in the family would wear sarees in the Gujarati style so as not to stand out. There were some people who did leave. At that time there was a feeling that they might have a better life across the border. Others stayed back for a strange reason – they were afraid that Pakistan would be full of fearsome Pathans. Beyond that, there were no political opinions.

What is it about those from the pre-Partition era that makes them tolerant? History is only an ancient, perhaps aching, memory. Where is the rage of the lost souls?

I ask my mother if she would compare the fall of the Babri Masjid with Partition. 'I was so young that only the thought of people dying frightened us. But when parochial fights used to break out between the Maharashtrians and Gujaratis, we realised that it was not only a Hindu-Muslim clash. And those we lived amongst were the same, they did not change. Partition was something that a group of people wanted. In 1992, there was no such demand. The two cannot be compared.'

Was she not hurt when, after the Mumbai riots, the local bania from whom we had been buying provisions for years suddenly became distant and even rude? 'A well is always open, it has no lid. So it is easy to drop insults.' She was not aware that Muslim-dominated areas like Bhindi Bazaar are referred to as 'mini Pakistan'. 'Let them talk. They are slighting their own nation by bringing another country in the picture.'

Another country. Such a simple yet potent phrase. How difficult it is for people to accept that this is how most Indian Muslims feel about Pakistan.

Despite this clear lack of identification with that country, I did not announce my first or even subsequent visits to many. There was trepidation. The couple of Indian Muslims I spoke to were disgusted with Pakistanis, even as they could not

The Indian Question – A Beginning

reconcile themselves to the idea of a Hindu India. For them it was not a question of options. One of them spoke about Pakistani arrogance. 'We once had this family from Lahore living with us and they behaved as though they were superior. They truly believed they were better than us. The fact is that they do not even know the true value of Islam.'

Conscious that as an Indian Muslim my role would be different, this was not to be just another journey. I was astride two worlds. Being Muslim was only a social advantage. There were times when I was made to feel like a rat that had left a sinking ship, though no one was willing to admit that the ship was ever sinking. There were a few people who thought they could still occupy India, that they could still win wars. The aggressiveness stems from a deep-rooted feeling of being let down. Which is why the questions are often trivial: Do you eat halal meat? Do you wear western clothes? Do you also worship idols?

I was trying too hard to hold on to my Indian identity. There were times when I resented being seen as one of them. At other times the 'otherness' hit me. I was puzzled. What was this utopia that lay across the border? At one level there was the genuine concern of people who understood the flaws in their own backyard. However, there were times I was faced with strange statements: 'What are you doing there? When we talk of India we only think of Hindus. You are one of us. We will take good care of you here.'

There are more Muslims in India than in all of Pakistan. How would they protect us? Pakistanis accuse us of suffering from the 'Stockholm Syndrome'; some have called us cowards, living with the fear of death and the filthy disease we are considered in the place we call our homeland. We had a chance in 1947 and chose not to take it.

Except for the Kashmiris, the rest of us are of little value as they have no points to score with us. Will we ever count? No. I know that. Because when the Babri mosque was demolished, Pakistanis destroyed temples to show solidarity; they did not come to the bastis where we the elite may not live, but the labourers, the boys working in tanneries, the domestics, and the little people do.

Crossing the border the first time became a matter of grave concern because while the older generation is secure, the young Pakistanis I met are curious, disturbed. They are looking for a connection and finding none.

It angers me. Our parents' generation participated in the Partition and we and those born much later have been divided. They regurgitate their historical experiences, but if we as much as visit the other side as more than curious tourists, we become suspect. I had an 'Exempted from police reporting' stamped on my visa, yet I knew that my every move was monitored.

Prejudice has become almost a necessary prerequisite to any communication. The more removed the post-Partition generations are from the timeframe, the more their need to assert the differences. It is not about territory any more, and therefore even more complex. For us, contemporary reality is important because this is our real history. People from the earlier era have seen destruction and its futility; we see it happening before our eyes and internalise it.

We do not have the luxury of distance.

That is the reason Pakistanis are wary of the South Asian identity much more than Indians. They know that aligning with it means being subsumed by India. They have their ghazals, their television serials where romance is

The Indian Question – A Beginning

wonderfully underplayed like a dewdrop on a petal, tingling but unseen. Yet, they are obsessed with Indian films and film stars.

I hate to say this, but on one occasion I did meet a man who wanted to make out with a Brahmin woman as revenge. Revenge for land, for atrocities against Indian Muslims. And sometimes on discovering that inter-religious marriages were not unheard of I was asked, 'Would the man in the street accept it?'

The geographical partition that took place has been replaced by a psychological partition. Those torn apart by bloodshed had their purging experience – death, destruction, homelessness, helplessness. Today the divide is uncertain. Issues are created by misunderstandings. If terrorism is a creation of politics, then why do people on both sides react so vehemently? And is a common culture only about language, food, dress, looks? Does culture not include civility and the ability to let each other be?

In a high-rise building on Carmichael Road, a posh residential locality in Mumbai, a party was on. I was expected to be there. As the glasses tinkled and the yoghurt dip and canapés were being passed around, someone asked, 'Where is Farzana?'

'She has gone to Pakistan...to find herself!' was the riposte.

This was how the Hindu mind, the urban, western-educated mind was thinking, the mind that asked me several times, 'So, what do you think of Pakistan?' even though I was born here, my mother was born here, I found my feet here, pay my taxes here. These were minds that always wanted to say, 'Go to Pakistan' each time I simply questioned the way things worked in India. Because that made me an outsider.

And when I was on the soil of the land of the pure, my impurity struck me. I was the emotional mulatto. The intellectual eunuch. The fence-sitter. The one who could not make up her mind. But when did I have a choice?

Section A

Cities, Ruins, Resurrection

1
Vestiges of Valhalla

She was a young woman, her head covered to maintain a superficial decorum, as stray strands of hair played on her cheeks. Pakistan International Airlines (PIA) conducts a second security check just before you board the aircraft. My hand-luggage was being scrutinised. She took out the bottle of Vicks Vaporub and sniffed it deeply. Then she pulled out the lipstick, its matt nude shade appeared to be too dull for her taste. Finally, her eyes fell on the carefully packed brown paper packages.

'Open!' she ordered.

They were taken to the table and each of the artefacts I was carrying as gifts was unceremoniously removed from its wrapping. There stood oxidised silver figures – a drum player, a woman with a mirror; enamelled plates with a smiling sun and static fish; wood carvings of the tree of evolution and the three wise monkeys. The latter brought a smile to the face of one of the male security staff.

'Yeh kya hai (What is this)?', he asked.

'It means speak no evil, hear no evil, see no evil.'

'Bandar keh raha hai (Is this what the monkey is saying)?'

The banter made me feel a bit at ease. I was the first to enter the aircraft. The captain was reading a newspaper. I asked him how long the flight would take. 'One hour and 30 minutes.'

Restless, I picked up a Pakistani magazine. *She* had glossy pictures with literal captions, not unlike our own Page 3 supplements. 'Samina Peerzada smiles for the camera', 'Tuku looks dashing'...

The captain got up, but not before asking, 'Aap ghar ja rahi hai ya ghar se aa rahi hai (Are you going home or are you travelling from home)?'

I had been mistaken for a Pakistani even before landing in that country. 'I am an Indian,' I said. I mentioned that this was my first visit. He told me I could join him in the cockpit. 'I will send a message for you when we are ready to take off.'

There was both excitement and fear. He was a distinguished-looking gentleman, his grey hair topping his boyish features lent an added charm. Was this a strategy to find out more about the Indian mind? I asked myself.

The seat belt sign came on. 'Bismillah ir Rehman ir Rahim' played on the sound system. It was a good thing that somebody else was praying for us. The flight steward came up to me, 'Captain saab has called you in.'

I walked into the cramped space and was asked to sit behind him in what looked like a barber's chair and swivelled madly, much to my embarrassment, till the engineer steadied it for me to strap myself. With a few words to the control tower, we taxied down the runway. As the aircraft picked up momentum and we soared up in the air, the captain said, 'See those slums? They are your tourist attraction.'

Before I could formulate a response, we had left those blue tarpaulin sheets way below us. Cottonwool clouds were breaking up like feather pillows. The pilot punched a few buttons and then stretched himself. He offered me a cigarette; I declined. 'This is a no-smoking flight,' I said.

'Ah, there is too much tension and we know what is safe.'

We exchanged notes. I was not travelling in my professional capacity, but it was not prudent to lie. He said, 'Please inform your government to let us deplane at your airports. We allow Indian airline pilots to do so, but we are not permitted to get out of the aircraft.'

'Any other problems?' I asked, warming up to my role as mediator.

'You know, I meet many of your actors, some have become close friends. But I don't get a visa to visit India as I am in government service, so we meet in Dubai.'

I returned to my seat.

The flight stewardesses wore smart-looking salwaar kameezes; not all covered their heads. They did not bother to smile. 'Slaalaikum,' they had uttered as one entered; the full-bodied salaam alaikum was like an exhaled breath. When they came round with the trolley, they offered biryani, kababs and different breads.

I went back to reading the magazine till it was time to land. I was asked if I'd like to watch the approach to Karachi from the cockpit. It was a gallant gesture. In those days it was probably acceptable, though unusual. After 9/11, it would have been impossible.

The captain brought out a piece of paper and wrote down his telephone numbers. 'If you need anything anywhere in Pakistan, just let me know. I hope you have your plans in place since you are travelling alone.'

I told him I had a return ticket and no schedule.

Karachi airport had a grungy look; the trolleys looked

worn, their wheels moving jerkily. Most of those waiting near the conveyor belts were families returning after meeting relatives. Their faces wore the confusion of having left something behind. But once mobile phones were switched on, they were back to the routine, giving instructions about food to be cooked, things to be done.

I was to clear customs. There had been a small error in my visa. Since I had initially not specified all the cities I wanted to visit, there were two signatures. The gentleman at the counter was perplexed rather than pugnacious. I decided to go on the offensive only to hurry this up: 'Why don't you call up Delhi?'

'Dilli se hamara kya taalukh (What have we got to do with Delhi)?'

'Your High Commission there issued the visa.'

'Theek hai, aap jaaiye (It's okay, you can go),' he said.

My baggage too was flagged off. It wasn't as simple as it appeared. I was to later realise the meaning of subtle tailing.

Right across the exit gate of the airport was a McDonald's outlet. Pictures of fat burgers and listless lettuce leaves peeped out from the glass door. It was clear this place had no memories.

Dinner was planned by some friends for the evening. They needed to get some 'stuff'. I hopped into the car. At the traffic lights, bangles made from fresh flowers were being sold. I thought we were headed towards some red-light area. In most parts of India these are worn by men who visit dancing girls; Hindi films have captured them with lust in their eyes as they moved their hands to their nose to inhale the fragrance. Here it was different, women wore them as embellishment. I pulled one over my hand and it rested snugly on my wrist, the tiny jasmine petals still slightly moist.

We stopped at the petrol station. A short thin dark man called Kanhaiyalal came towards the car and handed over a bottle wrapped in brown paper. Whispers were exchanged. This is one of the pickup points for alcohol – you call the dealer, he meets you. Often they deliver to homes, but the business is based entirely on trust. The locals depend on Hindus, Christians and other minority communities or foreigners for their quota. Illicit trade is not unheard of but can be expensive and might require trips to the interiors.

Shakeel, a young TV actor, was generous enough to offer to take me to Quetta to see how people live there. 'It is a different culture from most of Pakistan. You will meet my family, interact with the women and know.' The idea could not fructify because I did not have a visa.

We decided to get some food from the kabab stalls. Shakeel had come to Karachi with dreams. He had lived in a hostel during his college years; education made him rationalise his dream of making it big in television. On the way back he began to sing a ghazal. It was a magical moment. There was so much openness and honesty in his eyes. He was singing of himself, immersed in the words and his world.

When we returned, the drinks were being passed around. Suddenly, the doorbell rang. A large man in a blue Pathan suit made his entrance. It was a dramatic moment when I was introduced to 'Pir saab', a respected religious figure. For the first few minutes, there was some tension. He seemed accustomed to this group drinking, but to have a woman, that too an Indian, sitting in their midst, must have bewildered him a bit.

Shakeel held a glass of lemonade. 'You don't drink?' I asked.

'No.'

'Is it because of the eight lashes that is the punishment for a Muslim imbibing alcohol in Pakistan?'

He smiled, 'Then I should not even be sitting here. I just don't feel the need for nasha.'

Pir saab occasionally glanced at me and after a while there was indulgence in his look. I picked up the courage to offer him a cola from the host's fridge. It would have made for an apt scene in a Kafka play.

Next day I am at a television studio. The staff is young. They ask me questions like, 'Do you hobnob?' This is to check whether I am a vacuous socialite from Mumbai. They are clearly enjoying themselves. Someone mentions a drug dealer and diaries are taken out with much urgency to write down numbers. This group lives on hash.

We go to the editing room. A group is belting out songs in Urdu as the percussionist shakes his head more than he beats the drums. The language that sits like a kiss on lips is being contorted by wide-mouthed gargling. They have named the rooms 'India', 'Pakistan', 'Kashmir'. Are these divisions real or tongue-in-cheek? And why isn't a room named after Karachi, since there has been a demand for it to be a separate state?

It is a sprawling city that wears the mask of a town. I am initially taken in by its naiveté. It seems to be carved out of a large metropolis. And all it wants to remember are the neon lights.

It could well have been neatly sliced off from the rest of Pakistan had the mohajirs staked their claim with less force and more persuasion. The government seemed to have decided that it was better to give the old refugees and their offspring a place where they could keep their bad blood. The seminal autonomy gives it a separateness that represents only symbolic freedom, the ability to be different but forced to fall in line with laws and rules of the land.

Its first inhabitants must have been on the cusp of ecstasy, yet quite unsure. New freedom always exhilarates. It is only later that you have to contend with the slush, the flooded streets, the power breakdowns. The people looked happy. But collective laughter can be hollow. If a city could have eyes, then Karachi had a vacant look as though waiting to be filled in. I thought I would get to watch the fruits of an urban revolution. Instead, I found manipulated stability. Was it an oasis in a desert or a desert in an ocean?

India is named after the Indus river that runs along Sindh and Karachi is named after a fisherman, Kolachi-jo-goth. The city cast its net wide as it continued to bait immigrants. They travelled from India, from Punjab, from the hills, and later even from Bangladesh.

The origin of the word 'mohajir' is the Arabic 'muhajirun'. When the Prophet and his supporters fled Mecca for Medina they were referred to by that term to indicate their immigrant status. The 1951 Census of Pakistan simply states, 'A Mohajir is a person who has moved into Pakistan as a result of Partition or for fear of disturbances connected therewith.' While the Punjabis were tormented by bloodshed, they took to the new country, finding their roots. It was those who came from the plains of India who remain refugees even today. Whether it was the importing of their courtly tehzeeb (culture) from Uttar Pradesh or the education and secular values of Bombay or the canny business acumen from

Gujarat, their contribution was sought to be nullified by the feudalism that was seeking to get hold of the *system*.

Eight million people migrated to West Pakistan. During the early years of the nascent nation, more than half the industrial houses belonged to mohajirs. This continued well into the late 1960s. Their language became the language of the country. The founder of Pakistan and its first prime minister were both mohajirs.

After Liaquat Ali Khan was assassinated, Ayub Khan came to power and under the pretence of the 'basic democracy scheme' encouraged large-scale migration from the hills to the arid plains of Sindh, mainly Karachi. Being a port, the free flow of the Pathan drug trade was made easy. Gun culture usurped business culture. Cosmopolitan violence was legitimised in Karachi.

The city that prided itself on being the capital of a free country that had broken the shackles of the British as well as India was now denuded of even this figurative pride. Ayub Khan then decided that there was too much violence and immigration – something that he had encouraged – for it to remain the capital. A fresh city near Rawalpindi took shape. Islamabad became the seat of government and bureaucracy.

For a country that was born as the land of the pure for Muslims, it took no time for divisions to take place.

The suave and educated Zulfiqar Ali Bhutto, instead of standing up for unity, further divided the country. In the early 1970s he introduced the Language Bill, equating Sindhi with Urdu in importance. He brought in the quota system where Sindh, the land of his birth, was divided into rural and urban areas; this left the mohajirs with less than eight per cent of the jobs in nationalised sectors. Well aware that these refugees were wealthy and had private sector institutions to look to, he quickly nationalised businesses too. It was a horribly populist move, much like what Indira Gandhi had done in India.

I met Nadira Vazir, a contact I had picked up from Mumbai. She lived in Nazimabad. It has a fairly large mohajir population and the houses have the standard stamp of government residential societies, which they were when Karachi was the capital.

She was the sort of plain woman who enhanced her ordinariness by being studiedly grubby. Frail and tall, her features were hardy. 'My family lives in Kutch. I got married in 1962. My parents knew his family, they had moved to Karachi soon after Partition.'

They took their leather business with them; it was on a small scale and has remained that way. 'We are not rich. Our children were given a good education; my son now helps his father in the shop. He is married to one of us.'

Is that always the case? 'It is better this way.'

Did they not think of finding a match from someone in India, just as she had been chosen? 'My time was different, now there would be too many complications.'

Vazir Ali arrives. He has the haggard look of someone who has just got rid of a heavy sack on his back but cannot get used to its absence. He is wearing a bush-shirt with half sleeves over ill-fitting trousers. 'How is Bombay?' he asks me.

'A good city, you got your wife from there,' I jest.

'It is like Karachi, no? Both are dream cities, everyone working, working, wanting to become big.'

'How long does it take to become big?'

'Depends on luck.'

'Only luck?'

'Money also.'

'But if you are dreaming to make money then how can you have money to dream?'

'That is the whole drama of life.'

'And politics?' I was trying to gently nudge him into that forbidden area.

'No politics. We are happy. Small people are always happy.'

His son grunts as he shuffles his feet into rubber slippers. I am formally introduced to him. 'His name is Altaf.'

I take the opportunity to swoop down on this simple family. 'Oh, he shares his name with the other Altaf.'

Altaf Hussein of the Mohajir Quami Movement, now renamed the Muttahida Quami Movement (United Community Movement), ought to have been a hero to these small people. But there is palpable discomfort when I mention him.

'He is in London. The MQM has no leader here. We prefer to stay out of these violent groups.'

The son was just 14 when the mohajir students took to large-scale agitations. He remembers with his eyes even as he refuses to speak about it. Six years later in 1984, Altaf Hussein, sensing the deep resentment among the community, decided to give it a political form. His instincts, driven though they may have been by personal ambition, were not wrong. He spoke about a separate state, what he called the 'fifth nationality'.

While Pakistan was cut up again in 1971 to make room for the Bengali-speaking people of the East, the MQM works within the parameters of the Constitution. Despite being the third largest party after the Pakistan People's Party and the Muslim League, it has remained the dynamite that can be diffused.

Some have compared it with the Shiv Sena in Mumbai; they both have one strong leader and capitalise on students, trade unions and the underclass. The difference ends there. Karachi is not Mumbai. With its kidnappings and continual violence, it is more like an industrialised Bihar.

In opportunistic moves, Altaf Hussein has either been propped up or forged deals with different political factions – whether it was the army when Zia was in power, or the PPP under Benazir, or the Pakistan Muslim League under Nawaz Sharif. It is pertinent to note that these disparate alliances made no room for the promised separate state. It seemed like a lot of rhetoric.

This was bound to result in disgruntlement. A breakaway group that called itself MQM(H), the Haqiqi faction, was formed. But Altaf Hussein had consolidated his image – even his alliances were seen as quick-footed moves. It could be reasoned that he joined forces with the PPP as a response to the killing of 250 mohajirs in a Hyderabad bomb blast, allegedly by the Jiye Sindh Progressive Party. With Nawaz Sharif, it was a case of trying to consolidate his party while it was breaking up by talking the business lingo of 'the economy'. The image of Altaf was of one who had stood up to the Pathans, the Punjabis, the Sindhis and his own party men.

His life was in danger, so he fled to London in 1992. It is either a credit to his charisma or the genuine attempts by the party and the resentment amongst the people that the MQM continues to hold an important place in Pakistani politics. When Altaf Hussein returned in 2007, he brought along a trail of blood. His party has further consolidated its position as a convenient tool playing along and humouring those in power. Six decades after the country's creation, it unashamedly continues to strive to be a haven for refugees.

How does it feel to be called mohajirs when both the ideology and the land were created by them? Vazir Ali feels that the angst of youth was overtaken by survival. Without saying so, he conveys that when you leave something behind, you remain a refugee. He does not carry the burden. When he counter-questions me, 'How do Indian Muslims feel in India?' I know what he is driving at. The mohajirs constitute more than half the population of Karachi, yet they have been sidelined. Shopkeepers and professionals do not have a history; education and business acumen deny them romantic notions of a past.

'I have no past,' says Altaf. 'When mosques are destroyed in India, the mohajirs make less noise than the Punjabis and Kashmiris. Because we have nothing to gain. I only know I am a Pakistani.'

There is this touching story about Dr Eqbal Ahmed. As a child he toured with Gandhi and was told to read the Bible, the King James version, to learn good English. He and his brothers got involved with the Muslim League and went off to Pakistan, leaving their mother, who called them 'Muslim Zionists'. He met her years later – on her deathbed.

His father Rahman was killed in Pakistan; the stones from his tomb in his village had been taken away to help build homes. Dr Ahmed stoically accepted that it was good to see the dead giving life.

As I mentioned, I had to leave due to a visa problem. I sat in the coffee shop ruminating over the retired general's words still ringing in my ears: 'You need to be deported.' The manager came up to me and asked if I was a visitor.

'I am an outsider,' I said.

Ghulam Rasool, the driver who had come to fetch me at the airport, was disappointed to hear that it was my last day.

I told him to just drive me anywhere. He stopped in the middle of a road and asked me to step out with the camera. As cars whizzed past, he made me stand before a monument. 'Aap ghar jaakar keh tau saktee hai ke Karachi ka sabse behatareen nazaara dekha (When you return home you can at least tell people you saw the best sight in Karachi).' I did not know what I had 'seen' since my back was turned to it.

'Yeh Quaid-e-Azam ka maqbara hai,' he said. It was Jinnah's mausoleum that I had left behind. I craned my neck from the window to look at it. The sun hurt my eyes. Ghulam Rasool was telling me about his wife in a distant village, and his pathetic living conditions. Just one of so many unfinished stories.

I called up the captain; he had to take a flight but he put me in touch with a colleague. Captain Mumtaz-ul-Haq immediately invited me for dinner.

I had not bothered to open my bags. My luggage with its lock acted as a convenient barricade. The keys had to be somewhere. I was too dazed to change. Shariq, the captain's son, came to fetch me. It was dark and I could barely see how glitzy the area was.

There was a sprinkling of interesting people. A short, balding man with a shy smile was introduced to me as 'an eligible bachelor'. There was a doctor and the officer's wife. She pointed out the difference between Indian and Pakistani women in one pithy sentence, 'Our women have a glow on the face.' I cursed myself for not having taken the trouble to freshen up. That lost key had let me down. She must have read my mind for she said, 'No, no, I am talking about generally. Not about you.'

She showed me pictures of her daughter's wedding. Indeed, a beautiful woman. I saw faces in various stages of happiness, nervousness, faces captured on glossy print that now took on the mask of a nationality.

Captain Mumtaz had been in the army's flying unit for 10 years from 1966.

'Did you fight in the 1971 war with India?'

'No, I was posted in the city at the time, so I am not your enemy,' he smiled. In a small sitting room-cum-library, there are pictures of him in army uniform. In one, Prime Minister Zulfiqar Ali Bhutto is pinning a medal on his lapel. I turn to him.

'Don't worry. It is not for bravery displayed against your country. This was during the passing out parade.' His sense of humour and the genuine warmth in that house was infectious.

We went to the dining room. I was told that there had not been enough time to prepare, so the food was simple. The wife had by now warmed up to me; the glow perhaps had returned to my face. She personally served me. There were lentils, salads, pulao, but the scent of what was on my plate was overpowering. It was keema-roti (mince and chapati) whose fragrance took me back to my childhood. 'How is it?' she asked. With a lump in my throat I said, 'Like home.'

Less than 12 hours later, I would really be home.

Three years later, Karachi seemed to be eluding me again: bomb blasts hit the city. I was told to change my plans. 'You won't be able to move around, the whole area is barricaded.' The city is an equal-opportunity killer – French engineers, American diplomats, Shias, Sunnis, mohajirs, Bengalis, Biharis, churches, temples, mosques...a few thousand of the 14 million people may not make a difference to the landscape.

Nothing had changed. Fear was palpable, a shroud that seemed to cover the city. People spoke graphically about flesh flying and water hoses clearing the streams of blood. Some of the victims had names; most were nameless – someone's father, someone's brother, someone's husband. The descriptions seemed to act as a catharsis; they also gave them a reason to stay indoors.

Clifton beach wore a deserted look. It was evening. Ice-cream sellers and camels waited for children. The British had developed this area as a health resort. The waves made whimpering sounds as a prelude to the desertion that came after dusk. The winds were throwing up dust specks. The sand was not even-coloured, it had dark blotches. The evidence of the oil spill many months ago had probably not been erased completely.

An hour later, I was attending a get-together a short distance away. We were nibbling on titbits, listening to soft music in a smoke-filled room where the conversation was about Shelley and Frost. I walked barefoot in the corridor, examining the paintings. A nude woman took up most of one wall. One guest, a doctor, said she did not like it. She thought the woman looked pregnant. Someone else said that it looked like she was sitting on the pot. Only half her face was painted at the edge of the canvas, the rest invisible, perhaps to convey the pain of exposure.

In a short while, the two women had left. I was the lone female around, and knew only three people in that room: Khalid, Aijaz, and Fazal. We were at artist Riaz Rafi's house. Although he had helpfully permitted the freeloader Fazal to host the party at his house, he did not seem to have done it reluctantly. He had decorated the stairway with lamps and there was the sweet scent of flowers.

The doorbell rang and in sauntered a tall man with a shock of white hair. His face had a certain rawness. He sprawled on the low settee. He was introduced as Reza Pervez.

He mentioned that his sasural (in-laws' home) was in Delhi; he was married to Sadia Dehlvi. He started speaking in chaste Hindi; clearly a knowledgeable man, he was rather flamboyant about his knowledge. Soon there were heated exchanges between him and Aijaz.

Much as I disliked the cheap macho talk, being a silent observer provided me with valuable insight into the minds of the two people I was briefly acquainted with. Fazal was a man on the make and Aijaz was a collector – a collector of contacts; he called them friends to legitimise his desperate need for networking.

Next morning I took a taxi to meet a doctor acquaintance beyond Teen Talwar. The three swords stand like huge phallic symbols in the middle of a turnabout. It isn't the safest area to visit during periods of turbulence. It is pre-working hours; the streets are being swept, shutters are being opened. His clinic is in a lane off the mohalla.

It is a different world here, of subtle grey panels on the walls. Razaq Ahmed is a plastic surgeon. He shows me the room where the surgeries are conducted and where recuperation takes place. His clientele is mainly female. 'All of them want a straight nose, flat stomach and big bosom.'

I assumed these must be the rich, liberal women. 'I am expensive, but many of them take loans and quite a few are from conservative backgrounds. Often they don't tell anyone, not even their families. They make some excuses and come here.'

How was it possible? Wouldn't their absence be questioned? Apparently, there are easy excuses. Don't the husbands find out later? 'That is the irony. The men hardly notice. I think this is about competitiveness with other women in their social circle.'

What about his own role? How do they react to a strange man feeling parts of their body? 'It works well! Since I am the first one to see them in their new form, they want to see approval in my eyes, not just as a surgeon but as a man.'

Sometimes the attraction does spill over into his personal life. One of his patients, a Pakistani woman from Chicago, had come down to Karachi for the surgery. But they remained in touch and continued a long-distance romance. It was probably the sort of thing lacking in his life as he spent hours chatting with her online. 'One day I must have not signed out and my wife looked at the laptop and read the whole chat transcript. It caused a lot of turmoil. But I am glad it happened. Today I am closer to my wife, I take her out more often...Anyhow,' he changed the subject, 'is the violence here any worse than in India?'

This was a subject that often came up. Comparisons with India become inevitable. It's the same with Indians. When friends at home said things like, 'Oh, but only 16 people died in Karachi, our count was over a thousand', instead of expressing disgust, I began to contemplate. Was this merely a numbers game, the Bombayite's competitive spirit about everything? And what was I supposed to feel about Karachi, where I stayed in a hotel, my fortress, which had once been a target? How could I identify with a battle when I could not understand the Shia-Sunni divide at all? How could one Muslim group desecrate a place of worship of another Muslim group? And why were doctors being targeted – what had they done?

Dr Razaq tried to explain: 'Remember, this is about Shia doctors in Karachi. We are mohajirs. It is a battle of education versus feudalism. During your Bombay blasts, economic institutions were the targets; here professionals are.'

He and a small group regularly hold camps in the backward areas and smaller towns where he does what he considers 'more important work than beautifying people'. It is reconstructive surgery. 'Violence should not spell the end of vanity,' he says simply.

Innocent victims of bomb blasts whose skin and flesh have been torn off them are put together again. It takes weeks, months of recuperation, for self-esteem to return. They are targets of a cause they have no allegiance with, and are often clueless about. 'You should see the desperation in their eyes. They are confused. They must have been praying or going to school or just taking a stroll.'

Death kills; missing death by an inch destroys. Unlike the 'Salaam Bombay' banners that greeted the city of Mumbai after the blasts of 1993, commending the 92 per cent attendance in offices, Karachi is cautious.

Its individualist status is based entirely on its fractured identity. Urban terrorism does not need caves; it rides pillion on motorcycles in an open defiance of law, order and human decency. While it is a fact that people are pushed into action only during a crisis, one is forced to wonder whether it is because cities are often wrenched from their roots that there is little introspection.

A politician was discussing the blasts on a television channel. His most profound comment was, 'Iss shehar ko kissi ki nazar lag gayee (This city has been visited by the evil eye)!' Is this merely a fatalistic attitude?

Vestiges of Valhalla

The 'evil eye' has often been attributed to India's RAW (Research and Analysis Wing). There is no doubt in people's minds that their big neighbour is fighting a proxy battle. The difference is that unlike India, where ISI-bashing has been turned into a fine art form, the Pakistanis take it as one more terrorist activity. As in most sprawling metros of the subcontinent, the major divisions that matter are the ones between the rich and the poor. Karachi does not want to be like Singapore or Shanghai. It wants to be left alone. The Gwadar Project was being hailed in huge banners. It was a coastal town located in Baluchistan. After the Portuguese, the Baluchi tribes took it over and then the ruler of Muscat was handed over this town as a conduit port between Central Asia and the Arab states. In 1958, the city was back with Pakistan. In 2002, a project to build a large deep-sea port was started. The government of Pakistan intended to develop the entire area in order to reduce reliance on Karachi for shipping. This is probably one time that Karachi feels good to be sidelined. But it has caused unrest among the tribals. 'Tribal warfare is different from the bomb blasts that take place in the city,' I heard someone say.

I entered what looked like a spanking new bungalow. In a country where the army rules overtly or covertly, it wasn't surprising to know that the Air Force officer I was meeting had let out his other house to a gentleman from the civil services.

Is the defence area truly protected? Commodore Bismil smiled, 'Hanh, it is protected in the sense chori nahin hoti kyonki bade daaku yahaan rehte hai (There are no robberies here because the big thieves live here)!'

Was he implying Dawood Ibrahim, the fugitive Indian don who would qualify as the best-known mohajir? Once the United States declared him a terrorist, Indian right-wingers have often used him to bait Pakistani authorities. What has ethnic violence in a country got to do with world terrorism? He lived in Dubai for many years and cricket matches held in Sharjah often showed him in the company of film stars and society bigwigs. Journalists had access to him, so why did the Indian intelligence agencies not manage to trace him then? It was a Pakistani magazine that had exposed Dawood's Karachi hide-out, and that was when we woke up. The reason was simple. Everyone knows whose machinery is kept well-lubricated by the existence of criminals like him. The heartburn was due to the fact that the Pakistani economy and politicians would benefit instead of their Indian counterparts.

I kept these views to myself, but was interested in knowing the officer's version. He guffawed, 'You people have to deal with one Dawood Ibrahim. We have hundreds, one for each cause.'

We went for lunch to a trendy restaurant on Zamzama Road. This was a safe place, not only in terms of violence but as a mask to public fears. The lines of conscience divisions had been crossed beyond names like Allahwalla Chowk and life went on. Those who felt the genuine pain of friends lost and coffin cloth that had to be donated hushed their tears in the quiet of their subconscious. There was a refreshing lack of hypocrisy as no one made public gestures of jettisoning celebrations due to the tragedy, as many in Mumbai and other metros do.

Copper Kettle was filled with ladies who lunch, relishing the honeyed chicken wings, washing the food down with falsa juice. The restaurant has a burnished glow. I watch as a young couple walks in. The man is wearing jeans and a snazzy belt. The woman is in a full burqa; this was my first sighting of it in the city. While at the other tables there were working people, grabbing a quick bite, or groups out for a special time, this woman was taking painful morsels as each bite had to be eaten by lifting the veil just enough for the spoon to reach her mouth from the plate. At any other location, it might have seemed like a fairly normal thing; here she did become an object of curiosity, perhaps even disdain.

What was the man thinking when he brought her here? The menu of this place was largely continental. It would require quite a bit of use of cutlery; the young woman may have been adept at using it, but how logistically difficult it appeared to be.

There was the insensitivity of the goons who maimed and killed and then there was this – an emotional and social insensitivity.

What is real? Three years later, at the Gunsmoke restaurant in the same posh area, waiters are dressed like cowboys. You are encouraged to dirty the place, drop peanut shells on the floor. If you don't do it, the fellow will come and tilt the bowl for you. It doesn't quite work. In an Indian metro they would speak with a drawl. Here they continue to talk in Urdu. In Texas they wouldn't ask you if you wanted the beef 'Sakht ya naram', would they? Pakistan is safe. The only cultural colonisation is from India. Even if it comes in the form of an innocently curious question from an activist: 'Is it true that Amitabh Bachchan did not invite any Muslims to his son's wedding?'

The musician at the lounge was mourning, 'Saaranga teri yaad mein' as well-fed and bred Karachiites, unmindful of what the MQM had done a few kilometres away, relished steaks and fries. It was days after the horrific May 12 when

Karachi's streets were splattered with blood. Since this was one of several trips, I had realised an important thing: Pakistanis may attempt to talk about May 12, but they won't obsess over it the way Americans do with 9/11. No one is selling souvenirs; instead they are talking about 'imminent change'. Heroes are clay idols to be moulded.

Like all major cities, Karachi too has a shrine. It is dedicated to the eighth century mystic, Syed Abdullah Shah Ghazi, said to be the direct descendent of the Prophet. It is off Clifton on an incline that can be reached via steps crowded with beggars playing on sentiment. This is understandable, for most people visit this green and white striped shrine to ask for favours. Everyone is a beggar. The management collects a whopping Rs 80 million each year in the boxes left for donations.

Ghazi Baba has powers to fulfil wishes. However, like the dargahs at Ajmer and Nizamuddin, all feelings of peace disappear as one is assaulted to buy the chadar, a piece of cloth inscribed with Quranic symbols or verses, gold and silver threads hanging from it. There are flowers in wicker baskets, or large arrangements of lilies and roses that will be covered on the tomb; a munjavar (caretaker) picks up a peacock feather and runs it over the devotees' heads. There are people trying to pray, but unless you are a veteran you become a scapegoat being asked to pay. You are blessed with little packets of tiny white popcorn-shaped sweets that taste like sugar substitutes.

There are women here, mainly poor. If a woman seems to belong to a higher social class, then men forget worship. Malangs, originally Sufi mystics now mostly mendicants lost to the world, discover their hormones. This wasn't very different from my experiences in dargahs in India. At the Nizamuddin Auliya shrine in Delhi, a smart-looking man who had clearly said that men and women had separate places to offer prayers, had come into the women's section, thrust a register at me, pointed out the names, mostly foreign, and demanded money. It was a far more pugnacious attitude than that at the Ghazi Baba shrine. Also, there were no boards prohibiting entry of women or urging that 'men with empty heads' would not be permitted.

I made another trip at night. It was a Thursday, when qawwalis are rendered and can go on until the wee hours of the morning. I was accompanied by an acquaintance. Outside, bright white tubelights shone. Food stalls were thrown open. We were directed into a lane, a short cut. It was dark. People were sprawled on the floor; the trance had less to do with becoming one with God. There was the strong scent of crushed flowers, urine and marijuana. I could hear the sound of a harmonium being tuned and the tap-tap on the tabla. No one appeared to be in a hurry. Small orange glows could be discerned at intervals where beedis were lit. Someone was having a fit, a derangement arising from too much ganja. God was in the haze.

Rafi kept his promise to take me to meet an unusual baba. He is a child prodigy supposedly possessing faith-healing powers and has been adopted by Firdaus Haider, a well-known writer. She welcomes us warmly.

There is a boy, about 17; his voice is just breaking into adulthood. He wears a black cloth cap and a loose long shirt. Instead of the regular salaam, he bows a bit. He smiles sardonically; his upper lip has the faint trace of a budding moustache. The rest of his face is clean; his skin is the colour of biscuit.

We sit down on a sofa. Suddenly I hear a gruff voice behind me. He asks me if I heard anything. Yes, I say. 'Yahaan djinn hai (There is a spirit here).' It is spooky. I am now sitting at right angles from him with a holy spirit behind me on the white wall. Lost in thought, I hear another sound. He claps his hands and looks at me. 'Fikr nahin, worry not, I spoke to him to look after you,' he reassures.

'Who?'

'The djinn. He only comes when he thinks he is needed. You need him, you are lucky you heard him.'

He keeps flashing his fingers above my head. It is distracting. He makes a few general comments about me – things that are plain to the naked eye. Then he says, 'Men will cause you trouble.'

You could tell this to any woman in any part of the world and she would agree. I ask him whether I should stay away from them.

'Inside you there is a volcano. You are in this world but not meant for it.'

'Must I die?' I ask.

'Not yet. You should first let the volcano erupt.'

He tells me to stand and face the wall. 'Speak to the djinn and ask for help.'

I hear a huge rumbling sound and turn to where he is seated. He is not there. He is behind me.

He asks for my address in Mumbai. A few kilometres from where I live, he tells me, is a well. I should visit it when I return. The spirit of another baba lives there. I should utter some words and I will be released. The words he said were given by the djinn. My job was to act as courier.

Did all this have any place in Islam?

'It is about inner power. By the time I was 12, I could read the whole Quran by heart. I know the verses of all the Sufi saints. I was made for this.'

But Islam clearly mentions that djinns and talismans are not required. Faith is between God and worshipper. Even the Prophet was only a messenger.

'Salallahu'alayhi wa salam' (May the peace and blessings of Allah be upon him), he intones.

'Why do we say peace be upon Him? Who has given mortals the right to confer peace upon the Prophet?'

He did not reply. I persisted, 'Are you a prophet too? You also carry a message.'

'I am a fakir, a mendicant, I have no attachments. I will come to meet you in Mumbai. I don't visit anyone's house. Only Firdaus aapa and now you.'

'She has given you respect and a lot more. I have given you nothing.'

'It is about finding a soul.'

'Isn't that attachment?'

He had no answer. For a brief moment he looked like the boy he was, his voice a whisper.

Rafi and Firdaus aapa came in. They asked him to sing the Sufi saint Amir Khusrau's famous 'Zehal-e miskin makun taghaful, duraye naina banaye batiyan (Do not overlook my misery by blandishing your eyes, and weaving tales).' He sat there drumming his fingers for a long time. I moved to the floor, my right arm on the sofa, hoping not to lose touch with the djinn.

I heard the rumble again. This time it came from his throat. He sang loud, but there was a quiver in his voice: 'Cho sham'a sozan cho zarra hairan hamesha giryan be ishq aan meh

(Tossed and bewildered, like a flickering candle, I roam about in the fire of love).' The love the Sufis spoke about was invariably for the Self beyond the mortal self, for oneness with a cosmic being. He was stretching the words, throwing them high in the air – it was like the sky breaking into thunder. He did not seem to tire. He went from one to another. 'Kaahay ko biyaahi bides ray, lakhi baabul moray, Kaahay ko biyaahi bides...Bhayiyon ko diye babul mehlay do-mehlay, Hum ko diya pardes (Why did you part me from yourself, dear father, why? You've given houses with two storeys to my brothers, and me, a foreign land)?'

I felt the goosebumps, my face flushed. None of us was left unmoved; we had tears in our eyes. All of us except the man who had sung with such feeling.

This was disconcerting. There was something mercenary about this young man. When we were driving back, Rafi asked me what I thought about him. He had given enough reason for me to suspect him. That djinn's voice was his; he was playing tricks, like a magician. That wasn't too bad. But he was being propped up as someone on his way to sainthood. He had already managed to garner a few followers, people seeking release from the monotony of their lives. 'I would not trust him too much,' I said. Two weeks later, Rafi called me in Mumbai to say, 'You were right. He is a fraud. He had taken money in thousands from a few people and run away.'

'What about Firdaus aapa?'

'He spared her.'

She may have forgiven him but the hurt would remain. The hurt of being deserted by one she treated as her own child.

Commodore Bismil and his wife invite me to join them for a fund-raiser for the Petaro Cadet Academy in Sindh, one of the most respected institutions. On the way I am told that the only thing they are sorry about is that I will not be introduced as an Indian. They hoped I would understand. This was a closed Services group of old boys and new cadets. Although no one would be discussing the role of the armed forces, my presence would be seen as an intrusion. I completely comprehended the delicate nature of this situation.

We enter a place that has been taken over by cars; there are no signs of a function. After looking around, they find the open area. The uneven floor is covered with a red carpet; tables set at regular intervals are covered with white linen. As happens in most such gatherings, the men and women congregate separately. Bismil saab's wife is wearing a bottle-green silk kameez; discreet solitaires shine in her ears.

There is much back-slapping and queries about 'Which year? What house?' among the men. I sit there like a voyeur. These men do not look like they could live in bunkers. The stamp of being a part of the Services is not evident, nor is it an exclusive and swishy party.

The women are not talking about how far their spouses have travelled in life; they are discussing clothes, restaurants, music.

The food at the tables is like most buffet meals. It has no identity. Plates are being filled with pasta, covered with mutton curry, tandoori chicken; little pieces of cottage cheese in spinach are plonked at the edge of the plate and from the array of breads a couple are taken and added to the repertoire. Everyone moves gingerly to their tables. Bottles of soft drinks are brought in. Mrs Bismil gets me a vanilla ice-cream in a cardboard cup with a little plastic spoon. This is unbelievably charming. I had expected a starchy environment and a ho-ho camaraderie among big moustachioed men and dainty women in chiffons and pearls. I mention this later to Bismil saab. He laughs, 'You watch too many Hindi movies!'

After dinner, there is a music programme in the adjoining hall. A few dull speeches later, a singer comes on stage. There is applause. Someone even sings an Indian song. At one point, there is heckling. A bunch of young men are shouting and asking the musicians to stop. This goes on for a few minutes. An impressive-looking man, an ex-army officer of high rank, comes on stage. He is nattily dressed in a three-piece suit. He addresses the hecklers. He says that Pakistan has a lot to look forward to; this organisation is one that is trying to make a difference, but if this is what the new generation or the children of the old boys have learnt in life, then they are bringing shame upon themselves.

There is silence. The next singer sings about lost love. Everybody understands that. He gets a loud ovation.

We leave the function soon after. I thank my hosts for allowing me a peek into this aspect of the country. I had earlier given them a silk scroll; embroidered on it was the Taj Mahal. 'I wish I could see it now' and Bismil saab points a finger towards the moon. I had forgotten that the image on it also had a moon on a twilight blue background. He could not visit India that easily. 'It is strange we have to choose between countries that were one.'

The last dawn of Karachi arrives in the form of a cellophane-covered bowl of cornflakes ordered from room service. I need to do some shopping. The bazaars are abuzz with activity. Sadar is a crowded and dirty place, not unlike many in my own city.

The scent of spices is strong, mixed with that of summer sweat. People jostle and push. Empress Market is not as regal as the name sounds. In Mumbai I would perhaps never have shopped in a place like Crawford Market mainly populated by Muslims, but here I was a tourist. Beautiful onyx items were on display, in pumpkin green for the most part, carved in various shapes. Wooden collapsible trays make charming display items, for they don't seem to be of much practical use. A large piece of cloth is unfurled – its red, black and white print appears stark. This is supposed to be a trademark of Sindh. 'This is Indian,' I say, thinking about the fabrics worn by the women of Kutch or spread on beds or hung as curtains.

It could have turned into a futile cultural battle. The border of Kutch is easily accessible. The mute common heritage speaks through inanimate objects, immobile monuments haunted by the Mughals and the British. What was I trying to deny and what were they trying to reclaim?

Even Founder's Day in Pakistan commemorates Mohammed Iqbal and not Mohammed Ali Jinnah because the idea of an Islamic state was a gleam first in the poet's eye. This time I visit the Quaid-e-Azam mausoleum that is on a raised platform amidst a large expanse of emptiness. It is manned by immobile men in white; there is a regular change of guard. The room where the replica of the tombstone is placed has eight corners. Architectural whimsy has made the sepulchre a secular parody – Persian, Chinese, Turkish, African influences assault the arches, the interior design on the walls, the sweep of the stairs. The crypt is encased behind lattice-work; the true founder of Pakistan has become a bird in a cage. The reverence in which they hold him is as much as one would have for the builder of an apartment block.

Every time there is a leakage, a flaw in the plaster work of polity, his name is regurgitated with awe mainly to justify agendas he would never have approved of.

The ordinary people who visit the place of his memory are perhaps more sensitive. They come with the simple need for a large open space where they can relax and feel at peace. A gentle breeze blows. A vulture circles over the marble dome, wanting to swoop down on its cold flesh. What can be a more telling statement?

I feel reverence and tranquillity just watching the white structure against a deep blue sky.

At 9 p.m., I stand near the entrance of the hotel and call for a taxi. A cab arrives within seconds. The driver says, '*Aapko iss waqt akele nahin nikalna chahiye* (You should not be out alone at this hour).' I had deliberately wanted to go on my own.

'How would you like to spend your last day?' Rafi had asked.

'In silence.'

He drives us to Khalid's house. There is a short-circuit. In the dark we hold onto the railings and gingerly nudge our feet towards the next step.

Candles are lit. We sit on low cushions and place newspapers on the floor to act as table mats for the food ordered from the stall below.

The power returns. No one puts out the candles. Wax continues to melt. The flame flickers beneath the light bulbs.

2

Where Phantoms Walk

It looks like a landscaped park, symmetrical and green. 'You will only see trees there. Just trees, nothing else,' a trendy Karachi resident had told me.

Like all capital cities, Islamabad has an air of complacency about it, but somehow it cannot afford snobbery.

I had been asked to stay at a guest house rather than a hotel. Mezbaan House was in a little lane diagonally across a large market. Its owner was a Haji (one who has performed the pilgrimage to Mecca) originally from Bareilly in northern India. He had the soft, tender look of a man who would die happy. We rarely spoke. When I was checking in, an unkempt American was objecting to his passport being taken for copying; he said he would get it done himself, he did not want to leave it with anyone.

I chose the first room on the ground floor closest to the reception area. The carpet was frayed. Two upright chairs flanked a small coffee table against the wall. The wooden cupboard smelled of mothballs. A thin mattress was carelessly thrown over a double bed and a starched sheet with a print of tiny flowers hung loosely over it. There were two side tables – one had the telephone, the other a folded prayer mat. The direction of the qibla (Mecca) was clearly marked with a red arrow on what passed for a dressing table.

The bathtub was cracked, a crooked line running at the bottom.

I was getting a little self-conscious about how I was being viewed by the staff. They were most certainly curious and it took me a while to realise that I had to be constantly conscious about not being too outspoken.

Haji saab's son, the loquacious Irfan, worked in Muscat and looked like a prosperous Gulf-returned Pakistani. He smelled of strong and expensive perfume. One day he came and plonked himself next to me on the sofa; I was told that it was an unusual gesture.

He was happy with his lot – a wife, two children, a job overseas and a family-run business to return to if he wished. Was this the life he always wanted? 'It is important to go out. You get to see the world and look at your own differently.' His wife sat there, silent but observant. She was not quite sure where to place me, but she appeared non-judgmental.

I was enquiring about a possible itinerary to Peshawar. Irfan was a bit taken aback. 'Are you going there? Do you have to? Do you have relatives there? Is someone accompanying you? You know, I would not go there even with my family.' Family always meant spouse and he was telling me how unsafe it could be.

Without my realising it, he was building up information about me. He would casually throw questions my way: 'Is your cousin coming?'

'Cousin?'

'The gentleman who had done the booking for you.'

'He is a friend.'

It wasn't the smartest thing to say and Saqlain, who had made my reservation, told me, 'I had briefed the guys before your visit that my distant lady relative was to come and stay here. . .and I had got their assurance that the place was worthy. And what did you do? You called me your friend. It was not at all appropriate.'

Daman-e-koh, which means centre of the mountain, is in the middle of Margalla Hills. A winding road leads to it from where you get a bird's-eye view of the entire city.

Saqlain is afraid of driving there. He tells me that once a minister was found kissing a woman behind the bushes, so it is not a safe place. I find this excuse rather amusing. We decide to take a taxi. The view is spectacular. A low wall has been constructed and the steel chains that act as a cordon fall limply in neat semi-circles. Islamabad is a good example of a rule-book, measuring tape city, neatly divided into numbered sectors, each with its specific purpose.

We walk along the pathways; families are out for the evening. Nothing unusual here. As we descend the steps, I notice a few cops chatting; they are holding onto the bars of their motorcycles. Their eyes follow us. A hawker has set up a cart selling sea shells with inscriptions carved on them, shiny prayer beads and Chinese toys that make cackling sounds when you turn the key. Saqlain is getting irritable and tells me not to waste time. 'Get into the cab.'

We hear the whirr of bikes. He turns and says, 'I knew it.'

'What?' I ask.

'Those policemen, they are following us. I will report them to the higher authorities.'

'They are probably just returning to wherever they have to go.'

'No. Don't forget I work in a government department, I should know. It is you.'

'But I am dressed properly,' I say, pointing out my salwaar-kameez and dupatta.

'It is not the way you look, the way you walk!'

'What do you mean?'

'Women here don't walk like they own the place or display so much curiosity. You are too confident.'

'I have met many confident women in Pakistan,' I say.

'Oh, those types are different. They do not qualify as typical Pakistanis. They live in studios and act out scenes for the cameras,' he said, showing distaste for the TV actors I had got to know.

We reached the guest house. He insisted he wanted to hit those cops. He said he would return to the place we had just left. There was anger and helplessness.

Next morning there was a call from the reception. 'Police aayi hai (the cops have come). They want to meet you.'

I was assured that they did this on a regular basis.

I quickly grabbed a thick dupatta and opened the door. A burly inspector and two assistants came in. I had one suitcase on the floor and my tote was on the steel chair; my breakfast lay uneaten on the table. I was asked to open the bags. Then they told me to open the cupboard. I had got into the habit of drying my undergarments inside on a hanger as I did not want it displayed in the bathroom when the staff came in to clean. It was an embarrassing moment as the cops looked at those lacy things, still wet, between a couple of tunics. The rest of the clothes were still in the bag.

While his assistants were doing the checking, the inspector tapped on the tote. I told him I could open it.

'Lock *kyon hai* (Why is it locked)?' he asked.

I said these were gifts and I did not need them for the time-being.

He wanted to see my passport. He licked the tip of his middle finger, the touch of saliva making it easier for him to turn the pages. 'Aapke shauhar kahaan hai (Where is your husband)?' he asked.

'He is not with me, I am travelling alone.'

'Wajah (Reason)?'

'Bas, tourist hoon (I am just a tourist).'

He gave a wicked smile and turned to his assistants even while addressing me, 'Taajub hai, akele ghoomne aa gayi hai aap (Strange that you decided to take a tour on your own).'

I had to control the ire that was building up. I could understand them wanting to rummage through bags and cupboards, although there was no reason to. But the manner of the probe disgusted me.

Saqlain visited me later. He was scared. 'It must have been the instructions of the guys at Daman-e-koh. They are not supposed to do this, unless they are told to.'

He started pacing about in the small room. 'I cannot sit here. There is this Hudood Ordinance.'

'What?'

We called up his brother. Hamid laughed aloud when I asked him about it. 'Woh bilkul darpok hai (He is just being a coward). Nothing will happen to you. Besides, if you are educated, then all these laws can be worked around. Pay a few bucks and nothing can affect you.'

I told Saqlain about it. He explained the Hudood

Ordinance. It has to do with adultery – technically, I was married, according to my passport. I was quite irritated, 'Look, I am not doing anything wrong and, besides, why should Pakistani laws apply to me?'

'But I will get into trouble just for visiting you.'

'Then wait in the lobby.'

'There also they get curious. They want to know where I work and other details...I don't want to reveal too much as there would be other trouble because you are an Indian.'

I felt like I was in the land of Scheherazade, a fresh story being invented to protect itself from me and my nationality.

Every few years, Pakistan writes a new fiction. Islamabad does not suffer from the stench of power. Unlike Lahore, it is not the city of real and fake intellectuals and unlike Karachi, it does not seek to spread its wings. The torpor is evident even as one cruises along the tarmac towards the President's house. There is no feeling of obnoxious power. In Delhi, there is open acknowledgement of being somebody, here there is almost a feeling of diffidence. No one flashes business cards in your face with an air of 'Do you know who I am?' Could it be because the place at the top is so fickle?

I meet Ali Ranjha, a cousin of someone I had met in Karachi. He is a businessman. We are at the Marriott coffee shop. It is a Mexican theme evening. The waiters wear sombreros and jackets with tassels, two women in black satin gowns are singing. No one is listening to them. The crowd is mostly families out for dinner; a few men look like they could be important.

One observation I made is that the concept of looking up to five-star hotels is not as huge in Pakistan as in India. Even in the largest metros of my country, one sees people who feel and appear puffed up about their wealth, although they don't need to display it. In the cities of Pakistan I visited, the surroundings don't seem to matter. It isn't that they are not the flashy sort, but they prefer to host people and hold meetings at their houses. Perhaps it is a more tangible show of wealth and position and gives them greater control over their environment.

'Is Pakistan a good place for a businessman?' I ask Ali.

'Yes. I have the opportunity to settle in USA, Canada, Europe but I cannot leave Pakistan. I have seen about 30 countries. But dil Pakistan mein hi lagta hai (the heart remains in Pakistan).'

'What is it that keeps you here?'

'The sights and mountains and trees. I want to study streams and stormy oceans, why they are so restless. I read what is written by nature, for that is without any prejudice.'

'Where does all this fit into an Islamic nation?'

'This would not stop me from fighting for country and religion.'

'Is this good business strategy?'

'In the long run, yes! A country with self-respect brings prosperity.'

It seemed like an awfully circuitous route to achieve an ideal business model. The tortilla chips had become soggy.

Early next morning I went to the cyber café. In Jinnah Super, a stairway pointed towards Safaa Net. There were no cubicles, just planks of plywood separated the spaces on long tables arranged in a square across the whole room. There were a couple of foreigners; the rest were youngsters with headphones. I scrolled the 'history' of web pages visited. There were Pakistani chat rooms, and several porn sites. The names were self-evident. Swivelling in my chair, I tried to look at the people, all young men; some had pulled up chairs and were huddled together.

Speaking to a teenager in Karachi, I had bluntly asked him why he visited such sites. He did not bother to defend himself. 'There are two things we can do without spending too much money – go to chat rooms or go for a walk. We need entertainment and there isn't any here. I will be in this country forever. My parents are not rich. I went to an ordinary school and am now in an ordinary college. I learn by interacting with people from other parts of the world.'

'What is there to learn from porn sites?'

'That is just to take care of the hormones. You think in all those other sites everyone is innocent? Pakistani women too enjoy these interactions.'

'How do you know they are women and Pakistani?'

'From the language, and then with voice chat we can speak. You should see how they talk! The good thing is these relationships don't last. I use different nicknames.'

When boredom sets in, what do they do? 'We visit Indian sites. There are fights about Indo-Pak issues. We use the same language, same cuss words, and Kashmir is top in the list of topics; then we discuss films, cities, and politics.'

Driving through University Road, I spot large yellow banners saying in bold red letters: 'Help Pakistan and Kashmir against oppression by Israel and India'.

Ironically, it is August 14. Pakistanis celebrate the occasion lustily. It truly seems like a double celebration for them – freedom from the colonisers and freedom from those who were once their own people. Everyone greets one another. I stand aside. I do not have to carry the baggage of history but the past has often appeared wearing different Halloween masks.

I decide to pick up a few Jinnah lapel pins and pack them away as mementos for which there are no takers. Whom would I give them to? However, once I am out in the street late evening, I realise on closer inspection that the kids bursting crackers, tucking in special sundaes, are just children enjoying a holiday. The colourful lights that dot almost every building are just a reason to have fun.

I decided to pen a note for Saqlain. 'I sincerely wish your country well, but I also hope you can see the stars in the sky.'

Next day was India's Independence Day. The day that the modernist Nehru said was chosen according to Hindu astrology as being auspicious. It felt strange to celebrate it in a land that had been created with so much heartburn and anger. At home it did not really matter. A few paper flags and listening to one more speech by whoever was the prime minister. But here I felt an uneasiness. That chit of paper I gave Saqlain meant nothing to him.

Irfan was watching a few clips on television. 'You people do it very simply, there is no fuss,' he said.

At Serena Hotel, they were serving high tea. It belongs to the chain of hotels set up by the vast financial empire of the Aga Khan, the spiritual head of the Ismaili sect. The buffet table was laden with spicy Pakistani snacks, together with salads, canapés and pasta. It is a typical subcontinent thing where you have a little of everything, authenticity to cuisine or occasion being irrelevant.

It is a large hotel with strategically placed waterfalls and little nooks just off the lobby area with a view of the gardens.

At the restaurant, I ask the waiter where he is from. 'Hunza,' he says. He is an Ismaili.

Hunza is virtually an Aga Khani ghetto, although the community does not need one. It is largely apolitical, educated and wealthy. As in India, in Pakistan too the Ismailis avoid even commenting on political events. Soon after Partition, the then Aga Khan, Sir Sultan Mohammed Shah, the grandfather of the present one, Karim al-Husseini, had in fact issued an edict of sorts telling believers that in a family where there were two brothers, one should migrate to Pakistan.

Queen Victoria had conferred knighthood upon him and he was known to have sided with the British to quash a local rebellion. Pakistan is one of the largest beneficiaries of the Aga Khan's largesse, which is why in a country where smaller sects are treated with some amount of suspicion and derision, the Ismailis are given kid-glove treatment. However, unlike in India, they do tend to lead more isolated lives in Pakistan. I was confronted with the strangest queries by Pakistanis: do Ismailis practise bizarre customs? Isn't it true they never marry outside their sect? Are there special hush-hush goings-on at the jamaat khana (the prayer hall)? Is not the Aga Khan entirely funded by the community members? Isn't Ismailism more of a cult than a sect?

In the Islamic republic that Pakistan is, with its adherence to religious laws, a living spiritual head tracing his lineage straight to the Prophet should amount to blasphemy. However, no one is openly critical of such claims.

I was at the market, at a shop selling leather goods. I saw a picture of the Aga Khan, a small one in a gilt-edged frame. I addressed the owner with the Ismaili greeting, 'Ya Ali Madad'. He merely nodded. It is a small community and invariably the local jamaat khanas ensure that people know each other. I was an unknown face. I told him I was from India. He was wary of revealing too much. He was a post-Partition migrant. He had spent his childhood in 'Molla', the peculiar way an Ismaili pronounces mohalla and this referred to the area surrounding the largest jamaat khana in Mumbai. He remembered the deedar (the visit of the Aga Khan). It was obvious that this was sorely missing in Pakistan.

'Is it any different here?' I asked.

'Smaller community,' is all he was willing to say.

The Aga Khanis thrive in a multicultural environment and habitually adapt themselves to it, be it in India or Africa, where they are in large numbers. In Pakistan, they suddenly find themselves in a constricted cultural space, and since they are mohajirs they are double refugees – from the country of their birth and the country they have adopted for mostly economic reasons. I knew of relatives who were most uncomfortable during Zia's time when they had to cover their heads even in the streets.

Business is, however, good. Why Islamabad? I asked the shop owner.

'My brother runs our business in Karachi and we decided to expand, so I came here.'

How often does he return to India? 'Never been there after I came here.'

'Why?'

'Our whole family is in Pakistan, no one in India.'

He did not have what I was looking for. As I was leaving, he said, 'Allah Hafiz.'

Very pointedly I bid him goodbye with a 'Khuda Hafiz'.

Pakistan has adopted this unique form of farewell replacing Khuda with Allah because Khuda is not religion-specific and is a Persian word that was the prevalent usage in South Asia as well. Allah is Arabic and is most definitely about a Muslim God.

I was walking along the raised platform with shops selling everything from fabric, handicrafts to cosmetics. I entered a large pharmaceutical store. Inside was a veritable array of almost anything one might want. Souvenirs, stationery, CDs. One corner was taken up by small portable electronic goods. The salesman was sharp, he knew a tourist when he saw one. 'Yes, Miss?'

I ask for joshanda.

'Woh chhoti dukaan mein milega (The small shops stock it).'

Joshanda is a herbal powder that can be added to water or tea. It soothes the throat and acts as a decongestant. Islamabad is notorious for its pollen allergy. A peculiar ecosystem has developed where pollen dust flies all over.

'Which country?' he enquired. I replied in Urdu that I was from India.

His name was Iqbal, he said. He asked me my name and from then on insisted on addressing me as 'Miss Farzana'. A peculiarity is that most Pakistanis address women who appear even slightly educated as 'Miss' with or without the name and irrespective of marital status.

He noticed my empty wrists and showed me watches. These were fake timepieces, and so blatantly did they flash this fact that even the names on the dial were crooked. I pointed this out to him as I tried one on. 'For 250 rupees, what will you get?' he retorted.

He insisted it looked great, 'Aap ke haathon ke liye banaa hai (it is made for your hands),' he said, his flattery making me realise with rather deflated amusement that the fake was a good embellishment.

'I can get this anywhere,' I said.

'Yeh Pakistan ki yaad dilayega (It will remind you of Pakistan).'

'Yeh Taiwan ka hai (It is from Taiwan).'

'Magar khareeda yahaan hai. Jab bhi waqt dekhoge yahaan ki yaad aayegi (But you have bought it from here. Whenever you look at the time you will think of us).'

He then showed me cosmetics. Maybeline, Revlon, Max Factor, Gala of London. I asked him if he had any Pakistani lipstick. He pouted and shook his head. Then he brought out one and rolled it up for me. It was a pink, the colour of a baby's cheeks. It was of Korean make. 'Pakistani colour,' he told me.

The watch, I realised, had stopped. They did not have the batteries; he said he could deliver it at my address. I said it was okay. I walked out of the shop with a Taiwanese watch that did not work, a Korean lipstick, a Chinese torch and a decongestant imported from the UK.

'We don't make these, and anyway people prefer foreign things. They are more prestigious.'

Pakistanis often say that Indians are westernised. I had dinner that night in a trendy American restaurant called Arizona. Women were smoking, dressed in smart clothes. The men were more casually dressed, though a couple had tied bandanas on their heads. They were swaying to the music, which switched from Neil Diamond to Barbara Streisand with a Bob Marley thrown in. Humongous sandwiches with crisp fries were being taken to tables by waiters in tomato red shirts and black pants.

Although food is not a major concern of the people of Islamabad, there is a wide variety available. If there is Usmania, the hostel dining-hall style eatery with its bland arrangement of chairs and tables and no-nonsense way of serving food, then there is also the tiny boutique-like Omar Khayyam in the Blue Area, the business district, that serves Iranian cuisine. The entrance of the latter leads to a handicraft store stocked with carpets and jugs and a small series of steps takes one to the basement restaurant. There are couplets from the poet's oeuvre on the table mats and the famous painting of his with the saqi, the female wine pourer, immortalised in Persian and Urdu verse.

'La pila de saaqiya, paimana paimane ke baad' (Oh beloved, keep pouring the wine), he quoted in a voice deep with remorse.

Mushtaq Akhtar had his hair slicked back with too much gel as though he was afraid that even a strand out of place would risk his career prospects. He worked for a multinational bank. His career mattered, not only for reasons of security but because it gave him an identity distinct from his father's. He did not want to be a businessman.

'He is an amazing man,' he said. 'But I don't want to be that amazing. You understand what I am saying?'

I thought I'd make a cautious guess. 'Perhaps you don't want the pressure of being his son, you want to strike out on your own.'

'Absolutely right!' he said.

He was lying. His father was a man of morality and principles, and although the two are sometimes mutually exclusive, in his case they were finely meshed.

Mushtaq had married a second time; she was a colleague. 'It was liberating to meet someone who had no inhibitions, or so I thought. We would go out for lunches and drives. People did raise their eyebrows but I had the image of a family man. Soon we were deeply involved and got into a physical relationship. She started pressurising me for marriage, and I went and had a nikaah.'

Was it guilt that pushed him to take the step? 'It is more than that. I was an emotional wreck by then. I cared about her and began to feel responsible. See, there is this old-fashioned thing about the man being in charge. I was a little surprised that she changed from this person with no expectations to someone who wanted a commitment.'

After that she wanted respectability. He broke the news to his wife and father. He was asked to leave the girl or the house. He left the girl barely a month after the marriage. 'It was a humiliating experience for all of us. A huge mistake. You people think that it is so easy for Islamic societies, just say talaq, talaq, talaq – but it isn't. There are human emotions involved.'

The guilt made him quit his job. He took up consultation assignments. He had bought a piece of land a bit far from the city. He decided to build a house. 'My wife is very happy,' he would tell all his friends. He went to the site everyday as beams and columns were positioned to put together steel and concrete. The architects gave him a design for the rooms. 'There will be eight bathrooms!' he had laughed as he recounted the progress.

'What will you do with eight bathrooms?' I asked.

'What does one do with anything?'

He was building something, making it bigger, taking longer. He would return home late, too tired; his exhaustion became an excuse not to face probing eyes and lips poised with perennial queries. I did not know whether he was constructing something or destroying something.

We retained email contact after my return. It became less frequent as time went by. The house now had bronze bathroom fittings, the tiles were being glued to the floors, and a small garden was being landscaped. All his money was invested in a structure he would call home. Shame had seeped into his bones.

I called him late one evening. I could hear sounds in the background. 'We can talk later,' I said.

'No, it is always like this.'

'Where are you?'

'I am doing penance,' he said. 'I had joined this 40-day course and then extended it.'

For 80 days, he was getting away from it all. Yet he had picked up the phone. 'I don't want to lose touch with the outside world as long as it does not interfere with my conscience.'

'And what about your house?'

'It is ready and the family has moved there.'

'Wasn't that cause enough to stay with them?'

'I still had this feeling that something was lacking. Here I am discovering so much of myself.'

'You knew yourself; you were focussed, whether it was an affair, or getting out of it, or buying the house.'

'None of these gave me what I wanted.'

I told him about my next trip and wondered if we would be able to meet. 'Inshallah, we will,' he said.

He came to meet me. I was sitting in the lobby of another guest house, and saw the familiar tall figure, the loopy gait. This time he was wearing traditional clothes and a cap. He did not wish to linger very long and asked if we could go elsewhere. A battered jeep stood outside. His prized possession that he mentioned earlier. The rusting metal had a greenish tinge like there was fungus on it. Before starting up he said, 'I am glad you are not wearing jeans.'

'Why?'

'Because it would look so funny, I with these clothes and you like that.'

'What others think ought not to bother you, you have found God.'

He was quiet as we drove to the Marriott Hotel. He asked for a corner table at the coffee shop. Except for his clothes, his beard grown, moustache shorn off, he still gave glimpses of the old confidence.

We settled to talk over cups of tea served in bland bone china, the strings of the tea bags hanging out of the pot.

'Are you embarrassed?' he queried as he poured out some of the beverage for me.

'About what?'

'Being with me when I am like this?'

'No, but did you come here to see people's reaction?'

'I am beyond that now.'

'So you don't feel any anger towards the American war against terror?'

'Why should I not? Islam is not about offering the other cheek. See, the time I spent at the Tablighi Jamaat made me realise that I had been leading a false life. Do you know this movement started in India?'

'Does everything need to have an Indo-Pak tint?'

'I am asking you to realise the basic tenets of Islam; it is easier here, in India it must be tough.'

'Isn't it more valid then? Why do you need to spread the message of Allah in an Islamic society?'

'We are imperfect creatures and we have to convey that beyond Allah there is nothing. Pakistani society is going through a phase where it is getting influenced by the West. We have to protect it. I know how destructive that influence is, having worked for a multinational company.'

'You mean to say you would not have done what you did had you found God earlier?'

'Maybe I would not even have felt the need.'

He then started telling me about the sacrifices that the Prophet and his family made. He had certainly been converted to take the message forward and to follow the basic principles. 'Materialism is not a goal any more.'

'Why are we then sitting at the Marriott listening to western music?'

'It is all in the intent,' he said.

He excused himself. 'I hope you don't mind but I will go and pray. It is time for isha ki namaaz (dusk prayers).'

The Tablighis are not small in number; there are almost 80 million spread across different parts of the world. Pakistan's former prime minister Nawaz Sharif was a follower and a few cricketers too got the message due to the Jamaat. Mushtaq had mentioned being at a camp and leading a life of basic sustenance.

When he returned from his prayers, I asked him about his house.

'It has turned out well.'

'And those eight bathrooms?'

'Oh, they are there.'

'So, you are back to where you started. This 80-day penance worked as a spiritual spa, did it not?'

'It cleansed my spirit. What is wrong about that? And my wife was happy.'

'Well, she knew where you were!'

'That is true. Sometimes we do things for others.'

'So this is not about your soul, it is about saving your marriage.'

'Both. We are now expecting our fourth baby and I am still a firm believer in the principles imbibed at the Jamaat.'

What he did not realise was that he was part of a movement that was in fact denying an aspect of his existence. The Tablighi Jamaat is the 'superior' race born of the Wahabi-Deobandi movement. It looks down on the Barelvi need for a tangible devotion that has created symbols and saints. This is natural as Pakistan is an amputated nation, its limbs still carry the tissue and blood of its mixed tradition. The pure land had to become a pawn in the hands of a minority elite that had both religious fervour and money power. In a move that appears ironic, they declare themselves the *ashraf*, the high-born, even while discarding the lowly beliefs of the Barelvis, who are mostly converts from Hinduism. Ironically, Islam rejects the idea of class and the upholders of pure Islam are pushing that forward.

Several political considerations got meshed with the devotion. The Bengali Muslims were not wanted; the soft stance of modernism had to be rejected. Zia-ul-Haq became the natural hero. The barter system worked, it got them the necessary military training. It was perhaps one of the few times that madrassas were used for helping the Afghans fight the Soviets.

Islamabad boasts of a 'national mosque' that resembles a palace shaped like a marble canopy. The ceiling is high enough for silence to echo at 40 metres, while the minarets seem to hold the cover like an alabaster mirror to the sky. The prayer hall and the outer areas can accommodate up to a lakh of devotees.

In the daylight you find in it a pristine beauty. It does not overwhelm, but invite. As dusk settles on its form, tourists throng to it, as the feet of devotees are washed near taps. The long path has a wall, and many onlookers sit on the ledge. There are oglers and amblers.

However, the Shah Faisal Masjid exposes a dichotomy. The iconography that Wahabism, the superior ideology, abhors stands out in manifest obeisance to the Saudi ruler after whom it has been named, thanks to the money flushed in.

The Barelvis had protested against the demolition of the mosque of the Prophet's mother in Saudi Arabia. They even called the Saudis worse than Jews. Pakistan is caught in this battle for Islam. The monotheism that the religion has been so proud of is in fact a fractured identity. It cannot disappoint the Saudis, it cannot disappoint the West, it cannot disappoint its mohajirs, it cannot disappoint its large Pathan-Punjabi factions. It has to be with Iran, it has to be with Iraq and continue to admire Turkey and maintain some modicum of peace initiatives at all times with India. The position is uncomfortable.

Questions have also been raised about the role of the Tablighi movement in sponsoring people who may not be above board, including terrorists.

Mushtaq is unperturbed. 'Not at all. If that is the case then why point fingers only at the Jamaats in Pakistan? What about those in India?'

'I am not saying anything about Pakistan, it is a general perception.'

'This general perception you people apply to our madrassas and everything we do. We are an Islamic society and we have to follow its tenets.'

'Isn't most of it superficial? You went and shaved off your moustache, but you still look attractive.'

'Do you think so?' He was clearly pleased. He had been accustomed to such comments earlier and women would openly express an interest in him, his marital status notwithstanding. Did that happen now? 'No, even if they found me attractive, they would stay away. This is one of the results of my transformation, the way I dress and look acts as a barrier to such things.'

'You have not controlled temptation, just prevented it from coming close to you. Where is your transformation?'

He shrugged. 'I have found God, but I did not say I have forsaken the human in me.'

We were laughing on our way back as he drove at breakneck speed. He had the protection of his cap, my hair was flying all over my face. 'Why don't you cover your head?' he asked.

'It is God's creation.'

I had gone to one of those small currency exchange outlets with a stack of Indian rupees in thousand-rupee denominations. The young man at the counter looked at it, held it up against the light, and then banged the lot down on the counter. The owner arrived. His pale face contrasted sharply with his dyed raven black thinning hair. He was polite in a fawning way. 'Ab kya bataayein, hum kuchch kar nahin sakte (What can I say? There is nothing I can do)'. He said there was a big racket in fake Indian currencies and he preferred dealing in dollars.

I took a taxi to the Blue Area on the side where the major banks are. From the road the atrium structures reflected other buildings. The bank had closed transactions for the day. I needed the money; I wanted to avoid using my credit card. On the second trip, I had decided not to flash my Indian identity. Except for the guest house where I stayed, the hotels did not even bother to ask any questions.

Standing in the sun, I spotted a woman come out of one of the many buildings. She was wearing straight loose pyjamas and a smartly-cut tunic. In the sunlight, the transparent cloth revealed the contours of her legs. Her outsize sunglasses hid most of her small face. I looked at the place she had just exited from. There, in small letters, was a board that said, 'We also change money'.

The main business in that office was web design and software solutions. I walked in. Most of the small space was occupied by a brown sofa without a backrest. A tinted glass screen separated the inside room. The man outside asked me what I wanted. I could hear some whispers. He told me to go in. Behind the desk sat a large man with an aura of a film star. I was rather taken aback. He wore a striped shirt with short sleeves. His square jaw emphasised the smallness of his eyes. He was watching Hindi movie songs on the VCD.

He changed the money for me, though he did need a copy of my passport. He pointed to the dances on the screen. 'You know, this is what we don't have here.' His name was Nasser Alam. He belonged to the Punjabi gentry and although there was no connection with India, he felt a bond. 'I must admit that during the 1971 war when planes would rumble overhead and there was destruction around, I thought I would become a pilot. Not the best way to decide on future plans but this is how it was.'

When I was leaving, he asked, 'Will you join us for dinner? My wife would like it.'

I had no plans and I needed interesting insights.

He said he would come over to fetch me. We went to a Chinese restaurant. His wife Rehana was pretty, but looked too petite before him. While her husband was collecting the valet car park coupon, she asked me, 'How does it feel not living in your country?'

A bit surprised, I said, 'I do.'

'You live in India, don't you?'

'Yes.'

'So how is it your country? Shouldn't Pakistan be your country?'

'No. We have always lived in India and I see myself as an Indian.'

'When we think of Muslims in India we imagine them to be outsiders there.'

Nasser had arrived. He laughed at his wife's naiveté, 'Hum Pakistani ko eik bimaree hai ke Muslims ke barey mein har jagah tang rehte hai (We Pakistanis have this malady, that whenever we think of Muslims we get worried)...You know, most people don't bother about the Partition or knowing all that. The general concept is you are not well settled in India and depressed. I do not know if it is true or just propaganda. You tell me, what do Indian Muslims say about Pakistan?'

'Many have relatives here, so that connection is there... then we think about Sunni-Shia fights...'

'I honestly believe some foreign elements are behind this. Even during the Partition, the British cheated us by handing over some areas to India on Muslim majority basis. Even today our main enemy is USA, not India. That country does not allow us to function. Most people dislike army rule, and our elected leaders cannot work because they are not allowed to by the USA, which props up the army.'

'How can USA stop them from doing good for their own country? It may interfere in foreign policy, not in internal matters.'

'They have their vested interests and invisible hand. Can you see pain? So America has invisible influence. I would say enmity with that country is better than friendship. India will be next on the US list, and the reason your country is getting friendly with China is good because it will afford you better bargaining power with the Americans.'

And as always happens, he asked, 'What do Indian Muslims think is the solution to the Kashmir problem?'

'The ordinary Indian Muslims are not much involved.'

'It is sad, but also good. You know what I admire about your country? Every five years you can throw out the government. Don't underestimate this ability to elect leaders.'

'Democracy is not only about elections.'

'Think about a state where you don't even have that, or you have coups. To be honest, I would not want my children growing up here.'

When we leave, their daughter joins us for a drive. She is in her final year at one of the finer schools. At first she is curious about our film stars and tourist sights and Indian clothes. She listens to the latest in western music and Pakistani pop. How would she see an Islamic nation?

'We are becoming more westernised as a reaction. It embarrasses us to be identified with religion and madrassas. In school we all make fun of that Zafarullah Khan Jamali (then the prime minister), we draw cartoons of him and his protruding tummy. It is not like we don't have our say.'

'But isn't General Musharraf someone you could identify with?'

'No. Not any man in uniform. Pakistan looks like a puppet country with these military dictators. We are getting influenced by the media.'

'In what way?'

'He appears on TV like some actor.'
'He has stuck his neck out; his life has been in danger.'
'That was all staged,' she says with the certainty of cynicism and the confidence of youth.
'Why would that be necessary?'
'To make us believe in him.'

The bookshop was stocked with old marvels. I had to move sideways along the alleys. Thick volumes of Shakespeare jostled for space with self-help books. Most of the space was taken up by pulp fiction. I found Tehmina Durrani's *My Feudal Lord* in that pile. I had already read it, but picked it up, hoping I could engage the owner in a conversation. I held up the book and pointed to the lot where it had been placed. He smiled.

Most travellers get insights by talking to taxi drivers, I find them in serendipitous encounters and in bookshops. It is fascinating to watch who walks in, what they look for, how the books are placed, how the salespeople respond to your queries, whether the owner recommends anything — and why. I was fortunate to have met an educated and enlightened 'book-manager', as Qayyum Ahmed chose to call himself.

It was afternoon and the books seemed to be ready for a siesta. Flies droned over them as in a sweet shop. The discounted books were on a rack at the entrance, dog-eared, yellowing, the first pages with names and dates. 'Good price,' said the salesman wearing a pistachio green salwaar. This is clearly not a browser's paradise. Ahmed complains that larger bookstores have taken over. 'Now they all stock greeting cards, gift wrapping paper and stationery. There is too much competition.'

'What about Pakistani authors?'

'People buy their books only if they are a hit abroad.'

I asked him about the Tehmina book and its placement in the fiction category. 'Someone must have kept it there by mistake.' It seemed to have been a wicked error. The lady, draped in an ivory-coloured dress, her porcelain beauty fixed with matt foundation cream and just the right amount of ash around her eyes, had dedicated her debut book to the "six ex-wives of Mustafa Khar who have silently suffered pain and dishonour, and seen him get away with impunity. This time one of them is holding him accountable". In what was a scathing evidence of his attitude, she had quoted her former husband as saying, 'Tehmina, you are nothing any more. Once you were Begum Tehmina Mustafa Khar. Now you are just Tehmina Durrani. When you ring up people, you have to introduce yourself as my ex-wife.'

The book that might have been mere tabloid gossip in the western press ended up as a huge success. After its release, Tehmina could well boast that Khar would now be known as her ex-husband. But this is not quite true: she did sell her story on the basis of having been married into the orgiastic world of power. Khar was a well-known minister in the Z.A. Bhutto cabinet. Politicians have enemies who get vicarious pleasure from seeing them exposed. Her book did nothing for the awakening of Pakistani women.

Qayyum brought out a copy of Stanley Wolpert's *Zulfi Bhutto of Pakistan*. It was an old edition. 'He was a very good politician, the best.' There is perhaps some truth in the statement; the country has had a series of skilful politicians, no statesmen. Bhutto was an adept caricature of one, though. He was audacious, canny, and populist. As in life, so in death, he was a Shakespearian character, both the Caesar and the Brutus of Pakistani politics.

Zafar Salam is a Bengali Muslim. His wife Tahera is a Punjabi. I was introduced to them by a friend in the foreign diplomatic services. Although Zafar stayed back because of his wife, he rues the status of Bangladesh today. 'It has to do with the policies of power. Bhutto and Sheikh Mujibur Rehman capitalised on the people's angst. If the army was so bad then why are democratic parties not always successful? The politicians use the army.'

Bhutto, in a moment of self-righteousness, quit the government of Ayub Khan, the first of the military dictators, after the Tashkent Agreement following the Indo-Pak War of 1965. This was not for any democratic principles. He promptly joined forces with the next armyman to take over, Yahya Khan. The latter's reign ended with another war that was to split the country again. The Awami League would have at least had some say, but regional politics had gone way out of anyone's hands. Yahya Khan resorted to bluster. 'Kill three million of them and the rest will eat out of our hands.'

A lot of people were indeed killed. Zafar blames Bhutto. 'Most military men are happy leading the life of an army mess. It has always been these so-called westernised politicians who twist them. It was Bhutto who asked Yahya to arrest Mujib. It was a matter of time before he became the leader. He released Mujib and arrested Yahya, all in the name of false principles. It is because of such people that I don't feel guilty for staying back. They are the real traitors.'

Bhutto faked the communist credo by trying to marry it with economic revolution. He used the 'food, clothing and shelter' motto reminiscent of Indira Gandhi's 'garibi hatao' (remove poverty) movement that had made Indians sceptically wonder whether it was in fact garib hatao (remove the poor).

He was shrewdly using rhetoric to test the waters and see what would work a year before founding the Pakistan People's Party. His declaration, 'Islam is our faith, democracy is our policy, socialism is our economy. All power to the people' worked like an ice-pack in the heated atmosphere.

It was under the regime of the suave Bhutto that the National Assembly passed the resolution announcing that Pakistan would be an 'Islamic Republic' with a parliamentary form of government. He was going to feed the poor faith.

The machinations began once again in right earnest. Accusations of murder attempts gave the democratic rulers the power to change army personnel. Bhutto pushed up Zia-ul-Haq as army chief. The obsequious-looking general who smiled way too much knew what he was getting into. He wasn't a greenhorn. He had fought in World War II; his eyes and nose were sharp.

Zafar is surprisingly anti-Bhutto. 'He was willing to compromise for personal gain.'

'But at least he was secular,' I bait rather weakly.

'He was parochial and divided this country. He was confused.'

It was probably this confusion and lust for the spoils of power that made Zia frame him. Once again, the army took charge.

Bhutto was sentenced to hang to death by the Lahore court. Zia refused to commute the sentence, saying he had no precedent for doing so. As the noose went around his neck and the world stood shaken, Brutus transformed into Caesar.

Zia dropped the pretence of Pakistan's socialist leanings. He politicised Islam and Islamised politics and gave the country an identity for the first time in terms of ideology. The merits of that ideology are indeed debatable, but there was no obfuscation. In a country where many could not afford a good bottle of Shiraz, he gave them the Shariat.

Soldiers also make great politicians. Army rule in Pakistan is easy. When Indians talk of being a democracy, we must remember that we cannot have army rule given the vast and varied political and social landscape; our experiment with the Emergency proved it.

At every point in the history of Pakistan, the army has promised elections. It acts as a blanket of protection against any imminent war with India. This adds to the moral responsibility it craves to be seen as possessing. Zia sent troops to Afghanistan to fight the Soviets. It was an extended war and his rule lasted the longest – until his death.

His funeral, it is proudly claimed, had the highest turnout ever among mass gatherings in Pakistan. What were they mourning? Was Zia responsible for encouraging terrorism?

'Then why has no government after that been able to take care of it?' asks Zafar. 'What did Benazir Bhutto do for women? Did she do away with the Hudood laws that Zia had introduced where a rape victim has to produce four witnesses? And then she complained about male chauvinism even though she was brought to power twice.'

Tahera agrees. 'She fit in better in a socialite party.' I mention Tehmina Durrani to her. She smirks, 'Even the ordinary person was aware of Mustafa Khar's reputation; she knew whom she was marrying – a man who had married often, had mistresses and was ruthless.'

But she had gone beyond that and written about Abdul Sattar Edhi, whose charity work is spread across the country and does not suffer from any parochial prejudices. They call him the 'Angel of mercy'. Can one ignore her commitment to such causes?

'How many people will remember her for that? This is one more pastime. There is nothing new about the Tehmina types. It is so common in the high society of Lahore.'

These were nuanced segregations as cities opposed cities.

3

The Haunted, the Hunted

There is a bustle around the bus station. The Daewoo coach service in Islamabad runs at regular intervals from this point. The waiting area is crowded and unclean. Announcements are made. I am on my way to Lahore.

We have numbered seats. The interiors are much better, with windows darkened by curtains. Just before the bus lurches ahead, a hostess, like the ones in planes, arrives and hands over bottles of water and soft drinks in tetrapacks. There are the usual noises – of people arguing about luggage space, families fighting over who has to sit next to whom. Even before the journey can commence, snacks are passed around and the soft drink squeezed from its cardboard to the last drop as straws are pushed in. Then the carton is crushed into a misshapen convex.

Within minutes, there is silence, as most have fallen asleep. I am looking forward to the trip. I eye the roads with curiosity. As we approach Lahore, the canal comes into view. They say it was created as a buffer during the war with India. It stretches for a long distance and is supposed to be deep. Trees are reflected in the muddy waters; a few children dive in for a swim as a respite from the heat.

I check in at a mid-range hotel. It is new and one can smell the polish. My passport details are noted down. The receptionist asks if I am here on work. This is not the tourist season and it would appear a bit strange for someone to be travelling during this time of the year. I am given a large corner room; there are no windows, so the lights have to be switched on at all hours.

There is too much steel in the lobby, giving distorted mirror images of everything around. I enquire if there are any organised tours: the best way to see the regular sights. Fortunately, the Pakistan Tourism Development Council (PTDC) is running a tour that day.

The guide, Israr Ahmed, is a chatty sort. He looks a bit rakish. He speaks in the manner of guides – a broad accent that takes off from the local patois adding a few rolling 'r's to end with the soft tongue touching the palate fall of a consonant.

I am spared his experiments for I have the advantage of a common language.

The driver has a henna-dyed beard and thinning grey hair. There are three other tourists. Harold is a bulky German with thick hairless arms. One gentleman introduces himself as a Pakistani; I assume he is from another city. He isn't. He is an official of the PTDC, I discover later from Israr. 'I don't know why but at the last minute, just before we were coming to fetch you, he said he was joining us.' He keeps to himself.

The elderly man wearing a kurta with trousers is swarthy complexioned. 'I am American,' he says in a distinctly Indian-Pakistani accent. It is too early to probe what he has come looking for.

I am asked the usual question: 'Is Lahore like Delhi?' Both the cities reek of history, but while Delhi has internalised it,

Lahore holds it aloof, like a dust-laden scrapbook of memories. Delhi has let the cultures of both Hindu and Muslim rulers live in a symbiotic relationship; Lahore does not appear to feel any allegiance. It has moved on.

It has neatly stuffed the past into a treasure chest that has mere decorative value. But Indian and Pakistani Punjab suffered the most during the Partition. Lahore, at least in its tarred and cemented garb, has exorcised those ghosts.

In what might appear to be a sardonic take on its own creation, the national monument has been designed by Murad Khan, a Turkish architect. The Minar-e-Pakistan is best viewed through a small gap in the airy opening of the Badshahi Mosque. It is a tribute to the very formation of the country. The Lahore Resolution of 1940 passed by the Muslim League declared its intent for a separate state at this spot. It is an unhandsome structure from afar and stands out like a cold mercenary, scoffing at the ruins that overlook it. The tower does not rise from the ground but is built on a sturdy four-metre high platform that is star-shaped. It tapers like a pyramid to its full height of 60 metres. Even the stone floors and marble walls appear to fathom the immensity of the responsibility they hold of being in denial.

Lahore was initially a Brahmanical city. The first recorded reference talks about it as being named after Lav, one of the twin sons of Lord Rama. Muhammad bin Qasim marched into Lahore to begin the conquest of India. Then came Mahmud of Ghazni. The most decisive rule that lasted over two centuries was by the Mughals from the 16th to the 18th century.

For 14 years, Emperor Akbar made the city his capital. The Mughals were renowned for creating the most majestic structures. The Lahore Fort went through several changes and extensions by Jahangir, Shah Jahan and Aurangzeb.

The Fort is full of familiar rooms like the Sheesh Mahal, the palace of mirrors. A matchstick is lit and we see the magic of the flame shining in individual pieces of glass. There are niches where women kept their jewellery boxes. Most of the living quarters are rather small, as compared to the sweeping balconies with their low large windows and even larger courtyards and open rooms like the Diwan-e-khaas and the Diwan-e-aam, the ministerial and public assemblies. The women stayed indoors and appeared to have spent a good deal of time at the baths, which have large sunken tubs that could also accommodate the slave girls who would pamper them. The verandas served as their windows to the world outside as it was through chik curtains or cunning lattice-work that they watched dances, fights and various forms of justice and injustice being carried out.

Akbar had walked barefoot from Delhi to Agra at the shrine of the Sufi sage Salim Chishti to ask for a son. His wish was granted and he named the future ruler of Hindustan after the saint. The confluence of cultures was to be Salim's destiny as he soaked in the ambience of the Hindu heritage of his mother, Jodha Bai.

In Pakistan, they do not emphasise this. However, in a rather quirky manner, while the Rajput is sidelined, the slave girl Anarkali, said to be a courtesan, has a tomb consecrated in her memory.

As I walk through the magnificent gardens of the Fort I ask Israr, who has a master's in history and has studied in Austria, whether he believes she existed. He states, 'There is no mention of her in the *Jahangirnama*.' Like his predecessors, Jahangir was a meticulous recorder of events; it is possible that he was being selective. If she did not exist, then, interestingly, we are discussing an imaginary character standing in a historical ground that has entombed a fantasy. All reality from a distance appears mythical.

In the early days there was an inscription in Persian on her tomb that said, 'The innocent who is murdered mercilessly and who dies after enduring much pain is a martyr.' Israr mentions that like all Mughal monuments, her mausoleum was surrounded by gardens. Now it is a government building. On the remains of a nautch girl, legitimate business is conducted. The stone crypt pays obeisance to both God, by listing out all His names, and the beloved in a Persian couplet:

> *Ta qiyamat shukr guyam kardigare khish ra*
> *Ah! gar man baz banam rui yaar-e khish ra*
>
> (I would give thanks unto my God unto the day of resurrection
> Ah! could I behold the face of my beloved once more)

In another corner, almost shyly, it has been signed by 'Majnun Salim Akbar', the enamoured Salim, son of Akbar.

It is said that Akbar, incensed with the obsession of his son for someone of lowly stature, ordered her to be buried alive. The scene of her expressionless eyes numbed by now with grief as brick is laid upon brick has become part of cinematic legend. Though a film by the eponymous name was made prior to it, *Mughal-e-Azam*, released in 1960, became a huge hit. To recount the magnetism of the 'pomegranate blossom', a literal translation of Anarkali, the Indian director K. Asif expended 16 years and considerable money.

The two actresses who enacted the roles make for an interesting study in polarisation. In *Anarkali*, the 1958 version,

Noorjehan portrayed the doomed mistress. She had migrated to Pakistan after Partition and was hailed as the Mallika-e-tarannum, melody queen. Madhubala, the star of *Mughal-e-Azam,* was a Pashtun from Afghanistan and is to this day referred to as the Venus of Hindi cinema.

Beyond the celluloid saga of destructive love, another drama was played out between the actors, lovers in real life, both Pathans who had adopted Hindu names, as was the practice for several years.

Could anyone imagine Anarkali dragging Salim to court? Madhubala had done precisely that – sued Dilip Kumar for breach of trust when she realised he was not going to marry her. He stood in the witness box and told the judge, 'I love Madhubala and shall always love her.'

The youth of the time had been swept by this wave. The film had become a classic because our mothers nursed these minutiae and we were the experiments for their fantasies, made to relive some of those haunting moments dressed up in various *Anarkali* costumes. For years 'Madhubala *ki galli* (Madhubala's lane)' was a neighbourhood reality for me. She was dead but I could imagine her stepping out of the old bungalow a few blocks away any minute.

When it first hit the screen, people took the Rajput Jodha Bai, queen of Akbar, as an intrinsic part of the culture of the Mughal court and Hindustan. Almost half a century later, despite the sensitive issues, references to the heritage of Babar and Humayun are not even being noticed. It seems like we need imaginary characters like Anarkali to put the past in perspective.

The legend of Anarkali tells us that social class has always been more important; the poor man's religion has been survival and whatever moral means he may choose to do so with would still make him an outcaste. The sculptor who was to carve and chisel the statue for the arrival of Prince Salim remained as much of a minion as the nautch girl he covered with plaster as he could not have the image ready on time. By breathing life into a mute object, she courted death.

Religion in the subcontinent is about mass hysteria, not belief. Jodha Bai was the daughter of the maharaja of Amber; her royal blood condoned her religion of idolatry. It is said that the first ever mosque built in Lahore, the Mariam Zamani Mosque, was on her instructions. This was for the benefit of the Mughal princesses who would otherwise be forbidden from entering the male preserve. Despite its uniqueness, it is now a forgotten and forsaken structure.

The Badshahi mosque looms in brick red and white. You are supposed to be awestruck and this is managed by the practical visual access to it through a series of steps. The magnificence may not seem unusual for those acquainted with Mughal period architecture. What is surprising is that it was built during the time of Aurangzeb Alamgir. Known for his ruthless fanaticism and austerity – he wove skull caps for Haj pilgrims and copied out Quranic verses – this does seem like too much indulgence on his part.

As we go around, there is a man sitting on a cloth spread on the ground. He is wearing a red cloak inscribed with Quranic verses embroidered in golden thread; the white of his beard matches the white of his cap. He holds a pen in his hand; curled over it are prayer beads. There are sheets of paper and a small book of prayers. A bottle of mineral water stands in isolation at a distance. He reads people's future. More importantly, he lets people take his picture. He has become an attraction, a caricature of a bygone era.

Of all the Mughal emperors, Aurangzeb was the most spartan and ruthless. He did not spare his brother Dara Shikoh for his interest in meshing the cultures of India that included Hindu scriptures, and he imprisoned his father Shah Jahan, who spent his last days at the Agra Fort gazing at the Taj Mahal, his tribute to his wife Mumtaz Mahal, from the courtyard from where the Yamuna yawns in imminent slumber. Tourist guides take you to a stone bench where they say the imprisoned emperor sat to look at his beloved creation. The river is now sludge. Large black buffaloes stalk over it with heavy plodding legs.

The Shalimar Gardens in Lahore were commissioned by Shah Jahan. Built on three levels, it has symmetrically designed lawns, waterfalls, pools, and alcoves with scalloped awnings. It has been declared a world heritage site, and due to deference to this high status, few people seem to be enjoying it. There are some young men sitting aimlessly on the grass. A couple, the woman in a burqa, the man in a salwaar kurta, walk in purposefully. Two young boys wearing green tight turbans smile. They are from the madrassa; there is a strange maturity in their eyes. Unlike other kids who might enjoy playing, they have found God.

They pose for pictures and their expression transforms. The mouths stiffen. I wish to engage them in conversation. 'Hum jihadi hai,' they say. This isn't what people assume it to mean. Before I can probe their minds into the real meaning of jihad, to fight for oneself to be better human beings, to strive for a super-consciousness, an elderly man beckons to them. They leave, their heads down.

I recount this to someone. She says rather facetiously, 'Who knows, these could be future suicide bombers.'

The jihad of today had been a part of Sikh culture and is attributed to persecution by the Mughals. The fifth guru, Arjan Dev, was put to death by Jahangir's army. It was to be a bloody history. Guru Tegh Bahadur, who wanted to protect the Kashmiri Brahmins from conversion to Islam, met a fate far worse. He was cruelly treated and placed like an animal in a prison too small for him. Over 300 years later, the Sikhs would be massacred in large numbers due to the assassination of a Kashmiri Brahmin prime minister of India, Indira Gandhi. History repeats itself not only as farce and tragedy, but also as a macabre reminder of forgetfulness.

The Khalsa was an order started in 1699 by Guru Gobind Singh. It operated on the motto of do or die to defend God and land. These holy warriors were also insurgents. The Sikhs were consolidating themselves. After a rule that lasted 50 years, they lost to the British. During those years, they showed their enterprising spirit. For a warrior race, they seemed to relish a feudal lifestyle. The united Punjab gave them ample scope for that. The Englishman became the common enemy.

The Partition of India changed all that. When Punjab was divided, Lahore became the arena for the most bloodshed. No one expected this state to be cleaved. Punjab, Haryana and Himachal Pradesh together with Lahore constituted the province of Punjab. It was in Lahore that the first official demand for complete independence from the British was made by the Indian National Congress. It was in Lahore that the Sikh hero, Bhagat Singh, along with Rajguru and Sukhdev, was hanged to death for what were called 'terrorist activities'.

During the tour, Israr touches the walls of the echoing rooms inside the fort. He is explaining the intricate details about inlay work and of columns made out of single stones. Harold is transfixed. I look at these with the familiar cursory glance one gives a new cushion cover in one's living room sofa. I have been saturated with similar sights in Delhi and Agra and Rajasthan. But Israr is living a tale as if on auto-pilot; he does it everyday with the same dose of robotic emotion. He points towards little dug-up holes where a petal of a flower once was or a missing part of a star. 'These,' he says, holding on to the pillar as though it might fall from the revelation, 'were desecrated by Ranjit Singh when the Sikhs conquered Lahore and made it their capital. He took the marble from our mausoleums to build the Golden Temple in Amritsar.'

The gentleman in the kurta, who is part of the tour, wants to visit the gurudwara next to the Badshahi mosque where the remains of the fifth guru Arjan Dev have been placed. 'It is open only to Sikhs,' says Israr.

'I am a Sikh,' says the man. Without his turban and any other visible signs, no one would have guessed. Israr is embarrassed as he apologises for his comments and says, 'This is what history books tell us.'

Colonisers have always stolen; they need mementoes. History is built on these symbols. In India we blame the British for holes in the walls of our monuments. In Lahore they blame the Sikhs.

The Sikhs have an attachment to the soil that goes beyond emotions. 1947 exhumed the bodies of centuries-old saints, blood-curdling cries echoing in the trains where humans were stacked over one another like sacks, fleeing a country that was not their's anymore.

Satwinder Kohli is a Birmingham-based businessman. He has a droll manner. Tiny feminine teeth are scattered in his mouth. He is tall and built like a bull; he wears his trousers way below his navel so that the curve of his belly makes his legs look like fragile pillars propping up a dome.

His father Jasbir Singh, a man of some wealth in Lahore, found that slowly the prejudices were creeping in. The land he owned was a shelter; his house was attacked, the very house that had hosted many a dignitary was now an unwanted appendage. His Muslim friends who had lived with him were not as full of animus as were those who came to live here from what was now across the border.

He was young and his education and finances helped him make the decision to leave. Most of his money was invested in land and houses, but the little he managed to liquidate took him to a distant shore. 'My father did not want to just cross over and go to India. He knew there would be turmoil, there would be familiar people, familiar memories, so he left for London.'

He set up shop with the help of old friends. 'Had he chosen to stay in Lahore and there had been no Partition, he would have been as big as the Tatas and Birlas are in India today,' says the son with pride. 'He left me with a business I could expand only because of his vision. But he also left me with the bitterness of the past.'

Did he speak about it often?

'No, he never spoke about it at all. I had these elderly uncles and aunts around who had moved, first to India and then to the UK. They told stories of home. My father never did. His hurt was so great that once when I asked him to tell me about Lahore, he left the room.'

For the past 10 years, Satwinder has been visiting the city regularly. He knows everyone there is to know – politicians, judges, senior officers from the armed forces, bureaucrats. He has wealth and a common language. What they do not know is that he also has contempt. The business he has started is in a way his manner of hitting out at them, for telling Lahore that he is rebuilding his father's life, recreating it, a shrine they cannot destroy. 'Today, none of these people can refuse me anything. I pay them salaries and commission.'

He is not a braggart and, most times, he exudes an affability that sits rather well on his girth and benign face. His vengeance is economic and emotional. It is only when he mentions these things that I realise he is not wearing a turban, the primary identification mark of his religion. His hair is cropped short and he has no beard or moustache. He has an expensive watch but no steel kada (bangle). His adopted home, England, has made him play safe. 'I used to wear a turban when I was a kid, but I made the decision to discard it. Being a Sikh is my state of mind, my belief. I don't have to show it. I am doing well in Britain, am respected there, but Lahore feels like home. They don't call me Stan here. They address me as "Sardarji".'

Yet he does not like the people he deals with. 'All double standards. They will talk about culture but they only want status. They seek friendship and then hit you. Even when you do business, they offer you women. Not prostitutes, but their own mistresses. I am a man, I have my weak points. Once I was tempted, but destiny helped me. I later found out that the woman was HIV positive. That man must have known and deliberately done it. Cheating is a part of their life.'

The Haunted, the Hunted

Israr tells us that it is possible to be cheated at the shrine of Hazrat Daata Ganj Bakhsh, but it is a place one must visit. I have been told that at night it comes alive with the singing and dancing of dervishes. Large vessels serve food to the poor. I go during the day. It is a white structure in a crowded street. At the mosque, people are doing wazoo (ablutions before prayers) at a small open tank. A woman follows me, tugs at my arm and asks for money. I try to tell her I will give her something later; I am clutching onto my handbag as advised by Israr. 'Don't think that in places of worship crimes are not committed,' he had said.

The story is no different elsewhere in the subcontinent. This woman is insistent. I utter the line I use in my own country, 'Muaf kar do (pardon me)'. She snaps back, 'Bheek nahin maang rahe. Daata saab ke kab'r par aakar kuchch dena zaroori nahin hota? Sab dete hai (I am not begging. Don't you think that donating something at the shrine is important? Everyone does).' I am clearly angry now. There is a queue and I join it. She continues to rail against me. She points her hands in my direction and informs others about how unreasonable I am.

I put some money in a box and do not manage to see the tombstone. I walk away after mumbling some prayers that I recall from childhood. The lady does not follow me. Instead she shouts, 'Dekh liya? Kahaan-kahaan se aate hai log! Aur guroor tau dekho (Saw what you wanted to see? People come from just about anywhere! And look at her arrogance)!'

The choice is between feeling chastised or going away with guilt. I don't have to choose. On the steps is an old woman sitting quietly and praying. She is lost to the world, her fingers running over the prayer beads even as her hands shake. I am moved beyond words. Devotion lies in her form. 'Amma?' I try to break her reverie.

She looks up at me and gives me a toothless smile. I sit down next to her as passers-by move away to seek blessings and ask for favours and pay alms-seekers who blackmail them. I am learning the basic philosophy of life at the feet of an untutored woman. 'Baba ke paas aayi ho (Have you come to see Baba)?'

'I am here,' I tell her.

'Allah tau sab jagah hai. Kuchch maanga (God is everywhere. Did you ask for anything)?'

'Nahin, woh tau kaheen bhi maang sakte hai (No, one can ask for anything anywhere).'

'Haan.'

'Aap yahaan roze aati hai (Do you come here everyday)?'

'Ghar samajh lo, kaheen par bhi basaa lete (It is like my home that I can make anywhere).'

Hesitantly, I tell her we could share some food but I have to leave, so would she mind if I gave her money to buy it on my behalf?

A thin film of water above her lower lid is my answer. I place the rupees on her faded chadar in her lap; I do not want her to stretch her hands out.

'Allah khush rakhe aur murad poori kare. Hamari bhi tau sun lete hai (May Allah bless you. He listens to me too),' she tells me.

It is the silence of her needs that get fulfilled. Perhaps someone like me does pass by every day. Fulfilment of her wish to fill her stomach with some food to keep her alive is enough to keep her faith alive too.

The Haunted, the Hunted

I reluctantly visit the mausoleum of poet, philosopher Allama Iqbal. I must admit to a deep feeling of sadness seeing his memory consecrated here. What made him leave his beloved Hindustan? When did the poet become a politician? Sir Muhammad Iqbal is an enigma. His best-known work is sung in India and is a paean to it, yet he is the national poet of Pakistan; he was among the first of the leaders who spoke of a separate state for Muslims based on the purity of Islam, yet he supported Jinnah, whose interest in a separate state was based on secular principles; it was he who asked Jinnah to return from London to free the people. From what?

It is his words that resonate in India even today and the song played during the 'beating the retreat' ceremony: 'Saare jahaan se achcha Hindostan hamara, hum bulbule hai iski, yeh gulsitan hamara (Of all the places in the world Hindostan is the best, we are the nightingales of this garden).' It lost out on becoming India's national anthem by two votes, although it is far more popular. When the first Indian man in space was asked during a satellite broadcast by the then prime minister Indira Gandhi how the country looked from there, Rakesh Sharma replied, 'Saare jahaan se achcha.'

Somewhere at a juncture stands Kim's Gun. It has the roar of a lion, Zam-zammah being its original name. Many in India see Rudyard Kipling as a typical Raj Englishman taking a monocled literary view of India; the patronising sahib. In Lahore, which some commentators have referred to as 'the heart of Kipling's India', where he spent only five years of his life, the ancient gun has been named after the character in his novel. Only because his urchin protagonist Kim sat on it and went along to explore the innards of a museum with a Buddhist monk.

The museum is a dull place. A few people from other cities are visiting. I realise that in the few museums I have been to in Pakistan, the locals walk in and out as though strolling through parks; curiosity is merely an accessory.

The beauty of stoic Gandhara art meets the elegance of Mughal miniature paintings and evidence of lost glory. These relics could well be caged animals in a zoo as much as the general section. A boy of about eight spots a figure of a Neanderthal man. He leaps towards it, sticking his tongue out. The disinterest is infectious. I find myself ambling desultorily through the maze of busts, coins, flaky parchment.

The most riveting piece is that of the fasting Buddha. It is a masterpiece, renowned for its time and a departure from the usual beatific images. I marvel at its sculpted rib cage, a prince's penance. Behind me two men have positioned themselves. They laugh. One of them tells the other, 'Yeh Buddha itna dublaa kaise ho gaya? Yeh to mota tha (How is this Buddha grown so lean? He used to be fat).' The reference is perhaps to the laughing Buddha.

On the way out, there is a store selling souvenirs. A Frenchwoman comes in to buy a postcard and asks how many stamps would be required to send it home. The shopkeeper gives her a rough estimate. She insists on knowing the exact amount. 'Don't worry, Inshallah, it will reach,' he says.

'Oh, all I hear is Inshallah, Inshallah everywhere I go. *C'est la vie!*'

The old city is walled behind 12 gates. The heavy imposing entrance is like a sturdy package that carries something fragile within. The lanes and buildings and shops look like they'd crumble under the slightest pressure. It is the vulnerability of any marketplace that has lost its innocence but smartened up only as a defence mechanism.

The innards spew out the entrails of a garish life – colourful ribbons, shiny show-pieces, parandis that are braided into the hair and hang down the back like synthetic snakes. This is a place for tourists to experience exotica and for the poor to sell their wares.

There is a small open cart where a stove brews tea, milk turning a light salmon pink as it merges with the leaves. It is boiled and whipped with a large ladle and ebbs and rises within its aluminium confines. Cardamoms are held over this and opened up like eggs to fall into the concoction. The doodh-patti chai is ready.

An old man selling cheap trinkets is slurping tea poured out in a saucer; there is nothing that I really want from him, but over the fading rim of old bone china his eyes seem lost. I pick up a few plastic clips. He points out a golden one shaped like a butterfly. He does so wordlessly. I buy it. It would look quite appalling on hair, but does seem quite lovely by itself.

Further out, Anarkali Bazaar is the only surviving market that is two centuries old. Besides age, there isn't much it sells. I pick up a few net dupattas and a couple of white salwaars with shadow-work embroidery and tiny sequins encrusted on their stiff bottom bands; they fit tightly round the ankles. After one wear, the seams give way. They weren't meant to last.

Although these mohallas could be a part of old Delhi or Lucknow, they seem to be abandoned by their inhabitants.

The rich of Lahore do not visit these places. It is a city that has formed a hierarchy in terms of administration – neatly segregated parts of nine districts and a cantonment area.

Liberty Market is a large collection of shops arranged in a circle. There are several people selling naadas (strings) for the salwaars. It seems a peculiarity. I buy a whole bundle of 12 tied with a jute thread. It comes in handy for my new salwaars and also to wrap up packets just before I leave.

India is a better place for shopping, but the basic style and cut for ethnic wear seems to be dictated by Pakistani designers, at least for casual dressing. While there are women who dress in western attire, the use of sarees is not as prevalent as it was in the old days. I do pick up a few readymade 'ladies suits'. Trendy women experiment within the limitations, but what I find completely non-aesthetic is the slit in their kurtas. They are too big and reveal the line where the pleats in the salwaar start. This is as unbecoming as a bra strap or a panty line showing.

I was told to visit the khadi shop for interesting wear. Khadi is not just cloth; it is a movement started by Mahatma Gandhi, a man not liked much in Pakistan. There are amazing ways in which societies can get colonised or let themselves be inveigled by the charms of a hidden opponent.

It has been both an uplifting and edifying experience. I am attempting to understand why the claim, 'Lhaur lhaur hain (Lahore is Lahore)' that seeks to convey its exclusivity does not seem to reach out to me. This is the city of culture, history, trends; there is beauty. Almost everything has left me untouched.

I wasn't sure I would return. I did.

Hamid has stopped in Lahore on his way to Islamabad to get his visa and complete other formalities for his emigration to America. He is Saqlain's brother. Hamid has lived all his life in Faisalabad. He is in what he calls 'private service'. Unlike his brother, he does not have fanatical views. But his exposure to life and women is limited. He married early and is already the father of four.

His greatest adventure was sometime in the 1980s when he was in college as a first year student. He and another brother travelled by train from Amritsar and went as far as Mumbai. They had not told anyone at home and they had got their visas based on fictitious invitations.

'It was quite a high then. India seemed to be poorer than Pakistan, but it was more organised and people were simpler; there was less corruption than in Pakistan. Bombay even then was akin to western cities, but the class difference was more evident here compared to other places we visited. Now I read all this talk about India as one of the major players in information technology. I find it fascinating.'

Why did he want to leave Pakistan? 'Better prospects. We live in a joint family and there are bound to be small problems. I have to ensure a future for my kids.'

'Isn't there a future in Pakistan?'

'Right now, not the way I want it. I am sure I will return. We don't forget our values.'

He tended to see many similarities with India, quite different from his brother's attitude. 'I think it is his job speaking and not him.'

'But even outside political discussions he has appeared rather fanatical.'

'This is not fanaticism; it is the attitude of most people here. If you have not visited the country then the enigma remains, and we have an enemy.'

We drive towards Gawala Mandi for dinner. It is the food street, a large open area that is closed to traffic at night and becomes a pedestrian walkway. Tables and chairs are spread across as lights beam out from old homes. Stalls fan the fires over which lie iron prongs with pieces of meat; large vessels, their bodies like pregnant women, hold within their bellies unborn mysteries that have been marinated for hours, sealed with dough. This is the hub of the rich who want to experience the roads.

It reminds me of Khau Galli in Mumbai, a lane full of stalls that come alive mostly during the month of Ramzan. At dusk devotees come to break their fast, but many others visit it as a tourist and foodie delight. The tubelights are powerful.

At Gawala it is not so bright. Racks of flesh are hanging from hooks, some with slivers of blood still bursting out of dead veins. The stench is strong. I have lost my appetite. I break a piece of naan and chew on it as I sip on a glass of sweetened lassi, the curd churned to a froth that clings to the rim.

The city is supposed to be a gourmet paradise. The day before, I was sitting at Bundu Khan, one of the famous eateries. This is one of those over-rated restaurants that offer the wealthy a plebeian lifestyle for an hour or so. The seating is arranged both at the lower level and the terrace. The food looks cheap, but isn't. They charge you for the experience. Bundu Khan has become a brand name, and the moment a place has swanky cars and young men twirling car keys, a fad transforms into contemporary culture.

Unlike the North West Frontier Province, where most food is treated with a degree of reverence to its raw material, here, as in most parts of the subcontinent, there is a belief that the more chillies and spices you add, the greater will be the experience. It is almost mandatory to have colour in food, which means red chilli powder, and the richness of cuisine depends on how much taree (a term we used at home), oil or ghee, floats in small bubbles in the curry.

The speciality called halwa-puri is served at breakfast. It is a sweetened and fried mix of semolina, milk and sugar that sticks to the pan. I try it once. I think feudalism in Pakistani Punjab has a lot to do with eating habits. This is designed to make you somnolent.

We are walking down Fortress Stadium to the shops selling DVDs and CDs. Hamid is behind me. I wait, assuming he has stopped to look at something. He motions me to keep walking. 'Why?' I ask.

'Even when I am with my wife, we do not walk together. I suppose she feels shy and it just looks awkward, so I stay behind.'

I laugh. In India the concept of a woman walking two steps behind is considered regressive. Here the idea seems to have been turned on its head.

I want to look for the Pakistani television dramas that were so popular in India. At that time they used to be on VHS, large video cassettes that were held with awe; most Indians loved them, mainly because of the simple themes delicately handled and the beauty of the language. There was hardly any background music, but the ghazals playing during crucial moments or with the title stayed on and haunted. Although there was nothing dramatic happening, no suspense, we would wait to change cassettes. These were rented from the local library and invariably had scratches and portions blurred due to extensive and careless usage. That did not hamper our enthusiasm as we lived through the stories of *Tanhaiyan, Ankahee, Dhoop Kinare*. This was our link to Pakistan.

Living in Mumbai, where apartments rise vertically, we

would feel a tinge of envy at the sprawling houses that dot even a barren city like Karachi.

I pick up as many VCDs as I can. The popular ones are the comedies by Omar Sharif, whose humour tends to concentrate quite a bit on swipes at women. If art reflects society, then Pakistani tele-serials had indeed gone through a change. The music is loud; even in the old ones they have added a grating background score where the voices of the characters are barely audible. But I did find some rare music. The special feeling one has of buying the works of the maestros in their country cannot be described adequately.

The songs are not listed in English, but in Urdu. I feel lost. Hamid is surprised, 'You cannot read Urdu? What kind of Muslim are you? Okay, I understand, in India you don't have to learn the language.'

Urdu is one of the official languages in India. My ignorance has to do with upbringing, schooling and my own resistance. My roots are in Gujarat, like Jinnah's — who also did not speak Urdu. In school, the second language was Hindi, the third was the state language, Marathi. The only way one could remotely get acquainted with the Urdu script was to take some religious training. I was not interested, the only reason being the local muliyani (tutor), a female version of a maulvi, known to us was a rather forbidding creature always dressed in black. Enid Blyton had replaced god for me.

I learned to speak Urdu with some degree of confidence by picking it up from the works of poets like Sahir Ludhianvi, Ghalib, Mir, Zauk, Faiz, Faraz in the Roman script, and pored over the Lughat (dictionary) for hours to comprehend what Mehdi Hassan, Farida Khanum, Iqbal Bano and the rest were singing.

Hamid reads out the lines to me from a Habib Wali

Mohammed CD. 'Ae nigaar-e-watan tu salamat rahe...' I used to hum it with a lump in my throat for my country.

A woman in her early twenties enters the store. She is wearing tight jeans and a slinky short blouse that keeps slipping off her shoulder. Her face, except for a touch of transparent lip gloss, is devoid of make-up. This is rare among a certain class of women in Pakistan, especially Lahore. They are heavily made-up, the classier ones going in for the beige lips, dark eyes look; they use blushers on their cheeks quite liberally – pink, peach and even magenta blobs.

The woman at the store has clear skin that glows with good health. She smiles and starts looking through the pile of old records. When we are outside, Hamid tells me that she is from Heera Mandi.

'She? I don't think so. She was dressed so simply.'

'Business has not yet started, but she is from there, women do not dress like this otherwise.'

His world was indeed compressed.

I defer a visit to Coco's Café for the next night. I have been there briefly just to get a view on an earlier occasion. One reached the terrace climbing steep stairs; it is an old haveli. This is again a place for the rich. Shining copper bowls are brought in and the food has a roadside flavour. It is in fact bought off the smaller cafes on the streets. A pulley is used to haul the food up, clearly as part of the added attraction.

You can watch the lit up Badhsahi mosque and much of the skyline of the old city. The minute you enter the restaurant, cultures mesh. Large paintings of women adorn the walls. They are done by the owner of the place, Iqbal

Hussein, son of a courtesan. It is said that he does not know his father's name, but believes he was a painter too.

I look at the works on display. Like most artists and writers, Iqbal took his own environment and recreated it. The women look forlorn; they lack coquettishness. Was it the son trying to convey the real picture? An artist I spoke to does not think so. 'He is smart. He has cannily used his surroundings.'

At one level, it is quite true. He was a child of the mohalla and has got respectability for himself. No one is embarrassed to eat at his restaurant; it is the swish place to be seen in. He has made debauchery acceptable and legitimate within the confines of his eatery. You may not buy the services of these women, but you can buy the canvases on which their depravity has been hidden with oil and tempura caking and flaking.

He could have moved out, as many try to. Was it commitment to the place, a deep involvement with his past? Why does he draw these women? Isn't he an exploiter as well?

In the often exaggerated descriptions, a stark truth is ignored. Much like heritage sites that are seen with awe or sought to be abused, Heera Mandi is now not so much a playground for sexual gratification as it is a display of impotent power by the *nouveau riche*.

The lane below turns into the seedy neighbourhood it is. I cannot look at it as a westerner or a sociologist would with objectivity. I have worked among the children from the whorehouses in Mumbai. Seen their mothers at their morning chores, washing clothes near open taps, lying on cots outside while bargaining with vegetable vendors, visiting doctors. I have seen them get married, reformed, beaten up. They wear make-up that makes them look like performers at a circus rather than mannequins. Coal does not always transform into diamond and is not meant to in this 'diamond market'.

A large reason for the patronage of these women by the Mughal emperors was that they upheld the tradition of music and dance. Thumri and mujras became synonymous with them. Even singers and poets were given the status of invitees and keeps of the durbars. Respect was granted to them according to the level of pleasure the senses derived from their singing, dancing, attractiveness.

Today, if at all music is played in these houses of pleasure, it is film songs; the musicians do not even bother to tune their instruments. The discordant sounds of harmonium, tabla and ghungroo are not synchronised.

Earlier, the girls were polished into gems. Dance was associated with culture. Fouzia Saeed has written a detailed account in *Taboo: The Hidden Culture of a Red Light Area* as to why she got fascinated by the subject: 'The performing arts have always held an immense personal interest for me. At the age of 17 I wanted to learn how to play the sitar, but I soon came across the perception that it was not something that a "nice" woman should do. When I expressed my interest in dance, I came across the same resistance, and this sparked my curiosity as to why there was such a stigma attached to both these arts.'

That stigma persists, and although a few performances are held at the Al Hamra Centre, they have the stamp of rebellion.

Nausheen would have been one of the women on sale. A crooked fate saved her.

As she walked into the Avari Hotel to meet me, I saw her

from afar. Everyone in the lobby turned to look as her stiletto heels clicked on the granite tiles, their sharpness blurred on the surface. She was inviting glares her way. Her black and beige ensemble had an animal print. It was quite difficult to recognise which animal it was paying tribute to for there were stripes and spots with a sudden burst of an antler-like motif near the shoulder.

She had rolled up her dupatta like a rope round her neck. Her kameez was low-cut and showed a large expanse of chocolate brown skin between her throat and chest. I had seen flashes of cleavage in Pakistan, but this was unusual. Her large bosom drooped and on her short frame this appeared awkward. She seemed aware of it and would suddenly straighten up, her walk a duck-like gait. She spotted me and we hugged.

Stan, my friend from Birmingham, had suggested that I get in touch with her. 'She works for me,' he had said.

She told me, quite unnecessarily, that her husband was away. She was not married, but in the social circle she moved around in he was referred to as her husband.

Nobody, not even Stan, knew how many wives the 'husband' had. 'In Lahore, having another woman is a status symbol.'

'That is the case all over the world, in India too,' I told him.

'In Lahore it is under wraps.'

'Then how can it be flaunted as a status symbol?'

'Because it is a secret. But everyone knows there is a secret!'

Nausheen does not look like she can keep a secret, let alone be one. She took me to where the car was parked. She introduced the man who was driving as her brother. He was tall, fair and his eyes were the colour of sunlight falling on moss. She prattled on in Punjabi, but it wasn't the boisterous language one is accustomed to hearing. She spoke in the crude manner of truck drivers.

Her Urdu too was interspersed with a strong Punjabi accent to the point of being incomprehensible sometimes. She was making an effort to stop herself using foul words. Her attitude towards me had a lot to do with how much she was indebted to Stan. This car belonged to him.

She was the mistress of a highly-placed army officer. Although he told her that the house where she lived was hers, the papers were in his name. It was only natural for her to feel insecure; she was dependent on him for money, for shelter and for a precarious legitimacy. In a society where men can marry four times, why would they keep a mistress? Mistresses were cheaper to maintain and could be discarded.

She used this fear rather well with Stan. As he recalled, 'Whenever I went to Lahore on work, she would cry. Although the man she called her husband was my friend, I thought I could help. I suggested to him that she could look after my factory. I needed someone I knew. He was happy that she would be kept busy. A couple of months later she started complaining about commuting, so I bought the car. Since I travelled so often to the city, it came in handy and I was always staying at their house.'

Nausheen's life was made simple by the fact that she adopted emotional blackmail tactics. The man she had called her brother was not her brother. I was shocked to hear Stan tell me later that she had brought him along assuming that as a single woman I would like some company. She was in business.

One day after dinner, Stan found the maid at the house hovering near him. She was a young girl of barely 18. She was wearing nice clothes and tried to lure him with a smile.

Her eyes were vacant, though. Stan realised something was wrong. He later went into the kitchen and asked her why she was doing this. 'Her reply surprised me. Nausheen used her to entertain guests and took the money she was gifted. The girl got food and a place to live. I asked her if she did not realise that I was much older, and she told me, "Poor people have no choice". Next day I quietly took a bundle of a few thousand rupees and told her to leave. I said she need not be a victim of anybody.'

Wasn't Nausheen a victim too? Her story was as dramatic as it was devious. She came from a poor family where her father was someone who visited occasionally; her mother granted favours to several men. At an early age, Nausheen discovered that what she lacked in conventional beauty, she could make up for by behaving in a servile manner. Once she managed to trick the person, she had a slave for life.

It was complex. The wife of the army officer knew of her existence. And Stan knew both the women. 'The wife does not care because she knows he won't leave her. There is no clash of interest. Nausheen has to wait for days for him to get in touch, she is the outsider. This has made her smart. I have found that she has even robbed me of money that I might leave in the house.'

It is like many large houses, liberally furnished but devoid of character. Large prints, heavy curtains, big lamps, shelves covering entire walls. More than a lived-in house, it seems to be lying in wait, the prolonging of the wait giving it an exhausted look. It is a tired house with a small garden where weeds have outgrown the flowers. A few roses open up wide to reveal the dark underside.

Nausheen's mother comes into the room. She is fair and taller than her daughter. I know she was once part of Heera

Mandi, but I am not supposed to either reveal that information or bring it up directly. I get up from the low settee to greet her. She tilts my face with her index finger much in the manner of one appraising a product. She discloses nothing. It means I would not know how much I would have been worth.

Many people may find such insouciance discomfiting, even insensitive. But I have met women who work in these areas who do not feel exploited, who in fact turn into exploiters.

Isn't that the trail of Nausheen's life? She was saved but she does run a small industry without the label. She operates from a posh area of Lahore where no one can accuse her of seediness. The men who benefit from it are friends, people from high society. Rich men. Not everyone is like Satwinder.

Ammaji breaks into a smile when I mention him. At first she does not recognise the name, and then her daughter tells her I am speaking about 'Sdaanji', which is how she pronounces 'Sardarji'.

I am not a stranger any more in this house. Ammaji asks me about Lucknow, a city I have visited just once. She went there in her youth. From her Urdu, devoid of an intruding accent, I reckon her roots are somewhere in central India. 'Bohat shaan thi wahaan (There was a lot of opulence there)'. I tell her not much remains of that; it is a city rife with the politics of the underprivileged and how they are used and abused.

'Woh tau hamesha se hote aa raha hai (But that has always been the case),' she shrugs.

I tell her about Imrana, the woman who was raped by her father-in-law and how the Ulema in Uttar Pradesh declared that she should marry him. She is not shocked. 'Yeh zindagi hai. Duniya ko logon ne kotha bana diya hai (This is life; people have made the world into a marketplace).'

The world is on sale. It is difficult to resist the temptation, so I give her an account of my quick trip to Heera Mandi. 'Sab ki daastan hoti hai. Sirf eik cheez hai, wahaan par quam aur zaat ka koi matlab nahin hota. Sab kharidar hai (Each has a story. The only thing is that there religion and castes have no meaning. Everyone is a buyer).'

It is a moving moment. She is recollecting without recoiling the days of a place she was once in by removing herself from it. '*Wahaan*' – there – is a faraway destination she has left behind. There is no emotion in her voice even as her words are ripe with feeling. Like a story-teller, she weaves a spell about a fictitious place. Empathy replaces belongingness.

The person who is truly affected is Nausheen. She sits at the edge of a chair as though afraid that something will spill and the careful façade will crumble. She is silent, keeping watch like a bird of prey.

A girl brings in a tray. There are sweets; the tea is in mugs shaped like water pots village women carry. The girl waits for me to pick one up. I glance at her. She nods her head in acknowledgment. There is acne on her skin, a gathering of boils on her upper cheek; they have a bluish-pink tint. She leaves the tray on the centre table and stands there. Nausheen asks her to go and bathe. She touches her oily hair and laughs. 'Haan, baaji. Chaar din se dhoya nahin hai (Yes, sister, I haven't washed it for four days).'

Ammaji, Nausheen and the girl, all victims and exploiters in their own way. All for a legitimacy that society never grants fully to anyone. As Ammaji said, 'Ayyashi tau sabke khoon mein hai, riyaasatdar kuchch shaukh zyaada farmaate hai (Debauchery runs in everyone's blood, but the gentry make more of a show of it).'

The feudals in the city get a fancy education not merely to frame a degree on their walls. They strive to gain respectability through means other than wealth and hope. Today, learning sanctifies their position and is as much a social asset as the legacy of decadence.

Imran Khan lost it by marrying a westerner. The vehemence expressed by certain Pakistani women about his double standards regarding choice of bride was surprising. They were in fact a part of this conspiracy of hypocrisy. His was apparent when he rediscovered Islam through the political route. He began to criticise the foppish sahibs after he had tasted their wine and other weaknesses for years.

When he married Jemima, whom he transformed into a chadar-covered Haiqa, he was offering Pakistani society a version of the people's princess. High society jumped on the Bentley wagon. And they found a precedent to hark back on, no matter that it was a flawed one, to prove that the compromises were superficial: they said Benazir Bhutto gave up her slacks when she came to Pakistan. One small detail escaped them and Imran: Bhutto was head of the government and her position depended on how well she toed the traditional line.

This was made into a clash of civilisations: 4,000 miles, 20 years and a few million euros do not always create a chasm. But Jemima was being exploited to buffer a stereotype propagated by her country's media. Together with her marriage licence, they handed her a baggage of fake superiority because of her money, her colour, her nationality, her age. They were worried that if she was caught with a glass of champagne she would be awarded 50 lashes.

Pakistan's erratic electricity, water supply and the rumour that her husband did not even have a washing machine became tabloid chatter. She had become Blonde Power. Under the onslaught of Pakistani accusations of her being a Zionist conspirator, she wrote passionately about the Palestinian cause. She campaigned with her husband in the heat and dust and spoke Urdu and a bit of Pashto. She lived with her in-laws and shared her bed with her kids.

Among certain sections, Imran was reaping the benefits of his wife's martyrdom at the madrassa altar. There were others who just would not accept that.

Israr, the guide, who was completely in awe of Sonia Gandhi 'because she adapted to local culture', had refused to even imagine Jemima in such a role. 'Let her live here for those many years and become a part of us. Just wearing Pakistani clothes is not enough; the change has to happen from within.'

What happens within a society too reveals glaring disparities. One needs permission to visit the prestigious Lahore American School. I am not sure if it is because of 9/11, my nationality or just the regular precautions most American institutions take, their xenophobia transferred to even the establishments run in other countries. Some might say this is justified as they become easy targets.

Next day I go through the screening at the entrance. Chairs are arranged in a circle for the class. This is the informal session; the students are not wearing uniforms. Most of them are in jeans and t-shirts. Casual clothes are permitted, including 'long shorts' for the boys. The instructions are clear: 'Culturally insensitive or provocative clothing, outlandish hairstyles, slippers, torn and faded jeans, gym clothes, bandanas and caps are not permitted.'

This group I am with would qualify as cool. Some address their tutor by his first name; others prefix a 'Mr'.

It is difficult to gauge intelligence in such a short period of time, but they are curious about India; not as Pakistanis usually are but as they would be about, say, Sierra Leone. I had expected them to be more enquiring. They don't seem diffident, so perhaps it is just ennui.

They are more interested in American politics. I would not venture to be judgmental about this particular group, but it is not tough to take a guess that since 65 per cent of the teaching staff is non-Pakistani, they are being schooled differently. I am quite certain they aim to go overseas for further education and already have dreams of 'making a difference' to Pakistani society, of which they have an outsider's perspective even while being inside.

On my way out, it seems like a scene from one of those urban Bollywood films. Kids dressed in designer clothes – Gap, Adidas, Nike – standing outside a kiosk within the campus that sells McDonald's fast food and colas.

Outside the gate, there is a traffic snarl. Cars are waiting to take these students home. It is clearly a place where the rich will learn how to become richer. This is Pakistan sheltered from itself, a purer race within the pure land.

I call up the office of *The Friday Times*. I am given Jugnu Mohsin's residence number. She is the publisher and wife of its well-known editor, Najam Sethi. I tell her I am somewhere in the vicinity and would like to stop by. She does not ask any questions and gives me directions.

I reach a bungalow; two guards stand near the gate. I tell the driver to make sure we are at the right place. He tells me,

'Yeh to kothi hai (This is a mansion).' I can see that. I ask for the lady. I am told she has not yet arrived but I may go in. An ageing man accompanies me inside. We pass wood-panelled walls; it seems like a rather elegant place. There is a large room; four young people, three women and a man, are sitting at computers at the two far ends. A large glass door takes me into another spacious room. The walls have book-lined shelves. A big table takes up much space. Near the door there are a couple of comfortable chairs. The man asks me to sit and offers tea. He looks like an old family retainer, someone one can trust one's secrets and life with. He shuffles out.

I hear the phone ring and then it stops. He comes in again and says the call is for me. It is Ms Mohsin. She will be a bit late because she was expecting someone and could not cancel the appointment. It gives me time to watch the backs of the journalists typing. They barely look up or at each other.

This appears like nothing close to a newspaper office. The phone rings again. The old man motions me to pick it up. It is Jugnu again informing me that she will be here in a short while and to please have tea. I tell her I shall wait.

She arrives, looking a bit hassled. We shake hands. Her hair is wet, the soft curls shining. She touches them and says, 'I seem to have a bad hair day!'

Her face is glowing and her rose-bud lips are painted a dark pink. She orders tea. Thin cucumber sandwiches made with organic bread are placed on the table along with pistachio biscuits. This could have been a scene out of the immensely popular 'Social Butterfly' column in their weekly. I was later told that *TFT* is in fact considered an elitist publication, a fate suffered by those who do not strive too hard to appear overly serious. If anything, it satirises the very sections of society that are deemed to be the powers behind the powerful. I tell her that it is a lovely space to work from.

'Najam had this kothi. It is an old one and we thought we would use it as an office.'

The Friday Times is of tabloid size and has an editorial on its front page. Najam Sethi may be rich, but his political views have got him into trouble. Jugnu did not want to go into details. She just said, 'It was sheer torture. In May 1999, the cops came to our place and arrested him. Since they had tied me up, I could not call anyone for help. Later, too, it was traumatic; for five days there was no information about him.'

This happened during Nawaz Sharif's government; the accusations touted ranged from tax evasion to Sethi being an Indian agent. Like all media, *The Friday Times* has been under pressure to promote the point of view of different governments; Benazir Bhutto tried it, so did Nawaz Sharif. And to make their intentions clear, government advertisements dried up. Today the publishing house has a daily newspaper as well, *The Daily Times*.

Israr reads all the newspapers. I met him again in a happy coincidence when I wanted to check about a few things at the Pakistan Tourism Development Corporation office. In the intervening years, he has lost most of his hair. On a whim, I decide to hop into the van for a half-day tour. We are the only ones. He is not supposed to be the guide; he has been promoted to an administrative post and is tired of the meetings. His wife has a new job; she teaches at a local school.

This time as we are about to enter the Lahore Fort, he tells me that I should not pay the foreigner's fee. 'You can pass off as a Pakistani.' The man at the counter is confused. I am more confident on this trip. He knows that asking me where I am from would be an affront if I turned out to be from another city. I see him arching his eyebrows as he looks at Israr; Israr nods assent. 'What did I tell you?'

We sit beneath the shade of a tree. There is small stall where I buy us soft drinks and some savouries. Israr looks satisfied that he helped me save money.

'Is it because after 9/11 you have other enemies to deal with?' I ask.

'This last time during their visit Indians seemed to love Lahore so much that we began to wonder whether they wanted it as much as they want Kashmir!'

He asks me what Indians think of Pakistanis. Before I can reply he says, 'They think we are illiterate oxen...I know the common man does not think so, but there are some hi-fi types who have this impression. There was a man who said on Zee TV, "Hum tau Pakistan ko choona lagaa kar kha jaayenge!" It only made us laugh. You look at the people around. You can see young couples. We are a normal society.'

There is a silent challenge in his voice. As in an internal monologue, he is also trying to convince himself.

4

The First Frontier

The mattress felt like a cloudburst thundering past my head as it fell to the wooden floor.

That memory is etched on my mind even though one week later the world's attention would be diverted to slogan-shouting mobs, mobs holding aloft pictures of a man with saintly eyes and lascivious lips. This was the man who would show up the clay feet of the god that moulded him. America was soon to discover the word terrorism.

At the departure lounge of Islamabad airport I spotted her amidst an assortment of beards. They had told me that Pakistani women rarely travel to Peshawar, and never alone. They told me I wouldn't see female eyes.

I could not see her eyes. They were covered with trendy sunglasses. She acknowledged me with a crimson-lipstick smile. Wearing a thick chadar over smart culottes and a body-hugging kameez, she made no attempt to hide her curves as she held on tight to her modest covering; the tightening emphasised the tautness.

The baby in her arms tapped her bosom like a knock on the door. Her husband, an Afghan, was an exporter of rugs. They lived in Islamabad while his family stayed in Peshawar.

After discovering I was Indian, she told me about the sarees she had got for her brother's wedding and how she was the only one who wore them. She did not ask me whether I was Hindu or Muslim; no one in Peshawar did. And as a contrast to her was this pretty woman, Nadia, half German, half Kashmiri. She was travelling on work to the northern parts of Chitral with a male colleague. It was she who expressed astonishment over my travelling alone. Her broadmindedness seemed superficial. 'How come you decided to visit Pakistan?' I compared her attitude with the openness of the other, whose husband was praying the namaaz at the airport, who bought me lemonade while we waited. Who was the liberal here?

The plane was a Fokker. All hand luggage had to be placed in the front. The line-up of totes, haversacks, briefcases, plastic bags looked like unclaimed baggage. We took off with a jerk. The plane swerved like a heaving boat in a stormy sea. I looked outside the window and the starkness of the invisible sky was a serene divergence.

Peshawar airport was tidy, as though preparing for a funeral. I walked at a brisk businesslike pace to avoid drawing attention. A bespectacled young man came towards me, 'Farzana sahiba?' I was guarded. Who could possibly know me here? The man introduced himself as Salim. I had called up the night before asking if there were rooms available at the Khan Klub. The manager had said that they had full occupancy, but he would help me out. I was surprised to discover that Bilal had sent Salim to ensure I would be taken care of. As he was to tell me later, 'I started thinking what you were all about, coming from India, alone, without any reservations. Did you even know what you were getting into?'

I would soon know. I was taken to a large but ordinary hotel, a modern structure that was deserted except for two men talking in whispers in the lobby. The receptionist took out the registry book and asked, 'Lahore se ya Karachi se (Are you from Lahore or Karachi)?' Fumbling in my bag for my passport, I found it difficult to utter the word 'foreigner' to someone who spoke my language and thought I was one of them. 'Indian,' I said. There was a long pause as he gauged me. He had a cagey look in his eyes as he ran his fingers over the light green pages. Getting impatient, I asked, 'Do you have problems with Indians?' I knew it was not the right thing to say.

'Nahin, aisi baat nahin (That isn't so)...' he stuttered. I insisted on checking the rooms. Escorted to the third floor, even before I could enter, I spotted a grill door with a money plant creeping through the mesh. On a placard, written in bold, were the words, 'Private Admission'. I told Salim that I felt uncomfortable here. A quick call and we were at my original choice.

I had read about Khan Klub in travel books. There was something beguiling and adventurous about it. Two centuries old, it used to be the residence of what seemed like an old feudal family. Although the façade was weather-beaten, the interiors had been done up to suit contemporary tastes and whims. There were eight suites, named after gemstones.

Bilal, young and clean-shaven with a thin film of surma in his eyes, welcomed me. I was too relieved to bother to ask how his stance the night before of 'No rooms available' had changed to 'Of course you will stay with us'. I was given the keys to the Topaz Suite. It was only when I reached the room did I realise I had not signed any register. Bilal came up and told me about the problems. 'Look, this place is owned by a Taliban man. I am taking a risk keeping you here. Don't tell anyone where you are from. I will sign you in as my friend. Don't talk to anyone. Order dinner in the room. I have to go out now, but will speak to you at night. And keep away from that owner, he hates Indians.'

The window was half open, its hinges broken. I put my head out. Down below there were a couple of battered cars. Right across was a building, much like the one I was in, except that it was painted blue interspersed with panels in lime green. On the ground floor a shop was stacked with white sacks. A donkey stood nodding its head waiting to carry the burden. The pungent smell of spices wafted up towards me. I craned my neck to see what was next door. Several shut windows formed a crooked line. It was like watching bogeys of a toy train as it curved along steep tracks.

There was an air of spookiness about the faded brick-coloured walls, as though a past inhabitant would saunter in through the flaking plaster. An empty ornate vase made of brass stood on the carved wooden mantelpiece. On a low table was a big black telephone, its obesity more anachronistic than its newness.

A few steps poised like a ladder took one up to the bedroom. The bed took up all the space; above the head-rest lay a few books. There were two windows opposite. With much anxiety, I opened them. They overlooked the corridor where a dim lampshade made of broken shards cast eerie sepia patterns.

I rushed down towards the washroom to splash my face and escape from unknown history. The mirror was a battered bronze that looked like a portrait waiting to be framed. The water closet, the basin, the shelf were all in wood brown. The shower area was divided by a stone wall. A window opened out into a corridor similar to the one above. Afraid of the sound of footsteps, I switched off the lights and squatted on the floor, pouring jugs of water over myself.

It was time for dinner. Animated voices could be heard over the strains of the rhubab. There was a hub in the restaurant; foreigners wearing loose-fitting pajamas were seated on cushions. One man sat alone in a corner reading a book. I found a place opposite the musician. My mind was still preoccupied with the creaking doors and floor of my room. So lost in thought was I that it did not register when the waiter asked me, 'Aap India se aayi hai, na (You are from India, aren't you)?' I had decided not to hide my identity. 'Ji haan!' I almost screamed. He was solicitous and even offered to get me some Chinese food in a restaurant known for its frontier cuisine. I wondered why.

Lonely and insecure, I turned my gaze towards a boisterous group from Belgium on my left. A dark greasy-looking man with crater-like cheeks grinned at me. He changed seats with one of his group members so that we could talk. 'Suna hai aap India se hai (Heard you are from India)?' I nodded.

'Tou halaat kaise hai wahaan par (So how is the situation there)?'

'Kaunse halaat (What situation)?' I wanted him to be specific, although I knew what he meant.

'Mussalmanon ke (Of Muslims).'

'What can be wrong with us?'

Feeling chastened, he quickly added, 'I only asked, one hears stories. Are they true?'

I was saved from revealing a truth he would not comprehend when a tall man with a pruned beard and starched clothes walked in. There was a whiff of lazy authority about him. He was the owner, who Bilal had asked me to guard against. As I was leaving for my room, he enquired if everything was okay. I requested him to make arrangements for a makeshift bed to be placed in the seating area of my room.

A little later, there was a polite knock on the door and he himself appeared with one of the housekeeping staff, who immediately went upstairs. That is when the mattress fell like a cloudburst, dust rising from the floor. While my bed was being made, Maqsood saab asked me in lilting, halting English, 'So you Indian?'

'Hasn't Bilal told you?'

'He is only my manager, be careful of him. So you live in India?'

'Yes, I live in Mumbai and am travelling alone. I am accustomed to it.'

'Good, good. Just be careful of some of these fellows. I am an Afghan, I understand what you are saying, the others won't.'

At night Bilal called. 'Everything okay?' I was angry. Everyone knew I was Indian, so why had he told me to keep it a secret? 'These are my men,' he said. 'They are not the Taliban.' Did he expect Mullah Omar to pay me a surprise visit? 'Maqsood and all are no less.' I told him that he had come to my room and had a short conversation.

'Why did he come?'

'To make my bed...'

'That is not his job...he is a bad man. Why did you tell him you are Indian? He is not even the owner, he has taken this place on lease.'

Bilal's transparency was mystifying. In the course of such a short visit he was to propose to me, unmindful of my being older, demand the identity of the man who called me from Islamabad, ask to come over to my room late at night. He sounded slimy but, absurdly, I began to feel sorry for him. I had got talking next morning with Isabella, a Polish woman I met there. She worked in Tajikistan. I asked her whether Bilal had made any overtures towards her.

'No, never. Maybe he is curious about you.'

Within this limited context, I was trying to figure him out. He said he was made for love, he would never agree to an arranged match. 'Salim is engaged,' he told me, 'so he can have fun with his fiancée whenever he wants. I am lonely. There are no women around with whom I can talk romance. I want to be able to give gifts, go out.'

He would never be comfortable with a western woman; he would assume she had an immoral past. His liberal mind was seeking an evanescent sublimity even while desiring clandestine temporal pleasures. It made him so desperate that he was willing to send a car for me to return to Peshawar again after my next halt. 'We can then be together.' I was shocked. Wasn't he afraid of what people would say? Did he not think that his proposition could be offensive?

'I like you, what is cheap about it? And I don't care about people. But your heart is made of stone. Mera dil tau maum hai (My heart melts easily).'

Although it was not prudent to engage Salim in any such conversation, my being on edge all the time because of the calls to the room or the knocks on the door made me ask him later what the problem was. Was Bilal just acting, trying to test an Indian woman's reaction? 'No. He did tell me that you were not paying him any attention. The reality is that he is stubborn and wants to do things his way. His family is in the village which is not too far, but he rarely visits. He prefers to live by himself, sometimes sleeps at the hotel and also acts in serials at the local TV station. There is this thirst for achieving too many things and because he is educated and exposed to the glamour world a bit, he feels he deserves better.'

Next day, we worked out a schedule. Bilal vetoed the idea of my visiting the Khyber Pass. A Political Agent of the Khyber, a relic of the 19th century system where the British and the Pakhtoons had exchanged treaties, gives out tourist passes. Why? He was irritable. 'You ask too many questions. I am taking a risk.' I did not want a stranger to take a risk and, worse, not let me do what I wanted. He sulked, 'Do as you please.'

The romance of the Khyber Pass is such that it is a must on any itinerary. The permit is mandatory even for Pakistanis because it comes under the purview of the Khyber Agency. Spread over an area of 991 square miles, it is a bit like a corporation run by the Afridi tribes.

Khyber gets its name from a battle that took place in Madinia Munawwarah where the Prophet's son-in-law Hazrat Ali fought to victory. Legend has it that the marks of a hand on a huge boulder are those of Hazrat Ali, who it is said also prayed there. The Ali Masjid was built in his memory.

The Khyber Pass has been an invitation for conquest and hospitality. The Aryans, Persians, Greeks, Mongols, Huns, Scythians, Parthians, the Mughals and the Afghans, every invader and immigrant to the subcontinent has had to traverse through this stretch. The footprints have dug deep trenches in the mental terrain as well. No government can rule here. It is tribal law that prevails, a law that accepts a good fight as much as an honourable settlement.

Most westerners go to the Pass and ask for demonstration firings and take pictures of men with guns. Despite being aware of the superficiality of armed escorts accompanying visitors in a jeep for what seemed like the adventure of a safari rather than the Wild Frontier, I could not resist the urge to tread on the rugged soil.

I told Salim I wanted to get a permit. When we were far from the hotel he said that I was being watched. The cops had come to check and he thought they would follow us. 'Routine,' he assured me. But I was not registered in the hotel records, so how would they know? 'Remember that hotel we went to first? You did not like it there, so the manager must have informed them.'

If this was the case, then going to a government office would probably make my remaining days in Pakistan too visible. I told him to take me to an Afghan refugee village instead. Being from a city with the largest slum in Asia, with squatters all over the place, the idea should not have been all that intriguing. While Salim was genuinely concerned about the fate of the Afghan immigrants, I was looking at their houses. Mud constructions, almost like mini fortresses, spread across the unpaved road. A canal ran along the stretch and wooden planks served as bridges. Small gaps in the lanes led to the entrances.

Groups of men stood around gossiping, their rugged faces breaking into spontaneous smiles. Cattle and sheep were being taken out to graze on dry grass. Children with soot on their bodies were preparing for a bath in the canal. Some boys were playing cricket. A wall proudly declared 'For quality education' as the ball aimed high at the afternoon sky. A board with an arrow pointed towards 'Oxford Public School'. At the other end was a cemetery. Little green pennants with gold and silver tassels were flying listlessly in the summer breeze. These were flags on the graves of shaheeds (martyrs) of the Afghan War.

Just a few feet away, young girls in colourful clothes were making dung cakes; some sat embroidering large pieces of cloth spread on the ground. It could have been any village, except that even in the playfulness of the children one could sense a certain desolation.

Salim's house had a large blue gate. He rang the doorbell and a small slat was opened. Clothes were drying. Large water tanks took up most of the front space. A pretty young girl, his sister, peeped out. Inside the houses, women only cover their heads with a dupatta; they are not concealed behind a burqa. An elderly relative brought it out for me and demonstrated how it was worn, laughing at the ridiculousness of it all. This is what amazed me — she found it funny.

There were three young girls in the house. Fahima was to be married soon. Ali, the brother, was lounging on a coir cot when I entered the room; he said he would miss his sister. She had not met her husband-to-be. Wasn't she worried? Did she have no expectations? She giggled, which is when Ali intervened and said, 'A girl has it better than us. In the street, if there is an older woman with her who has seen the boy, then he is pointed out, so even through the burqa she can see what he looks like. We men are not so lucky.'

Ali was tall and well-built, his features chiselled to near-perfection. What was life like for the young men? 'If we don't want to get into any trouble, we just stay at home, there is nothing much to do outside and if we hang around too much people start calling us names. I just lie on this cot all day.'

Was he not frustrated? 'Of course, I am. I will ensure that my children have a different future. But we cannot change things as they are. We have been brought up this way. With all your education, can you go to the Khyber Pass? It makes me angry that those foreigners, the whites, can go, but you who are more like us cannot. There will be so many questions asked.' He requested his brother to take me there and to say that I was a cousin from Karachi or Lahore. 'Those women are not much different. They dress like you.'

The room had a television set, a music system, and fine crockery; they were a comfortably-placed family. There was a basement to keep them cool in summer and warm in winter. I was allowed to take pictures. The father had even granted his daughters permission to have their photographs taken, but they were too shy. Endless cups of green tea, like mossy liquid, were served. There was no chariness that Salim and Ali were chatting so openly with me, sitting cross-legged on a cot. Both the brothers liked their free-spirited young aunt, Naheeda.

We went to her house a few doors away. The chachi truly turned out to be quite an unusual creature. She had been educated in Islamabad. How did it feel to move to Peshawar? Was there a cultural difference? She spoke with a remarkable degree of confidence. 'Initially, I could not understand some things, but now it is better. I do not wear a burqa even when I go out, so people have become used to it now and they don't care. I also insisted on planning my family, or else in these seven years I would have six kids...now I have three. People here like to have children around the house.'

She smiled indulgently as a naked little one, the youngest, kept jumping on the bed. We sat in a small, dark, unkempt room. There were some Afghani rotis and curry in an aluminium bowl on a table; the older children would occasionally tear large chunks of the bread and dunk them in the gravy, holding the rag-like bits over their open mouths as the liquid left trails of speckled brown on their chins. Naheeda shooed them away.

She had not let childbirth and housework mar her looks, although some chubbiness had settled on her cheeks and chin. Her head was uncovered and her black hair was tied in a loose braid. 'I want to work too, but I get no time. The schools are far, so I have to drop the children there. Women rule in the house. If I were under any restrictions, do you think I could talk to you in privacy? My husband is there praying, he could have stopped me.' Just then he called out to her. She returned within minutes. 'He has asked me not to let you leave without having lunch with us. He has to remind me to be a good hostess, I just talk so much that I forget basic manners.' And what happened to the education she had acquired? 'In future I don't know, but for now my children will benefit. And it shows in the way I conduct my life. No one can boss over me.' While her husband and mother-in-law were busy with their afternoon prayers, she did not feel it necessary to join them.

I had to leave. 'If you cannot eat with us now, come later. Check out of the hotel, stay with us, it is safer here. There people will wonder. Here we can protect you.' I felt truly humbled by such a spirit of acceptance.

We were hungry. I told Salim I wanted to eat at an authentic Kabuli restaurant. Breads were being baked on upturned woks. The place was packed. I was the only woman in there. A scraggly-looking man came up to us and parted a curtain; the few men having their meal immediately got up and moved out without a word. Chivalry was unspoken and not brandished with a flourish.

The sofa felt wonderfully comfortable after the long drive. The moment I raised my eyes I found Ajay Devgan staring at me. Stuck on the wall, his photograph typified the Afghan obsession with Hindi films.

We had a hearty meal. There was a stew, some barbequed meats and sautéed vegetables. The food did not leave you feeling full, cooked as it was with a touch so light that even flesh had a feathery texture. Bowls of yoghurt served as dessert.

Driving back to the city, we passed another route. This was Hayatabad; it was called the mini Islamabad due to its well-structured houses, trees peeping out of high walls, bursts of floral colour in the balconies. The inhabitants were invisible. Who were they? Salim explained, 'Mainly Afghans, the ones who have made it big. But they can only rent the houses, not buy them. There are two million Afghan mohajirs here, so they say Peshawar should be theirs.' But what about the guns and drugs? 'The problem is that Pakistani laws do not extend beyond Torkham, so our government can do nothing. If they commit a crime, our rules do not apply.' Yet there is sympathy for them in many quarters. 'Our hearts are with them, though our minds may not be.'

It was difficult to understand how the Pathan heart could

even fathom a jihad against the Russians – was it an Islamic jihad they were supporting or an American one? Salim sounded genuinely concerned: 'The Afghans do not have it easy. They have to work hard to make money. They may be a burden for the rest of Pakistan but not for the Pathans.'

Next day I promised myself I would explore the question that had been left unanswered.

When you enter the smuggler's market in Bara – the other being Jamrud – it is not glitzy. Alleys lead to pale buildings greying at the edges; flies squat on plump fruits in so relaxed a fashion it might seem as though a durbar was being held to squeeze out every drop of juice. 'You get everything here, except maybe cars', said Salim. When we arrived, it was fairly early in the morning, people were still getting their shops ready. Some were fanning the dhuan (thick incense sticks and coal pieces burning in a small copper pot) to ward off evil, even as under the table there might have been some devious items they would sell.

Cheap and fake cosmetics are available together with branded ones. You are not supposed to know the difference. I picked up a bottle of Issey Miyake and asked for a tester. The salesman became tetchy. 'Aapko khushboo se matlab, achha hai tau bas (You should be concerned only with the fragrance, nothing else).' At one-tenth the price of the original, he was certainly right.

There were carts outside with Korean toys, Japanese gizmos, sweets, green tea, spices, but it was essentially a cover-up. The real stuff was what could not be seen. I tried to understand the gun culture. Was it so easy to get arms? Apparently, it was. If the Pakhtoons have benefited, it is by getting weapons, corroded rifles left by the Russians. Interestingly, the Afghans want to appear more respectable and are preoccupied with beautifying their homes and fitting them with the latest amenities.

The mujahideen, as they came to be called assuming they were 'holy warriors', were above the law. Primarily because they came in handy for Pakistan's Inter Services Intelligence, the ISI, that trained and armed them. It must be remembered that the country had to deal with a huge refugee problem after the Afghan War. Most of those who crossed the border chose to stay in the frontier regions even after the war was over. And this was seen as an ideal give-and-take deal. Besides, the drug trade of the Afghans is diverted via Pakistan, so again there is a mutual need. There are several contradictions. While Pakistan has to keep an eye on the Pathans in its armed forces, it got caught in the Afghan problem. Salim mentioned how some youngsters would go back home to avenge the death of a family member or a rape or the destruction of property and return to Peshawar to work and make money, often to sponsor another vendetta. It is said in these parts that every Afghan is a mujahid.

Salim's family is an old one, where things like education matter. There are others who have homes in Peshawar but choose to live in the more mainstream cities.

This is in sharp contrast to the widely-travelled and suave Waquar's brother who retains the Pakhtoon stamp, choosing to live in the village. In a sense, the tribal identity was a cocoon against a communist Afghan regime next door. For the Pathans, military rule in the rest of Pakistan does not count; they feel they are on a cusp.

We enter the university town with its neat avenues. The red brick façade of the 70-year-old Islamia University is awe-inspiring. Water fountains and perfectly-lined trees, like obedient students, dot the landscape. Salim is doing his postgraduate studies here. He looks like a nerd. A small, built-like-a-boy Pathan, he wears steel-rimmed glasses. What would education mean to him in the given context? 'It is a personal choice. This car too is mine, it does not belong to the hotel. I work as a tourist guide because that too is knowledge for me. I try to speak in English to improve mine. And this broadens my world. I don't want to go out and earn big money, but I want to be equipped to improve things here. I will marry the girl chosen by my parents and it will be early, but it will also give me a sense of security.'

He takes me to a bookshop where there are volumes of Osama Bin Laden's biography. This was pre 9/11, so that is the only place I saw his face. I picked up a copy and was riffling through it when the shopkeeper came up to me and said, 'It is okay only if you are interested in the man. Otherwise it is useless.' This was in the heart of Pathan territory, which was to later display complete loyalty to this man. I was told instead to look for books by Khushal Khan Khattak. He and Khan Abdul Ghaffar Khan are the true representatives of Pathan culture, Salim tells me. One is at the traffic signal, a statue in bronze, the view impeded by a lamp-post, the other 'not available'.

Khattak, a 17th century poet, was also a warrior. His verses resonate with the convergence of mortality and resurgence:

The nature of the world, you see
Is like a raging elephant

But when one mahout loses his life
Another always mounts its back.

His deification is easy to understand.

The Khan Abdul Ghaffar Khan factor is more complex. In India he is remembered as Frontier Gandhi. How did a man who founded the Khudai Khidmatgars, in the spirit of a Sufi asking men to serve god to quell the religious fundamentalism that was becoming politics, fit in here?

He did not. His politics was probably as divisive as that of many other mainstream leaders. 'God's servants' tried to emulate communism and brought the Afghans in. For him, Partition was not about India and Pakistan, but 'Pashtoonistan'. His eldest son Wali Khan had once said, 'We have been Pathans for 3,000 years, Muslims for 1,000 and Pakistanis for 40.'

Until almost a decade after Partition, Peshawar remained a fortress enclosed behind sturdy walls and 16 gates. The Afghan War, ironically, made 'Pashtoonistan' a forgotten dream recalled only when Ghaffar Khan died, having left instructions to be buried in Jalalabad, not Peshawar.

Salim does not know that a map had been drawn, flags been designed for this separate state. But even to an outsider, he introduces himself as a Pathan, not a Pakistani.

We pass the much talked about gaudily decorated rickshaws. The rough terrain transforms into what seems like an outlandish performance as one watches burly men driving these effeminate-looking vehicles.

But then the origin of the word Peshawar itself lacks pugnacity. It derives its name from the Sanskrit 'Pushpapura', the city of flowers. Prominent is the scent of poppy in its most potent form. Walking through the bazaars, fragrant smoke curls in statuesque poses, much like the antiques in the stores.

The Qissa Khawani Bazaar is no more a storyteller's paradise. Like the Khyber and Meena bazaars, it markets a made-to-order past that has been carefully rusted in the corners of freshly carved curios. It does not matter how old they are; they seem to speak of a more genteel life of music, wine and a relaxed lifestyle. Embellished decanters, small models of musical instruments, a striking drum and rhubab painted a candyfloss pink tied with a plastic string, hookahs, bookstands, jars, a whole menagerie in burnished copper...there is little place for religious symbols.

Ready-to-wear garments with intricate embroidery are surprisingly cheap. In the main market, none of the women are wearing veils, let alone the regular 'shuttle-cock' burqa, the derisive appellation that derives from the mesh through which they can see the world. This is their territory, and obedient fathers, husbands, sons carry the parcels as women haggle aggressively. I see no sign of passive womanhood here. Perhaps the intellectual and emotional subjugation makes them spill forth in a cathartic verbal fusillade in the marketplace where they rule. They buy henna cones in non-traditional colours like magenta, gold, electric blue. Many are trying out high-heeled shoes embossed with fake crystal.

We leave the noise and reach the Mohabat Khan mosque; it seems forsaken. A lone figure is praying while several bodies are lying in deep slumber on the cold mosaic tiles. The only religious relic of the Mughals in Peshawar, it is all filigree and calligraphy. A young lad has followed us to the terrace from where the expanse of the city can be seen. The ivory of the mosque looks out on the stillness outside – of baked mud buildings and sandy roads. 'Fire coming,' he says, explaining the fire that partly destroyed the mosque over a century ago. He speaks in English with a Pashto-American accent.

He is not a guide. His agenda is to direct us to his uncle's shop midway down the steps. I ask him whether he is happy chasing foreigners. He laughs, 'They buy anything, and think it is antique.' I walk towards the store. A quick look reveals mostly Buddha figurines. I am struck by the contrasts of an idol being created in the environs, though not the sanctum, of a mosque and a lusty Pathan chiselling an image of calm and austerity.

Buddhism is no stranger to Peshawar, though. There is a Stupa and the school of Gandhara art thrived here.

The destruction of the Bamiyan Buddhas by the Taliban was not a major topic of discussion. The West had raised its voice against it to score points. The Taliban were about power, not religion. Despite it being a repressive regime, it stolidly stuck to its principles, refusing to toe the line drawn by the West or cater to tourists. Like in all revolutions, the Taliban had decided to efface what did not suit its ideology.

Besides, there was no Buddhist population whose sentiments they were trampling upon, something that Hindutva proponents in India, who had jumped on the ideology gravy cart with a comparison to the fall of the Babri Masjid, ought to know.

Next morning, I am ready to leave. When I go down to make my payment, Bilal tells me, 'You don't have to, after all your name is nowhere on our register.' I insist. He blinks away the tears.

Salim drives me to the airport. We are quiet. He asks me if

I had met Daniel. 'He is an American journalist. He is waiting for a visa to go to Kabul. He is so frustrated and upset. He had come with hopes, but God knows when he will manage. Did you not speak to him?'

'Who was he?'

'That tall guy at your hotel.'

When I was paying Bilal, I had heard a voice say, 'Nice bracelet.'

'Thank you,' I responded a bit too late. When I turned, I could only see his receding back. He was the one who used to sit alone and read a book in the dim light. I did not know this Daniel. I did not know which Daniel he was.

Salim loads the luggage on the trolley. Time for another parting. He says, 'It is rare to meet Indians, and your being a woman travelling here alone, I feel so proud that I could show you around.' We again start on the subcontinental version of hospitality. He reluctantly takes the money, and gives me his cellphone number. 'When you are in Pakistan and need anything, please call me.'

That moment came three years later.

The car was a red Corolla. Ismail, the driver, was a large man in a starched Pathan suit. He ran his hand over his beard as he surveyed my bags. This time it was to be a road journey. We had left Rawalpindi around 3 p.m.

On the dashboard there was a tiny DVD player; the monitor flickered as large breasts loomed and took up most of the screen space. Then a male face became visible, the head covered with a loosely tied turban, one end left hanging down the shoulder. He was telling the girl something. She had a startled but inviting expression in her eyes. I could not understand the words, but this seemed like a prelude to wild lovemaking. It was to be my first and last glimpse of a Pashto film.

It wasn't at all surprising to see such generosity in demeanour and deed, for cinema expresses subconscious needs. The audience, all male, sit in darkened auditoria only to affirm that their fantasies are right. As I discovered, the Pathan is not afraid to express love or lust. That is the reason the fight for honour is often centred on women.

Ismail stared at me through the rear-view mirror. Seeing that the film had only momentary appeal for me, he switched to another DVD. Shahrukh Khan was cavorting in the mustard fields with Kajol. This was a song from the Hindi film, *Dilwaale Dulhaniya Le Jaayenge*.

I looked out of the window at the fawn-coloured landscape. The Bala Hissar Fort stretched with aloof disdain. Babar, the Mughal emperor, had built it in the 16th century. It somehow did not look incongruous even from a flashy red car on a road tarred to sleek perfection.

Ismail's eyes were riveted to the screen. He did not speak much. Did he understand what was going on? The language was comprehensible but what about the social and romantic dynamics of such films? These might be as difficult for him to fathom as any Hollywood production. I tried to put my question more simply: did he enjoy these films? His nod was non-committal. Just at that moment Shahrukh Khan was feeding the birds in an attempt to impress the father of the girl he loved. Ismail laughed. I thought he must be finding it a rather inane thing for a hero to do.

'Do you like that?' I asked.

'Woh Pathan (he is a Pathan)' he said by way of explanation. 'Dhalhip Khumar bhi Pathan (Dilip Kumar — a veteran Indian actor — is also a Pathan).'

Since we seemed to have made inroads into Pathan parochialism, I wanted to know about Imran Khan, who occasionally took to wearing tribal dress in the manner of a schoolboy participating in a fancy dress contest.

'Imran Khan Lahore mein,' said Ismail, informing me about his location.

That staccato sentence sealed the fate of the cricketer-politician at least in this part of the world. The Pathan seemed more accepting of one of his own in a distant land who claimed no allegiance rather than someone who belonged but had lost touch with the soil.

We reached as afternoon was giving way to dusk, a pink pall making the city blush. Peshawar seemed to be ready to welcome me again. I did not understand the reservations people had the first time I had decided to make the trip and I did not understand them now. The comment, 'Our women don't go there and we don't even take them as a family' kept replaying in my mind.

What were the fears of the urban-dweller from the plains? He saw the Pathan not as a rustic but as someone who had infiltrated the cities and brought with him a subversive and violent culture. Even the lowly guard knew the power he had due to the weapon in his hand.

On my last visit, the security man at Khan Klub was said to be a Taliban supporter. As I was setting out for the day, Bilal had stopped me, 'Wait!' and then with a flourish held one end of my dupatta and asked me to cover my head. He was playing out the parody in full view of the one being satirised.

The First Frontier

When I had wanted to tip the guard as a goodbye gift, he refused to accept it. I thought I had offended Pathan pride. Later it transpired that he disapproved of me. Salim enlightened me, 'He knew you were a Muslim from India and thought you would be like us, but with Bilal's act of holding your dupatta he saw you differently.' In his mind I had transformed into a western clone.

Bilal had since then moved to his village. No one knew anything about him. His arrogance and flamboyance would not have let him reveal that he had copped out. He did not have money or a strong identification with the tribe. While he sought one, he tried hard to shun the other. He probably took his isolation along with him, a fragment of the imaginary land he inhabited.

This time I could not stay at the Khan Klub, it had been shut down for a while. I was taken to a guest house with a British name. It was owned by an overly genial Pathan. The room was large with pallid doors and cupboards. The floor had not been swept in days. Sprawled near the bed was a raggedy rug, its blood red having congealed with dust and shoe-marks of guests from a while ago. Not too many visitors recently. No drama here, I thought to myself.

I walked out to the small garden, a patch of wilting green. Jamal Khan, the owner, joined me. He had heavily-armed guards manning the emaciated gate.

'Why is Peshawar so guarded?' I wanted to know.

'It is self-defence.'

This astonished me. His explanation was most fascinating. 'You see, Pathans have this culture where you must avenge anyone who harms someone close to you, even if the person is a guest. So if one Pathan knows that the other is well-equipped, he will desist from harming you in any way. It is a social necessity.'

I tell him about the quote I had read that said if a Pathan makes a mistake, he is stuck with it forever. He agrees. And how do they take revenge? 'The jirgas call a meeting.' The jirga is a hastily-assembled village court.

'Who is the chief?'

His face crinkled with amusement. 'There are Maliks but they are not the only people in charge. Even I can take part in a jirga.'

Malik is a prized title and nothing more. It boosts the vanity of the landed gentry to have a say in the affairs of their tribe. This has also given legitimacy to those with new money who have become prominent in public life. Most political demonstrations are organised by them, and the only way they can keep the reins of power in their hands is not by modernising but by appealing to tradition, which they themselves lack.

While the Pakistani army has had to curb the overworked testosterone levels of the Pathans, it was the democratic regime of Zulfiqar Ali Bhutto that left behind the debris of a capitalist miasma.

He is largely responsible for the Pathan support of Communism, for he could not identify with such ideological dissent that was taking place in the tribal belts. In the 1970s, Wali Khan, who had political control of the North West Frontier Province, resigned in protest against the repression that the Pakistan People's Party was indulging in.

While American arms and support were coming to the rest of the country, the Frontier was playing with rusting Russian guns. This made its fight all the more poignant. The Afghan-Pathan combination was lethal in its potential for martyrdom. The Pakistani establishment had to start playing games long before the United Sates officially attacked Afghanistan to find a cave-dweller.

Kalashnikov is perhaps the only Russian word people in this region know. It is loaded with nostalgia and remains a symbol of vengeance. Vendetta is more a psychological state that can explode into reality at the slightest provocation.

'Revenge is allowed?' I prodded Jamal Khan.

'Not only allowed, it is important for our honour. We are an accepting people. Anyone can live with us, but there has to be mutual respect and trust. If we are stabbed in the back, we turn around and shoot. At least, we are expected to. Most of us would prefer a non-violent settlement.'

Pakistan has decided to keep the Federally Administered Tribal Areas (FATA) from any progressive reforms. Under the Frontier Crime Regulation, even the jirga's verdict is not binding. The Political Agent can slash it and the final decision is taken by the President of the country. They have no recourse to the regular laws of the land and in a practice reminiscent of the dark ages the family members of the guilty are often punished together with the convicted person.

The Army does not hesitate to attack madrassas. The mullahs don't play any role in the jirgas.

What about jihad for the ordinary Pathan? Jamal Khan threw up his hands in the air. It could have been a dismissive gesture to convey that it either meant nothing or it was all in the domain of God.

The God I had found less evident the last time had become more visible. The Taliban regime in Afghanistan had been decimated. This was America's gift; Islamophobia was forcing people to look for roots. Religion under the Taliban was about morality; now it was a question of identity.

On this visit too I expressed a desire to go to the Khyber Pass. Salim shook his head. 'It won't work out, you are wasting your time.' I had time. We arrived at the Home Department. The offices had not yet opened. Instead of going elsewhere, I insisted we wait outside. The security guards arranged their faces into impassive barricades.

After almost an hour, we went to meet the man in charge of issuing permits. He took out a slip book. Salim looked surprised.

'Identity card?' he asked me. He was a portly fellow whose belly rose upto his ribs and folded over the desk as he extended his hand to take my details.

My identity card was blue: my passport. He did not touch it. He merely read the words: The Republic of India.

'Yeh nahin ho sakta (Not possible).'

'But why? Look at the visas; I have visited before, your High Commission even stamped "Exempted from police reporting"....'

'Muaf kar do, Indian log ko permit nahin dete (I am sorry, but Indians are not given permits)...'

Salim said I was a Muslim.

'Fark nahin padhta (That does not make a difference).'

I was in a defiant mood. 9/11 had happened. The Americans had demolished civilian property and lives in Afghanistan. Pakistan was held to ransom. But westerners could still visit the Khyber Pass.

'Yeh kuchch aapko ajeeb nahin lagta (Don't you find this strange)?' I asked him.

'I am only a small person here,' he said. 'Aap hamare mehmaan hai, khushi se chai pilayenge, lekin pass nahin de sakte (You are our guest; we will be happy to offer you tea but not a pass).'

I got up from the chair but not before telling him, 'Chai tau hamare mulk mein bhi pi lete hai (I can drink tea in my country too).'

We drove in silence towards Chowk Yadgaar, the central square and arena of many a political rally. More than any other place, it was here that Osama was heralded as a world hero.

Like all heroes he had become an ossified poster on greasy walls, the seasons having wrought havoc on his visage as scratches ran across his cheeks like wrinkles on skin.

He had grown old in the somnolent air.

We decided to take a round of the residences in Mohalla Sethian. I was told the houses are ornately decorated with mirrors and carvings. One could see evidence of it in the balconies that looked like aging courtesans, decaying but still coquettish.

These were the homes of the old business community. It could have been a scene out of Satyajit Ray's *Jalsaghar*, the music room. The debauchery lay not in the doing, but the intent.

Salim invited me home again to his village. Keen to see the changes, I readily accepted.

On the way, children came running towards us, more confident than they were the last time; many were girls. Their hair had baked and browned in the sun. They went to school. As we passed the same roads, I read out the names, 'The Ockenden Venture Jahad Primary School', 'GTZ Befare Basic Education for Afghan Refugees, Primary school No. 153, Camp no. 2, Kabarian'.

The teacher inside was young. There were no classes to take, but she had stayed back to complete some work. 'Al Jehad' was written in English on a cardboard pinned to the wall. Is that all that is taught here?

'No, I teach mathematics. Other subjects are there too, but the children have to help with housework, so they are not regular.'

'And why this al jehad?' I prodded.

'Just another term,' she shrugged. And then added, 'Isn't the Quran also about knowledge?'

One boy took me to a small shop where he worked. He opened a glass jar, put his hand in and brought out a toffee for me. I bought some. We sat there, a group of children and us, sucking on sweets. My mind wandered to the shuddering thought of their faces one day being trapped in posters.

We left them reluctantly to reach Salim's house. I was greeted warmly by his mother. Two young women I had not met before came out. Both Salim and Ali were now married. Salim was the father of a two-year-old boy. Their quarters were on the first floor. These had been constructed to give them privacy and more space. They shared a common bathroom, but their rooms were different. Salim's wife had brought along silver-plated jugs and plates; they adorned a glass showcase. The bed had a red velvet spread over it. A sofa and chair upholstered in suede were against the other wall. Ali's room had glass crockery and a printed bedsheet.

These were gifts the wives had got from their parents. Salim's mother assured me that if it reflected any disparity, it was more to do with how the girls' families wanted them to live. Below, the hierarchy ceased to exist. The younger daughter-in-law was openly curious. She asked me about India, the big cities, people, and films. Salim's wife stood silently. Being older and richer was her psychological advantage.

Ali, who used to spend his time lying on the cot dreaming about change, had found an educated partner. But the revolution in his mind had called for a ceasefire. He had become reserved. The earlier intensity in his eyes that I remembered so well had dimmed.

'How is your aunt Naheeda?' I asked about the woman he had admired so much for her rebellious spirit.

'She wears a burqa now,' he stated without emotion.

She wasn't there, so we could not meet. I wanted to know more about her. Ali was a reluctant raconteur. Unlike earlier, he did not sit with us. We were in the same room I had sat in three years ago. The coir cot now had foam mattresses. The glass-fronted shelf housed a model of the globe, two cups and saucers, a showpiece that arched towards an egg-shaped bowl. Perched on it, rather incongruously, was a pair of Ray Ban glasses.

I did not find any religious motifs. Salim's mother volunteered the information I was seeking. 'We keep those inside.' She turned her hand upwards and then touched her heart. Her God lay within.

Our non-verbal communication interspersed with monosyllables conveyed much more than sentences would.

Naheeda continued to intrigue me in her absence. I asked Salim about her. 'She gives tuitions to the children in the neighbourhood.' Nothing could stop her and nothing did. The veil was just another garment, I reasoned.

They called up their sister Fahima. I was touched that she dropped everything to come and meet me, if only for a few minutes. I saw her enter through the same gate she had opened for me the last time. She was wearing a burqa that she removed at the doorway. We embraced like long-lost sisters. She seemed to have found happiness.

She asked me to hold her baby, barely a few months old. I took out some money, folding the note to fit into the child's tiny palm. At that moment India, Pakistan, Pathan, Muslim, Hindu all were forgotten as a soft innocent balled fist closed in on a common tradition. The little fingers curled over mine.

Section B
Inside Outside

5

The Kafir Mussalman and the Confused Muslim

Shujaat Rizvi was travelling on a fake passport. 'Not fake, just a second one,' he said. We had met in Sri Lanka, he was a Pakistani. The sand beneath our feet was warm and the water felt icy as a contrast.

We were about contrasts. He wore full-length trousers as he walked at the edge of the shore. I returned to the deck chair and watched as the sun reflected on the swollen waves. His receding back was a silhouette as the wind made his shirt cling to him. On his way back, he stopped to talk to me. The first thing he said was, 'Do you need to show your legs to watch the sea?'

'I am not showing my legs, you are seeing them. And Islam asks men to lower their gaze...'

'This is not about Islam. Look at those men...' he pointed towards some labourers who were sitting at a distance.

'They are quite accustomed to seeing women in beach clothes,' I explained.

'But you are not one of those women, you are Indian, you are Muslim.'

For perhaps the first time, my legs got a national and religious identity. These were Indian legs, Muslim legs.

I wanted to walk away. He stopped me. 'I guess it is your life, maybe you people don't mind all this.'

Social approval mattered to him, but what was his contraband passport about then? Were values limited to clothes and behaviour and not about ethics?

'The only country I can travel to is China,' he said dryly. And then he asked if I'd visit Pakistan.

He was attractive in a roguish sort of way. His moustache covered his upper lip completely so that when he spoke it appeared to be a sneer. He was very dark and a thin scar ran down one cheek like an exclamation mark.

The day I landed in Islamabad, he decided to take me for dinner.

We reached an Italian restaurant and headed towards its *alfresco* section. Most of the diners were foreigners, perhaps from the diplomatic corps. Champagne flutes glowed on the checked table cloth.

It was a nice place but the mosquitoes were bothering me, so we went in. There were no guests inside. We sat across from each other, a flickering candle between us. It was a mellow moment. 'Would you have ever married a Pakistani?' he asked.

'Never thought about it, but perhaps...'

'It is easy to get you a Pakistani passport and even an ID card. All that can be arranged.'

'I said I did not mind marrying a Pakistani, I did not say I would live in Pakistan.'

'This is a better place. You can walk with your head held high. You don't have to suffer during communal riots. This is an Islamic country. There is no pretence.'

The Kafir Mussalman and the Confused Muslim 133

He was curious about Muslim women in India. When I told him about relative freedom of movement, at least among the urban, educated woman, and cross-religious alliances, he flared up. 'I have no hatred against anyone but if they would try to act smart I would wish them to be burnt alive. I do not think Indian Muslims can get equal status by marrying their women to Hindu men. It is nauseating to even imagine about all those stinking Hindu rats they would be sleeping with.'

He could not understand that relationships were not based on religion. 'With such westernised and modern views, do not tell me that the man would say Islamic prayers before, after and during their intimate moments.'

He hit me at a vulnerable time. I was getting divorced from my Hindu husband. I had not converted. The timing of both my marriage and divorce were tied up with decisive happenings in my country – the Bombay riots and the Gujarat riots. Much as Shujaat's words hurt, I was battling with the identity question. In India there had been a religious resurgence, starting with the demolition of the Babri Masjid. The riots that followed were hell for me. I had been visiting the affected areas, seen smoke billowing out of markets and homes. In shanties, the police had climbed roofs and started shooting. I was shown bullets in the walls, holes in bodies stinking of clotted blood because they were afraid to go to the doctor. The women had come out in the streets and fallen at the feet of the cops.

For the first time, I was scared of something. I was afraid of the light as it curled up into balls of fire, as sparklers singed the unsuspecting skies. And the sounds in the distance were foreboding. Home had become a refuge for ideas. Words like acceptance began to be patronising slaps on my face. The doors became victims of possible annihilation, to be fortified with prison-like grills.

All my imagination could not describe how I felt about the little boys I knew going out to make petrol bombs or spending the nights patrolling on their terraces.

Questions were being asked. Should I go ahead with this marriage? Now that the situation had changed, would it be the same? they asked. I had smiled weakly for I did not know how the deeds of some goons in the streets could affect my life. The crucial months of preparation were tinged with apprehension, of returning home in good time laden with silks that did not feel so soft anymore.

Would the city give me back my innocence, my unquestioning acceptance?

And would this elitist innocence really count when I was being told the first time I met the extended family, 'Touch everyone's feet'? This was 11 days after the Bombay riots, when I had seen the congealed remnants of death and destruction on crumbling walls. Just 11 days after the full import of the term 'Muslim' was rammed into me, my hands were being urged towards 'their' feet; I managed to skirt my fingertips near kneecaps, hoping to retain my dignity.

I cringed at the thought. I looked at the face of the man I was to marry, for traces of the non-conservative who I had assumed understood me. My culture that I had internalised did not permit bowing before any human. It did not strike me that my resistance was an alien concept to him.

My marriage had suddenly made a fairly common inter-religious alliance into a chip on my shoulder. It had got tied to an ideology that I did not fully comprehend just yet.

And just how Muslim was I? Born in an Ismaili family came with an aadha Mussalman (half a Muslim) label, anyway. We were religious eunuchs whose spiritual head, the Aga Khan, owned an island and horses.

I never did read the Quran, did not fast, and did not pray. Taking drags of existentialism, my gods were as ephemeral as smoke. Therefore, marrying a Hindu-Jain was perfectly normal to me. Or so I thought. In the elite circles to which I belonged and the even more elite circle into which I was to wed, the Chantilly clique have their own delicate prejudices. No brandishing weapons here; just a little throwaway comment about the 'other kind' suffices.

As I entered the new home, I was carrying brand new baggage, a new label. The Kafir Mussalman. The atheist Muslim.

Shujaat's knowledge was based on news and prejudices, mine on experience. His prism only showed him a Muslim utopia. Was this about the Quran? The Vedas? If this was not about religion, then what was it? Nationalities?

'If you don't have a problem about nationalities, then why would you not live in Pakistan?' he queried.

'I cannot live even in America.'

'I think your attachment to your country is like a bad habit. Like smoking, it can cause cancer. That is why you should have married a Muslim, preferably from a Muslim country.'

The personal regret of my marriage gone wrong had crossed beyond that. Shujaat told me that according to Islam I did not even have the grace to choose an Ahl-e-Kitaab, a Person of the Book, which is sunnat (legitimate) in the religion.

'The moment you are ready to regret and do penance, you will be purified because now you too are considered a kafir. I am sure Muslims in your country would feel the same.'

I wished to deny it, but it was at least partially true. The story of regret, penance, purification had visited me in various garbs. Ashfaque had been married to a Hindu. He was going through his own retribution. The first thing he did on getting the divorce was to go for the umraah (pilgrimage). He said I was fortunate to have met him. In what he took to be a charming gesture he presented me with a copy of the surah-e-yaseen; he also said that wearing the hijaab would adorn me with enigmatic sex appeal.

Shujaat found this acceptable. 'This is the reality you do not want to face. You must appreciate that a lot of thought goes into simple things. And if someone misbehaves, believe me, people can kill for such things. We do not burn women alive as you in India do.'

'I do not deny the ills in my country. But if a society is so stable in its uniformity, then why would there be a need for honour killings? Isn't someone abusing another's honour? Did you not tell me you almost got involved with an Indian woman while you were abroad?'

'Not just an Indian woman, but a Brahmin one. There was this desire to have an affair, a short affair.'

'So, would you not become impure?'

'This would not be about love but hate. It is like war. You don't love the land you occupy.'

Towards the end of our conversation, Tarique Alam had joined us. He is a Pakistani and seemed as disturbed as I was. As he told me later, 'Shujaat does not represent Pakistan or even a decent human being.'

Tarique is now married to a Hindu.

We first met when I watched him amble along the aisle of the aircraft that was to take us from Karachi to Islamabad. He had puppy eyes and the languorous walk of a panther.

The Kafir Mussalman and the Confused Muslim 137

He came and took his seat next to mine. He was dressed in all-black on a hot sunny afternoon.

I tried to start a conversation. India opened doors immediately, but he did not want to appear overly curious. We had not yet revealed names. Instead we had begun to discuss poetry, metaphors and finally the metaphysical merits of the cupcake that was served with tea.

He had studied and worked in the US. He was visiting his family. After a while he said, 'I am escaping from Karachi, I am sure you are escaping from something too. I will travel to the northern areas with friends and clean my mind of all the rubbish it has collected.'

He said he would be in Islamabad for a couple of days and gave me his number.

Our chat had been wonderful and he was non-judgmental. I decided to call the next day.

He was completely at ease when he came to fetch me, greeted me in the lobby, and sat next to me in the taxi.

I could see that Tarique did not truly belong. He did not care much for defined parameters of thinking. However, there was something he seemed to be holding back. 'I could be just another kathputli (puppet) in life but I do not mind it. Maybe, there are two sects in this puppet show, and I belong to the sect that has chosen to enjoy the show. Should people be scared?'

I did not know about his fears and apprehensions then. He later told me about Naina, a Nepali, whom he met at a conference overseas. They kept in touch and that slowly transformed into love. He asked her to visit him in Malaysia where he got a job. Though he was certain he wanted to marry her, there were many questions that bothered him.

'I agree to understand her culture and will be there to be a part of it because I know that it is a big step for her to take. At the same time I do expect that she will convert from her heart. It may take time, but I can bring about the transition and make sure she feels comfortable.'

'What about her?'

'She is afraid as it would mean a big change. It is cultural rather than religious. She has no beliefs at all. She has lived in a hostel with Christian girls and does not visit temples. The other issue is that she belongs to a prominent family and she thinks it may hurt them that their daughter is marrying a Muslim.'

Would she convert out of true conviction? If not, then what purpose would it serve? He gave me the usual reason. It would make things smoother and the children would not face a conflict.

The day after Naina landed in Malaysia, he took her to Karachi. They got married in a simple ceremony. He shared his thoughts with me. 'There were many times when we both felt this was not possible but somehow we succeeded and overcame the barriers. We were not the first humans from distinct religions getting married. I wish these complexities did not exist at all. Aren't we supposed to be rational beings?'

They have not yet visited Nepal, but they go to Karachi. The arrival of a daughter has made things easier. 'I think she is the delta region and somehow the river is flowing in the right direction.'

Naina is a beautiful, soft-spoken woman whose life revolves round her home. But she has definite views that she expresses. She also looks distinctly different. Does that draw attention in Pakistan? 'Some say she is from China, some say from Japan, and some say she may be from

Afghanistan. The key element I learnt way before I got married to her is not to worry about what others are thinking. That has made my existence within me and around me simpler. I wish somebody experiences what I have; it is tough but it is fun. Today, she is very welcome in the family.'

'Had she been an Indian would things have been different?'

'I think the Hindu is a stigma for Muslims, anyway. One group of Muslims perceives them as worshippers of many gods and the other may put them in a different compartment. They are definitely not seen as the same as us. These individual minds have little knowledge about civilisation and refuse to accept varied thought processes. But several Muslims and even non-Muslims attach the variable of Buddhism when discussing Nepal. That somehow softens their stand. I am still intrigued about it!'

Would she have been able to live in Pakistan? By the time Tarique and Naina had married, another such case was in the news.

Divya Dayanan and Aman Khan met in Ukraine, sometime after 1995. She was from Kerala in south India; he a Pathan who lived in the village of Mardan in the North West Frontier Province. They got married in July 2003. Her case was brought to the notice of the Interior Ministry. Both are doctors, but he had to reiterate, 'Neither I nor anyone else from my family has a criminal background'.

Under what circumstances did the marriage take place? She made a sworn statement about surrendering her Indian nationality and converting to Islam. She said, 'I converted because I found some truths in Islam.' In her arguments she had implied it was unjust that after coming to an Islamic state and becoming a Muslim, she was being denied citizenship.

Did she convert because she was marrying someone in an Islamic state or because she found some truths in the religion?

Her fear of being deported too raised many questions. She said, 'If they force me to go back to India I will have to convert back to Hinduism.' Why was she afraid of re-converting to Hinduism? For how long had she known and experienced Islam? And how conservative could her parents possibly be if they sent her to study medicine in Ukraine in 1995, when she was barely 16?

Was it right to politicise the issue? Indian and Pakistani culture may be similar, but the cultural conditioning is different. It is wrong for any couple to talk in terms of thawing of relations between India and Pakistan to help their case. 'It is I who took a personal step towards better relations between two neighbours by marrying an Indian woman,' Aman Khan said.

Did he woo her as smitten lover or as an ambassador of his country or as peace-maker?

The only one qualified to talk about bringing the two countries together was their little son, and he was too young to speak. The doctor said without any hesitation, 'My boy is a Pakistani. Would it really help my case and persuade the Pakistani authorities to allow me to stay here with my son and husband?'

Was it all about a case?

Was she brainwashed into seeing the truths in Islam by Aman? Would she be just another hostage then? Tarique had a more philosophical way of looking at his own life. 'I think we create boundaries for ourselves, physical and emotional. Most of the time we completely rely on some external stimulus to be happy. This dependence makes you reactive. And that is what causes problems and confusion.'

I thought being out of the country was an advantage. Tarique could speak the way he did because of his exposure to a world outside the borders. This is not how it always happens.

People can carry the borders with them, draw lines outside their doors wherever they live. I had met a Pakistani family in Seattle, a couple and their two college-going sons. In this suburban home they had created a cocoon.

The older son did everything possible to rebel; these were seen as aberrations. Until one day, when he announced he was in love with a Hindu girl. He would bring her home and take her to his room. His culture was different from that of his parents.

The father told me the problem was not about religion, it was the girl. She was using the boy's popularity and was just a groupie, said the mother. It took a while for me to understand that all these explanations would not have been necessary had their faith been strong. The moment of truth came when he said, 'Do you know she comes from a rabid family; her brother has the "Om" sign as his screen-saver.'

A family friend had even offered to use tough talk to get the girl off the son's back, but this was the time when right-wing parties were on the rise in India; money was being pumped in from zealous Hindus abroad into the coffers to keep the ancient Indian culture alive. At such a time there was bound to be fear.

Fear wore the garb of obfuscation. I was shown a copy of the Quran where the son had marked several passages. 'He used to be involved in Islam, he knows a lot,' spoke paternal pride. Now he had turned away. He would do anything for the girl. Even become a Hindu.

A complete kafir. The rest of us had to remain on the fringe, branded with half an identity, half a handful of our shores and beliefs.

Cross-cultural alliances always cause some turmoil. In the departure lounge at Mumbai airport a young woman just out of her teens was speaking on the phone. I could sense that she was trying to fake confidence. She fidgeted and kept checking her handbag.

'First time?' I asked her.

It wasn't, and Nafisa was surprisingly forthcoming. It wasn't a holiday; she was going to meet her father for the second time in two years. She was born in Karachi. After her parents separated, her mother had chosen to return to India, her homeland, with her daughter who was then four.

Was she looking forward to the trip this time?

'I have a brother, he had visited us. He set the stage for my visit to Pakistan. I would have liked to travel elsewhere too, but had to stick to Karachi. There was some curiosity to meet my father.'

Her brother did not seem like the men she knew. As she recalled, 'He was also very conservative. I kept away from him. My mother was giving him too much attention; I was jealous.'

Her mother was meeting her son after years. She and her husband had parted ways when Aamir was 14.

'How was Karachi?' I asked.

She could not comprehend the emotions that must have come into play at the time. One day she and her estranged father went out. 'He gave me a hug and was in tears. I felt no emotion.'

'He spoke about his time in Delhi and Bombay; he had a good memory and he spoke well. But there was awkwardness. As an adult when you look back you feel there was a void, but then I was happy in my world. It was just a meeting and moving on.'

The Kafir Mussalman and the Confused Muslim

Was it the situation or the environment? Didn't she feel different?

'To visit for two weeks is fine. I wear a dupatta, leave my jeans at home, it is easy to adjust for this much time. There are no barriers. But there is a huge cultural difference. If I were asked to uproot myself from India and go and live there for even two years, I would not. To think of even marrying and settling there is impossible.'

There were too many emotions involved for her to cogently understand the barriers.

Sadia was a Pakistani acquaintance in Mumbai. She had married an Indian Muslim and adopted the child of a relative. In the few interactions we had, one sensed that she was investing everything in the baby. The life of luxury she led was not too different from the one she was accustomed to back home in Lahore.

One day we heard she had disappeared. Her husband received divorce papers by courier from Pakistan. The adopted baby was returned to the original parents. How could she wrench herself away? Was the child merely a symbol she had used to imbue her obliterated persona?

What really constitutes the spaces we occupy?

Bertha Anderson has lived in several parts of the world. She has passports of two European countries. Her father was from the mountains of Pakistan and her mother a Belgian; she married someone outside both her identities.

She visited Pakistan for the first time in 2004. She had come to meet someone at the guest house where I was staying. Dressed in tight jeans and a T-shirt, a scarf carelessly thrown over her shoulder, she did not look Pakistani. She smiled warmly, her dark lips that otherwise appeared stained took on a luminescence.

With a spontaneity that continues to characterise our friendship till today, she asked me to join her for tea. I went to her place and she took me to her room. She was going for a party that night and opened her wardrobe to show me what she would wear. It was a black sequinned gown with a knee-high slit.

She was a single mother; her son studied overseas.

What made her visit Pakistan? Roots? 'I have come here as a part of an NGO, not to seek roots. Roots keep you in one place. We go everywhere, no borders, no religion, no countries.'

'Then why Pakistan?'

'I cannot say I identify with Pakistan. But I do like its culture.'

'You spend your time in the tribal areas where there is destruction, what culture do you see there?'

'My work does entail seeing poverty and death. There is violence against women. In tribal areas there are human rights violations; it is a closed community. When people need help they don't get it. I get protection from the government.'

'Does it not mean that even the work you do is dictated by the government?'

'I am not working for money, so I won't be rewarded by people or the government, but by God. It is an opportunity to learn about a new way of life.'

'No discrimination?'

'I have been so involved in my work that I did not see it, even if it was there. I live alone, drive alone; so many European women live in these areas. No one can touch you. I am an open book. I am respected, maybe because of my passport. If I were a local woman, perhaps it would have been different.'

She sticks to the UN Club for her social outings. 'If you

mix too much with locals then they will want to know too many things, they keep scratching for information.'

'Just information?'

'Okay, okay, I know what you are asking. Yes, some men want to get close. I wear western clothes but so many young women here also dress this way. We should not misuse freedom. At one party this diplomat came and told me, "You are looking so sexy." I was wearing a long coat and a big dupatta. I asked him, "From where you saw how sexy I was?" A woman here should challenge people or they will walk over her.'

The first time she stepped out of the airport, they asked her why she was in Pakistan. 'I realised the important thing is to have contacts. I did not argue. I just said I will call up General N. They kept quiet.'

She admits though that a colleague was poisoned in Afghanistan. 'See, this is sad, you come to work and people get jealous.'

'Is there suspicion?'

'Of course. All our telephones are tapped. They think NGOs are spies. They also read our emails. It is a police state.'

That is the reason we maintain prudence. 'The name of India is involved with a lot of emotions.'

'Where do you feel you really belong?'

'Right now, here. Tomorrow I don't know.'

I told her about Amrita Pritam. I told her about longing. Her love for the poet Sahir Ludhianvi when the land was not divided. In those days people kept separate tumblers for Hindus and Muslims. Amrita, who lived in Lahore then, had recalled, 'Neither my grandmother nor I knew that the man I was to fall in love with would be of the same faith as the branded utensils were meant for.'

Love, like regions, does get branded. This one remained a mirage. She then met the Pakistani artist Imroz, who assured her, 'There can be no one else...no one...you are my daughter...I your son.'

He remained with her till her death, in the same house in the posh Hauz Khas area of New Delhi where I met her a few years earlier.

She wrote in the poem My Address, 'Today I effaced my house number and the name of the street where I live. I wiped away the direction of every road; and still if you must search me out, just knock at the door in each street of each city of each country. It's a curse, a benediction – both...and wherever you find a free soul, that is my home!'

6

The Marginals

'Long, hot stretches of sand...' she hummed. I heard the imaginary waves. 'I have never been to India, but my father was born in Goa.'

Sabrina was born in Lahore. Her father taught at a school. Her grandfather had brought the family here a few years after Partition. This seemed like an unreal migration. She does not understand. 'Why do you say that?'

'Why would a Catholic family move to a Muslim country?'

'In India too we would have been a minority.' In fact, at the time her grandfather made the move, they would not have been considered Indians, for Goa remained under Portuguese rule until 1961.

She shuttles between Lahore and Karachi. Did her father ever compare? 'He remembers, and then we have albums.' The pictures show a crumbling old Portuguese house, a piano, four-poster beds with mosquito nets.

Sabrina does costume designing for films; the profession lends her glamour. She has short hair and a fringe that falls on her forehead. I tell her, realising how facile it sounds, that she looks like any other Pakistani. 'But I am,' she says.

At that moment I become conscious that I am projecting my minority mindset on her. These are the statements and queries posed to Indian Muslims more than to any other community.

She has an obviously recognisable Catholic last name – D'Mello. Why did her parents not choose a more Muslim first name for her? 'Whatever I am called I would remain Catholic. I don't try and hide the fact.'

Is there a need to assert it? For those answers I spoke to her brother, who lives and works in Islamabad. Jeremy has a gym-toned body and the face of a boy. How does it feel being a Jeremy in a world of Jaffers?

'I am a Pakistani,' he says with unnecessary aplomb.

'Homogeneity kills imagination,' I tell him. 'Why assume that cosmopolitanism is not culture? Why do we stratify culture to necessarily have the benefit of an authenticated, uniform history?'

'I did not say I am not a Catholic. I go to church.'

'And you are frisked.'

'I think it is a wise move. After 9/11 we have to be more careful.'

'So your community is under threat?'

'Everyone is. Aren't mosques bombed? And are missionaries not killed in your country?'

'Can you discuss Christianity in social gatherings like Islam is discussed?'

'Why should I? I am allowed my drinks, I carry my name and I go to church. People are fair.'

'Is it fair to be measured by another's yardstick?'

'It happens all the time. And today we live in a global village.'

The global village is really utopian. So, we must look at it through an idealistic prism. How many dissimilarities can it

The Marginals

accept and encourage? How much dynamism is possible without causing a storm? Is tolerance a patronising term or does it encourage dissent? Is dissent welcome or a nuisance? Why is it all right to be judged by what America does?

'No. But are Pakistani Christians the only victims?' he counters.

While being unmistakably positive, his views were those of the elite, of the less than two per cent of the Christian population; not the sort sheltered beneath tomes of rational thinking, but the expediency that common sense forces upon those tethered to a geographical identity.

The story at French Colony is different. It wasn't Jeremy who told me about it. I had mentioned to the manager at the guest house that I did not see any slums. 'Go to F-7/4. Any cab driver will know.'

You cannot immediately see the largest slum in Islamabad. From the main street there is a wall that appears like a fortress. The hutments can be reached by climbing down a few cemented steps. It is like a basement mall of poverty. Ghettoes are a reality for any minority group and the ghetto can be physical or emotional.

A few women are carrying water jugs; they are dressed in salwaar-kameez, their heads covered. Children scamper around. Some men are smoking. From their tone, I realise that they do not use the typical Catholic patois that is so unmistakably theirs in India and more specifically Mumbai.

His bloodshot eyes appeared at odds with his stance. His speech was slurred, his arm extended. His blotchy skin folded like an envelope on one side of the cheek. He was dressed in a white shirt and grey trousers. A cross dangled from a chain round his neck. 'Give me ten rupees, please,' he pleaded. 'I am suffering from cancer.'

The ten rupees would not cure his cancer, but it might help him get his tipple for the day. He barely looked at the note and went away. Defeated by destiny.

French — or France — Colony has become a stereotype of the hash-booze image of the community of 700 families. This is often how they supplement their incomes since many work in what in India are called 'untouchable' jobs. Surprisingly, in the casteless Islamic society, they are derisively referred to as chooras (scavengers).

Although the fact that the likes of Jeremy will not be branded should reveal that this is a class demarcation, it is also true that were Jeremy or Sabrina not to fall in line they too would be lumped with the sobriquet.

The lines of division have only been consolidated further since the battle of the crusade between Osama and Bush. This brought the Christian community in Pakistan into sharper focus.

As in India, many of the poorer Christians are converts from Hinduism; the missionary zeal still pervades parts of India. Conversions from Islam to any other religion would be an impossible scenario in Pakistan; it carries the death penalty for men and life imprisonment for women. In cases of crimes against them, the police disregard even detailed eyewitness accounts.

Is there fear? Jeremy admits that it exists. 'There is inequality in the laws, but not socially. If one of us contests an election, Muslims are not allowed to vote for a non-Muslim candidate.'

Isn't he perturbed about the notorious blasphemy laws? Bishop John Joseph committed suicide in front of a courthouse in 1998 to protest against the trial of one of the accused. The Pakistani Islamic blasphemy law, 295-C of the

Pakistani Penal Code, states that the crime of criticising Allah, the Prophet or his teachings would be punishable by death. Jeremy is surprisingly stoical about it: 'Why must anyone criticise what is holy to another religion? How would I feel if someone said something against Christ? And many of those arrested are Muslims.'

There was the famous case of Dr Younus Shaikh who spent three years in prison for maligning the Prophet's name. He was sentenced to death but due to widespread appeals and retrials, he was acquitted. His release was hushed up for fear of fundamentalist backlash. He left the country, maintaining till the end that he was falsely charged. A doctor and lecturer, he was perhaps being made an example of.

It isn't only other religions that suffer. Ahmadis have been declared heretics. If they wish to perform the Haj they have to provide a written declaration stating that Mirza Ghulam Ahmad, the founder of their sect, is a 'cunning person and an imposter'.

President Pervez Musharraf, when asked whether he would object if his daughter wanted to marry an Indian, confessed in an interview to *The Nation* newspaper in Pakistan, 'If it's a Muslim Indian I wouldn't. If it's a Hindu Indian I would certainly object.' He said the same would apply to any other cross-religious alliance. 'There are cultural differences involved and there are societal differences involved and therefore that is the reason when I said that I would not like my daughter to be married to a Hindu Indian. It doesn't mean that I am intolerant.'

Taking the argument further, he said, 'Our heroes are their villains and viceversa. Our culture is absolutely the opposite.

They consider cows as their gods. We slaughter cows and eat them.'

The image of an animal-worshipping society is so ingrained that most Pakistanis do not realise that only three states in India are vegetarian and there is routine animal sacrifice.

The first Hindu I met in Pakistan was in Karachi. There are around 3 million in the country. I was walking aimlessly in the market and reached a dead-end. Shops dotted both sides. I went into the one on the left. It was cramped with fabric, shawls and a few stitched garments.

I found an amazing intricately embroidered kameez, the shades of desert women reflected in its mirrors sewn along the front. It was heavy, so I kept it back on the rack. The store owner urged me to take it, 'Aisa maal nahin milega (You won't find this kind of stuff easily).'

It is a good thing that on such travels one's antennae are always up. The word 'maal' was so resonant of India and Mumbai, I couldn't help but greet him with a 'Namaste'. He looked uncertain. I am from India, I told him.

'Hindu?'

'No. You are?'

He nodded. His card said 'Nand Kumar Parmar'. He was not a migrant, his family always lived in Karachi. They decided not to move to India, though many relatives did. They are in Gujarat. When movement between the two countries was easier, they did business together. Why did he stay back?

'*Ghar hai* (This is home),' he said.

There is the belief that most of the Hindus who chose to remain here must be rich. There are wealthy Sindhis and Rajputs, they live well. They install small idols in their houses, hoping to retain their separateness. This causes questions to be asked. They have real gods, with faces, elephant trunks, with several arms and heads; this is magic. They don't have one holy book; they have many that sound like fantasy stories.

Unlike in Islam, where the month-long fast is a test of human endurance, Hindus fast for the long life of their husbands, or to get favours from specific gods on specific days. And then there is the image of astrologers. In most parts of Pakistan where there are shrines, there will be Sufis and fakirs reading people's future. Many of them survive solely on this special skill or by selling blessings in little silver boxes. These taweezes are worn round the neck or the arm to keep you safe.

This is not a residue of the pagan roots of Islam; it is a subcontinental intrusion. Pakistan will of course not admit to it. Rich Hindus can be left alone and ironically it is their minority status that affords them this immunity. Politicians, realising that they cannot depend on them as a vote bank, try and indulge them in a convenient barter for preservation. It is conditional. When Justice Rana Bhagwandas was sworn in as Acting Chief Justice of Pakistan on 24 March 2007, he had to take the oath of office in the name of Allah and a Quranic prayer: 'May Allah Almighty help and guide me, (Ameen)'.

I am driving through what is a Hindu locality. There is a large building that seems to have been stripped of paint. The remains of what must have been a blue shade blink in the sunlight. Clothes hang from balconies; the structure is patterned like an old haveli, though it is an apartment block. Some houses have thick cloth tied to the railings that imitate awnings.

In a lane, there is a trader's office, a Konica photo studio and a bookstore selling Islamic literature. A short distance away stands the Swaminarayan Mandir. An open gate leads to a small compound. A tree partially impedes the view of the yellowing temple. A wooden bench is placed against the wall. A board reads out the name in three languages – English, Hindi and Urdu. The symbol of 'Om' in white stands out on a circle in brown. A smaller gate is visible and a saffron pennant is poised listlessly near a short flight of steps.

Jeremy is married to a Hindu. She happily converted to his religion. 'Hindus have too many castes, so she made this choice.' After pausing for a long time he said, 'But I don't think she would have become a Muslim. There is too much bad blood, too much of a past.'

The past gets quantified. The indoctrination starts early. School books and the socialising process of children tell them about another faith that is less than theirs.

During my second visit to Peshawar, I had seen two Hindu men in the lobby. The elderly one was dressed in narrow pyjamas, quite unlike the broad Peshawari salwaar of the region. The younger man, his son, was blowing smoke rings as he paced about on the dull carpet.

Kushal Meghani was a reluctant raconteur. 'It's a good life. We buy spices and dry fruits from here and market them to the other cities.' They live in Karachi and make monthly trips to oversee the business. As he was leaving, he said '*Allah Hafiz*'. Why was he mimicking Muslims? Does he want to remain unnoticed? 'Each has their own way to survive,' he shrugs. Their silence finds voice in a Muslim friend who had said, 'The wealthy Hindus don't care about their community. How can you blame us if some politicians destroy temples when some mosque is destroyed in India?'

'But don't you have a stereotyped image of them?'
'Don't they have one of us? Do you think they love Islam or Muslims?'

More often, it is not religious differences but monetary considerations that awaken the minority conscience. Minoo Bhandara, whose Murree Breweries was shut down in the 1990s, is one such example. The reason was not his minority status, but because Asif Ali Zardari was eyeing the market.

Bhandara's sister is the noted writer Bapsi Sidhwa. Her fiction is rooted in history, as in *Ice-candy Man,* where the Partition is seen through the eyes of a Parsi child, and a Zoroastrian sensibility that she is not afraid to flaunt, as in *Crow Eaters* where she had 'fun portraying [her] community'.

When the Parsis had fled against persecution from Pars in Iran to Sanjan in Gujarat, the king had asked them to abstain from missionary activities and to marry only within their community. In contemporary times, the latter has caused obstacles. The Parsis in Pakistan face problems similar to the ones they encounter in India. They will not permit an offspring of a mixed marriage into their fold.

I met an old couple on one of the flights. They live in Mumbai's Dadar Parsi Colony and were travelling to meet their son in Karachi. This seemed rather odd. 'He was working for a multinational and they posted him there,' said the woman.

'Do they have Parsi colonies in Pakistan?'
'Yes, but he lives in a cosmopolitan area.'

I found it unusual that in a Muslim majority country, the mother was telling me proudly that her son was not living in a Parsi ghetto. He has retained his culture, and that includes tying his kusti (sacred thread) three times round his waist to signify good words, good thoughts, good deeds over his sudreh (a muslin vest) and muttering a prayer. This is his heritage from the moment he is initiated into the faith, not at birth but after his Navjote ceremony at the age of eight.

The Parsis in India are the westernised elite; they remain so in Pakistan. But there are no special eateries, as one sees in Mumbai, where they put up signs that read, 'No smoking, no combing hair, no discussing politics'. For a community that was supposed to completely submerge – they did say they would be like 'doodh mein shakkar', sugar that would dissolve in milk and yet sweeten it – they stand out.

Unlike in Mumbai, where even the vultures that prey on the mortal remains are disappearing, in Pakistan a Parsi can at least die with his faith intact.

Minority paranoia cannot be wished away. The Constitution defines a Muslim and a non-Muslim. It declares Islam as the state religion of Pakistan and the Holy Quran and Sunnah to be 'the supreme law and source of guidance for legislation to be administered through laws enacted by the Parliament and Provincial Assemblies, and for policy making by the Government'. This goes against the honourable intentions of the Objectives Resolution passed on 7 March 1949 that stated, 'Wherein adequate provisions shall be made for the minorities freely to profess and practise their religions and develop their cultures.'

Is culture the chattel of religion?

I was visiting Taxila. It is a part of Rawalpindi district, 30 km from Islamabad along the Grant Trunk Road. Although the terrain is pretty much the standard macadamised one, with factories dotting the sides, the bus-stops look like pagodas.

It suddenly appears to be a different world. While the museum houses important artefacts from the Greek to the Gandhara period, it is the stupa and its environs that haunt. Fittingly, the guide Rahim is a small man with a sparse beard like dry grass. He could well have attained nirvana himself – he speaks about the Ramayan in fluent Urdu. Takshashila is the name that originated from Taksha, the son of Bharat, brother of Lord Ram.

It became a centre of high learning. Sanskrit flourished, and knowledge went beyond books. Rahim points out one large block of terracotta. On it are sculpted various forms: bows poised, arrows pierced, animals speared. Some of the ruins have been resurrected. His expert eyes can tell the old from the new, however hard the attempt to age it. What has faded in the sun cannot pose competition to what has been faded under light bulbs.

It is said that Kautilya, the Machiavelli of the Mauryan dynasty, composed the Arthshastra here. All statecraft must ultimately fall to the conniving ways of Time.

From Darius to Alexander, the Persians and the Greeks did leave some influence, but these are not intrinsic. Taxila is essentially about Mahayana Buddhism. There is a large sculpture of the Buddha seated in a yogic posture, the face half-smashed and the stomach a hollow. You can put a coin in and your wish is granted, I am told. History swallows many riches and a saint in penance has metal coins that will be disembowelled.

To reach up here there are two small streams in which twigs float. A herdsman is getting his bullocks to climb the steps. 'Harrr, harr,' he shouts as he gently uses a stick to prod them from behind. Besides those sounds and the occasional flop-flop of falling twigs in the streams, there is calm. The expanse stretches in brown speckled with strands of green, like a bald head sprouting dispersed hair.

The fact is that when you have disparate elements they will have disparate needs. One often wonders at what point in time the urge for a separate identity really arises. Khushwant Singh offers an explanation for Punjab: 'The seeds of Sikh separation were sown by the Sikh's own gurus when they gave them their own temples, their own scripture, their distinct appearance, the common casteless name, Singh'.

Is there place for secularism in an Islamic society? Or atheism? Atheists remain the invisible minority; they have no heritage to uphold. No blasphemy laws apply to them. Non-belief is a private wound that you nurse quietly.

I had got this interesting note from a Pakistani even before I visited the country: 'When I was a child I remember I used to think a lot about God and admired his power and grandeur. Then I thought I should find out whether this guy exists or it's a hoax. I did it this way. I decided to talk to God and I said, "I will call you an s.o.b. If you respond then you exist and if you don't then you don't exist, then I am your creator not the other way round, and if you hurt me for calling you s.o.b. then you are an s.o.b. and not God." Nothing happened. I therefore concluded he didn't exist or I left him with no choice except to remain silent. Ever since I have imagined him like a guy at some distance from me and sort of angry with me for calling him such names. If he is concerned about what I do or think then rest assured I will always be doing the right things but it will be me figuring out what are the right things, not him telling me what is right or wrong. And if he punishes me for this when I am dead or while I am alive then frankly my dear I don't give a damn.'

The writer of this note today calls himself 'Allah's chosen one'.

7

Changing Faces, Static Masks

At first it did not look like a party. There were people seated in isolated bliss, characters in quest for a moment, a phrase or a stigma that would define them.

I had met some of them earlier. The host Zafar Ehsan was a musician. There was stasis in the air and no music playing; when people spoke it was in murmurs, two or three forging ephemeral bonds.

There was an eclectic mix of invitees and gatecrashers. The alcohol was just as varied – Campari, vodka, gin, wines, Scotch, rum...

The writer's face was sharp and beautiful. There was stillness in his eyes. 'I don't write,' he said.

'But you are a writer,'

'I am also alive,' he smiled.

He was killing himself, slowly, relishing it as he did the glass of neat whiskey that burned his entrails.

Life had not been good to him, I was told. He refused to touch any food. It interrupted his communion with drink.

A man in bermudas walked out from one of the rooms. He had an evil grin and a distinctive nose. His hair was knotted at the back.

'My grandparents are from Jallandhar,' he said.

'Are you a Sikh?'

'No, but they all tell me I am. I look Indian.'

He thought the connection warranted that he should serenade the guest. 'Aaj jaane ki zidd na karo...(Do not insist on leaving today)' he sang a stanza from the famous ghazal.

'I have just arrived,' I said.

'Aane walle hi jaate hai (it is the ones who come that leave),' he replied.

He left.

Who was he?

'A failed actor,' I heard him say.

Fazal Saeed was the only one who moved from one person to the other. He had sparse hair on the top of his head but the luscious locks in front seemed to give him much pride. Ever so often he would make a scissor-like movement with his fingers and push them back; they'd fall over his eyes again. He could not stay long enough in one place. He came across as desperate.

He lived in the West but had moved to Karachi to feel 'at home'. No one quite knew whether he was still married to the woman he spent a few years with; she is talented and among the most admired people in her profession. His story is of deceit, about how one individual has managed to mislead his whole social group.

By day he is a respected man; at least he is in a respected position as head of an organisation that works among the dispossessed. He makes full use of it. Under the guise of helping people, he exploits some.

Almost every morning he walks the lane near his house and looks for domestic helps called maasis. When questioned about it by his friends, he says, 'I believe in equality.' He also feels, in a twisted sort of way, that he is empowering these women. He does not have a lot of money; he uses his contacts to enrol such girls in some vocational courses run by NGOs. The organisations think he is doing a great service, the helpless young women keep quiet due to the stigma and because they have no other recourse.

Although many know about this aspect of his life, no one has exposed him publicly. His delusions as well as his dalliances provide vicarious satisfaction to those around him. It is a relationship of convenience, although it seems unreal for they are better known. Someone said that many of these men are lonely and need drinking buddies; like old poets they seek an audience for their verses.

He is an aging man trying to hold hard to a forgotten youth. He is constantly dropping names of famous women. They are aware of it, and they don't care.

Why this silence?

He knows their secrets. They have conspired to keep each other's lies hidden.

She lit a cigarette, holding the flame for much too long. Her short compact frame has been squeezed into a tight kameez through which one could figure out the foam in her padded bra. She had acquired a toy boy. Shaista had given up on men. Initially they would get intimidated by her academic prowess and then would begin the role-playing. If she could break through the barriers of thought, then why did she not demolish these roles? It transpired that she was a victim of her own fantasies.

Her lover was with her that day. Her eyes followed him even as she pretended to be deep in conversation. He was busy networking. She had met him in Germany. He was several years younger and one could see that she found his behaviour juvenile. After spending years in the US he had got a job in Berlin. He had given it all up to return with her to Pakistan.

Within an hour I realised no one seemed to trust him. Junaid came and sat near me and asked about India and music. 'I have come here to learn to play the sitar. I used to be a part of a small percussion band in the US. Now I will stay here and learn classical music. I would love to visit Benares.'

He did not have to pay for anything. He lived in Shaista's house, used her car and, since she travelled often on work, did as he pleased.

This included using her name quite blatantly. 'He is an embarrassment to her,' said Zafar. 'I had not invited him, but he insisted on coming and bringing a few new friends. They are all on the make. They know they will meet interesting people here.'

'Why is she in such a relationship?' I asked.

'She has been hurt several times, now she thinks she is in control because he is dependent on her. Ultimately, she is the one to get emotionally disturbed. Do you think a man will leave everything and come here?'

'He is learning music.'

'Where? He is lying.'

'What will he get out of it?'

'Contacts and the thrill of being with a known person. I am close to her and she told me how shocked she was the first time they became intimate. He had gasped, "I cannot believe I am sleeping with The Shaista".'

'Yet she chooses to stay with him?'

'Ego. She too has it. She was upset, but then it is not a normal relationship.'

'Is this common in Pakistan?'

'Why do you make it sound like Pakistanis don't do regular things?'

'I don't mean that. There are social and legal restrictions.'

'These apply to the poor. A rich or educated woman, if she is discreet, can buy her freedom.'

'At the price of personal hell?'

'True. See that woman there? Do you know who she is?'

Kamia must have spent considerable time doing up her eyes. Long strokes of mascara curled her lashes and made her look like a surprised child.

She took pride in saying she had walked out of her first marriage with only her clothes on. She never mentioned the fact that she went to a place where her wardrobe was designed by those who make the rich and famous look rich and famous. The raw beauty that had made her look like a tribal woman doing hard labour now with the passage of years gave her a tinge of transvestism. She always over-dressed. Too many bangles, too long earrings, chokers that hid her bird-like neck.

She spoke breathlessly as though time was running out. She sniffed often, like one looking for a prey. With age catching up and several insecurities besetting her choices, she was in love again. Those who knew her well spoke about how she was fraught with anxiety. After two bad marriages, she wanted a third.

'It is a need,' said Zafar.

'Ego again?'

'No, in her case there is anger.'

Her rage emanated from her inability to make her earlier relationships work. So she seduced a young man trying to get into film direction. She became careless, sending him perfume-soaked letters. Gossip did the rounds. He cringed. It wasn't only morality; he could not make a commitment. She threatened him with suicide. Late one night she went to the house of an acquaintance with a piece of paper. Her hands shook as she handed over the note to the lady. 'Please give it to him,' she pleaded. He had disappeared.

Are women always victims? Zafar has been the recipient of some amorous aggressive advances; one such lady is smart and educated.

'I was disturbed when she challenged me, saying she has never tasted defeat in these matters. To me this is the only unsavoury attitude in the episode. However, I spent a lot of time trying to explain my position to her, knowing that she is not the sort to go around distributing her attention and favours. She ought to be granted that dignity.'

Omar's situation is slightly different. He was being hounded by a close friend's wife. She was always in purdah. He often visited their house and started getting signals from her. How did he know what she looked like? 'She has her photographs displayed all over the drawing room.' And then one day, his friend told him, 'Your bhabhi (sister-in-law, a term most men in India and Pakistan use to address the wives of their friends to ensure that no hint and possibility of lust creeps in) cooks good food, come home for lunch.'

At the table, she served the food, but Omar suspected that something was going to happen. Soon enough, she feigned illness and suffocation and pulled up her veil. Both men were shocked. As he recalled, 'I thought she would want to do that but to actually go ahead was surprising.' He conjectured that she was an immature girl, and he sometimes felt sympathy for her when she got aggressive on the telephone. She called him when her husband was away.

She did not seem like an innocent at all – she knew her game too well, and the purdah provided her with a safety net. Besides, he was a bachelor with no responsibilities, so he was an easy target. She was feeling suppressed within the confines of her 'happy settled' life and was probably a frustrated wife, and the best way to hit out at her husband was to shower attention on his friend.

'Why would she take such a big risk?' he asked, unable to accept my explanation.

Omar, who had definite views about what he called 'those broad-minded, confused women', had only sympathy for the veiled woman's confusion, her openness. 'She is not a slut... just a young lady with her dreams gone wrong, a helpless person. Some girls have no maturity and not much say in marriages in this country. But let me tell you she would never go to any physical extent with anyone except her husband, no matter what. That's the way the social set-up is here.'

It did not strike him that most women in our societies have arranged marriages and it would not be considered proper for a woman to call up her friend's husband, whom she barely knew, to discuss her frustrations. Did he never wonder why there was the need for purdah at all and why she stayed indoors?

'These women prefer to stay indoors. Women are respected here.'

Omar had been happy to discuss his life with me, but he could not come to terms with the fact that I was unlike the women he knew. The first time he introduced me to a close friend of his who shook my hand, his response had befuddled me. 'Why did he have to do that? Pakistani women would not allow it.'

'It was only a handshake. And I am not a Pakistani woman,' I remonstrated.

'At least he should be aware of how to conduct himself. Did he not see that I said "Salaam alaikum" to you, could he not get the hint? And do you know that in all the years I have known him, I have not even met his wife? These are double standards.'

On another occasion, we had gone out for dinner with his friend Waquar. This gentleman was worldly-wise and having been told that I had travelled a bit, started recounting anecdotes. One such experience was about a Lebanese woman he knew who would visit him at his house when he worked and lived in Karachi. 'Even urban society is such that if there was a knock she would have to leave from the back door.' I said it must have been quite humiliating for both of them.

Driving me back, Omar expressed his distaste for what had transpired, 'It was so obvious that he was sleeping with her and getting great pleasure telling you about his sexual escapades and you were listening to all that!'

I reminded him about the time he had invited a girl to his apartment when he was studying in America. But he had a justification that made him look honourable and noble in his own eyes. 'She was not attractive in any way. She would talk to me about general things; she was probably lonely and wanted someone to speak to...I thought I should invite her for a cup of tea to my apartment so that she could feel comfortable and I'd introduce her to the other friends living there. Is this a crime? And this was not in Pakistan.'

On another occasion, he and his group of friends had been sitting around waiting for a fellow student who was in the shower. She was known to be uninhibited. She came out wrapped in a towel. They laughed. Omar smirked and teased her, 'Ok, let us see you drop that towel now.' She did and came and sat before him on the floor, completely naked.

What had that moment meant to him? 'It wasn't enjoyable. I was testing to see how low she would stoop. It was only a challenge for me.'

This was the typical male attitude. The standards he applied for others were vastly different.

He was respectful towards women in a warped sort of way. He defended some of his hollow masculine acts by saying that there was no sexual intimacy involved. He was steeped in a guilt so deep that everything above that was crass. His one early attempt at sexual contact with a woman whom he had paid for had filled him with shame. The mere recollection of it sickened him. He invariably chose the blanket of self-righteousness and denial. He had remained celibate most of his life.

'It does not mean that I am a woman-hater. I always found women stupidly arrogant who want men to run after them and beg them for love, therefore I discarded most or they gave up on me. I like mature and composed ladies, but they are hard to find and harder to have access to.'

I ask Zafar if women and men are on hold, in a state of suspension. 'It is a fight between who they are and what they want to be.'

Some have given up, some are making an attempt to savour the dregs, and still others have become adept at playing the game of life.

A well-known actress makes a late entry. There is no drama surrounding her arrival; a few acknowledge her. She is carrying a large bag and toying with two cellphones. She unties her hair, brings it in front and lets it cascade down

Changing Faces, Static Masks

her shoulder and down to her navel. After a few minutes she coils the dark strands and ties them up. This alternate tying-untying goes on all evening. She has a serpent-like sensuality.

She tells Zafar that a prominent producer has been persuading her to do a role. There is a phone call; she refuses to answer it. It rings several times and she silences it, interspersed with laughter. Zafar asks why she does not just tell him she cannot do the role. 'Nahin, usko maarne se achcha hai ke woh sisak-sisak ke jiye (No, instead of killing him I'd like to watch him live in agony).'

She is bright and lethal.

It is time to eat. I get up and my saree gets caught in the jagged leg of a chair. I feel hands arranging the pleats.

'It's ok, thanks,' I say.

He stands up. 'Hi, I am Joss. I know about drapes, I am a fashion designer.'

He gives me about 15 business cards. The design is dramatic.

'He is gay,' Zafar tells me. Much as one hates clichés, in Pakistan as in India and the rest of the world, certain professions have been taken over by homosexuals. Joss does not flaunt it, therefore I am surprised when I get to know that one of his partners is Junaid, Shaista's toy boy.

Two days later I call up Joss. He invites me to his workshop. His room is done up in red and black. Clothes are displayed on one end – lehengas, toga-like gowns, off-shoulder blouses. The workers in the annexe are cutting, sewing and embroidering.

'I like colours,' he tells me. There are metallic greys and shiny turquoises, fuchsia and purple. He brings down a gown in chiffon with a slip that reaches the knees, the legs would be visible through it; the fabric is embossed with gemstones.

'Where would people wear this?'

'Weddings.'

'Don't they go for more traditional clothes?'

'Depends on who you are. This is a stand-out kind of outfit and the person must be able to carry it off.'

'A thin person?'

'No, someone with confidence.'

He shows me magazines where he has been featured. I ask him about high society gossip.

'Even if people talk, they know they need you and will have to meet you again.'

That one statement purged the underbelly of a movement that silently expresses its differentness and hypocrisy. While men hurriedly grope each other and satiate what is seen as illicit passion in a few minutes, the tomb of Malik Ayaz stands with pride in the middle of the commercial hub of Lahore. He was such a devoted and good lover of Mahmud of Ghazni that it is said the king became 'a slave to his slave'. He was invested with power and the story of their ideal love is celebrated.

It isn't merely the laws that prevent gays from expressing themselves openly; societal pressures do play a role. Even when Zafar, a supposedly liberal person, mentioned Joss's orientation to me, there was an element of aversion. Why did he have a problem?

'What he does in private is of no concern to me, but I don't like it when they use our parties to find partners. How do you think he met Shaista's boyfriend?'

They have no choice. While in small towns and villages, these may be considered a part of growing up and dismissed as exploitation, the supposed anonymity of the city forces them to operate under a flimsy camouflage. The knowledge of who is gay is covered beneath the even greater knowledge that it must be hidden.

Changing Faces, Static Masks

What would exposure mean? Arrests and a jail sentence, unless the cops are kept happy, in cash or kind. This is a replay of what happens in India, but the metros like Bombay and Delhi have established strong groups that openly fight for their rights.

Joss is too privileged to want to fight for rights. He can get what he wants and he does not wish to legitimise his sexual preference. He might even get into a marriage of convenience and it is quite likely that his wife could be having an affair with another woman.

Lesbians just go on with their relationships. But it is rare to meet completely gay women. Irham, a consultant, is open about it. Dressed in khaki slacks and a black t-shirt that offsets her creamy complexion, she narrows her eyes as she lights the cigarette with practised ease. She does not want to look like a woman. 'I dress the way I do because initially it was to convey my sexual preference when I was in the US. But it is also true that I got tired of being feminine, the androgynous look is more appealing to me,' she says.

Are the stereotypes the same then for male and female gays?

'Unlike an effeminate guy who would immediately be recognised as gay, there aren't any such specific ideas about lesbians. Yes, there is a term called mahi munda, a tomboy, for those who are not in touch with their feminine side.'

Is it role playing? 'Not necessarily. A Butch woman can convey it but not all Butch women are the active partners.'

She parties, drinks and is surrounded by people who take the Happy Pill. Tongues loosen, inhibitions are lost and on the dance floor orientations are revealed as the tactile gives way to a tacit understanding. 'Most lesbians will not admit to it even after that. They hide under the garb of bisexuality.

At parties you may find someone that catches your fancy. There is a certain look, but since women also like to check each other out for their clothes, their beauty, often it can be an error of judgement or someone just deciding not to reveal their preference.'

Is it different for men?

'Generally, in society men occupy so much space, so it is not much different for homosexuals. I know that in Lawrence Garden in Lahore they have codes and signals. They have huge parties and hundreds of gays get together and have a great time. I asked one of my friends if any gay women are invited and he said no.'

When she returned to Pakistan in 1997, she got her first contact through someone who knew one of her partners in the US. 'It was a stroke of luck. I have been lucky because I am open.'

Those coming out of the closet are small in number. 'Sexuality is not something that is discussed openly as it is, except for reproduction and gynaecological problems. No one talks about desires. Heterosexual women may gossip about men they like because in our society we are supposed to get married, so it is okay. There are very few women even I know about who are gay for sure. There is this elderly couple who have been together for years. They were both married, got divorced and became partners. One of them is a scholar, but she was not comfortable talking about her orientation although she knew I was gay. The reason often is that if they talk about it they risk outing their partner. There is a stigma attached and also it might work against them in their profession. Their legitimacy is in trouble; cultural norms come in the way. Gay women have internalised it.'

Changing Faces, Static Masks

The legal ramifications are not so harsh. Pakistan's first known lesbian couple had threatened to commit suicide earlier in 2007. Shumail Raj had undergone a sex-change operation and married Shahzina Tariq. They were arrested and put in separate jails. They spoke candidly about their love and human rights organisations fought a spirited battle on their behalf. They were charged with perjury, not homosexuality, because there is only provision for the crime of sodomy. They are free now.

Is it more difficult for women who are not educated? Do they get exploited sexually by other women? 'It is about power so it can happen with women too.'

Are there any support groups? 'It is not so organised. There is an email group and one small organisation in Karachi that I know of.'

One would think that homosexuality is an ideology too. 'I wonder why we don't talk about ideology and politics. A person I spoke to said there are other important issues, this is an elite agenda. I feel I am becoming a part of it; we tend to settle into cocoons as long as it does not come in the way of what we opt to do.'

Does religion come in the way? There is a belief that you have to be a liberal cut off from faith.

'When I was coming out I thought I could not be gay, pray and be a communist all at once. There are many gays who pray and fast; they have struck a balance between their religion and their identity. I wonder though what happens when two women are together and one is religious. What would be the equation? I think that is one reason they don't want to discuss the politics of it.'

She believes it is easy to guess her orientation. I knew about it before I met her, but when we went out for meals or shopping or to visit my friends, it appeared that people saw her as just another westernised urban woman. Short hair isn't uncommon, although hers is really very short and often spiked with gel. She wears no make-up, a big masculine watch, and black no-nonsense sandals.

How do people react? 'I don't announce it in conservative company, and most of Pakistan is. There is curiosity. When I was teaching, a lot of students were asking around if I was gay. A couple of times I have heard people say, "She will infect you". Being gay is considered sex outside marriage as well as being same-sex, so it is a double sin socially.'

She told her mother a few years ago. 'She did not speak to me for four days, but then she said I should be careful because of AIDS. I was surprised she even knew about that. My brother who is married is also gay and he understands. Surprisingly, a sister who is religious has also accepted it. And they know about my partner.'

She is in a long-term relationship but has seen other women. Male gays do often tend to be promiscuous. The same is not true of women. 'Women tend to be more monogamous, except me. I am scared of settling down. I want more fun. See, I came out only ten years ago so sexually I am just ten years experienced. I need to explore more. I am against all kinds of institutions. I don't believe in the permanence of anything in life. Even if I were straight it would be the same. I have an aversion to settling down.'

And fidelity? 'Loyalty goes beyond monogamy.'

8

Dissent and Defence

The boy outside the music store did a little jig. The sound of the song playing inside was foot-tapping. A few men standing outside watched with amusement and began clapping. This was in Islamabad. The song was '*Main Jat yamlaa pagla deewana*'. The little boy was still innocent, but what about the men? Did they not realise that in the film *Gadar* their country had been belittled?

When the Pakistani crowd rushes towards the protagonist Tara Singh, he single-handedly fights them and manages to take his family away. This prompts Akhtar, the mohajir turned mayor, to declare in loud tones, 'Ek Jat ne tum sabko hijra bana diya (A Jat has made eunuchs of all of you).'

Even as a non-Pakistani, I found the movie objectionable and a distortion of history. Its intent was quite clear – to denigrate that country.

When Tara Singh crosses the border to claim his captive lady love – the message conveyed is that Pakistan is a prison – his probable acceptance into their fold becomes a battle of wits; the quasi jihadis are not ready for peace, unlike the Indians who welcomed the heroine Sakina as one of their own. A crowd has gathered, Tara Singh is asked whether he will convert. He agrees. Then he is asked to say 'Islam zindabad'; he does. 'Say Pakistan zindabad', they taunt him. He does that as well. Finally, to push him over the edge, he is prodded to say, 'Hindustan murdabad'. He protests and asks why wishing Pakistan well must necessarily mean wishing doom upon his country.

An ordinary truck driver starts talking with great authority about politics. He quotes the Rashtriya Swayamsevak Sangh line when he gloats about the Rs 65 crore India gave Pakistan during Partition.

Contrast this with the family the heroine lost to Pakistan. It is wealthy, but feudal. It is a strange way of telling us that only the rich could make homes there, and all the poor Muslims were left here and must be eternally indebted to India for protecting them.

By showing a mad man in Pakistan at this particular time holding aloft the Indian flag to say 'Hum azaad ho gaye' and singing 'Saare jahaan se achcha', *Gadar* only tells us that we need to be victorious over a small country to even today be considered free.

It is about how we can retain an enemy-state status. And because the line between the aggressor and the victim is blurred, we have to find ruses.

The major obstacles in formulating a Pakistani identity are the country's fantasies and Indian hegemony in the region, both real and perceived.

Most cultures evolve. The heritage that Pakistan inherited, it has spent most of a lifetime denying. Pakistani nationalism seems to exist primarily in opposition to India. How to be a Pakistani has a lot to do with how not to be an Indian.

The flaw in Pakistani nationalism is that it does not recognise a moderate or a median path. You are either a conservative or a liberal and both come with very rigid stances. Ideas get ossified.

It is a telling statement that the idealists are cynical. 'What is nationalism?' they ask. 'What is Pakistani culture?' they query incredulously.

Defining Pakistani culture would mean asking who represents it best. It cannot be an empty shell. We are talking about a nation that has been wrenched twice, once from its roots, the other time when a branch was chopped off. There has to be a category that symbolises the fractured remains. 'The one that the ruling class wants to sell,' is a point of view.

The genuine voices of dissent have been more victims of military dictatorships than religious fanaticism.

The sacked Chief Justice Iftikhar Muhammad Chaudhry's pictures were everywhere. He had begun to stand for protest, a protest that has become commonplace every few years in Pakistan. Usually when someone decides it is time for their version of a coup.

Unlike the common perception, the press as well as the people are open and talk about these things. News reports and editorials are extremely critical of government policies.

The electronic media has become a creepy-crawly aspect of Pakistani society too. Images of not just dead bodies, but people dying and breathing their last, have been captured on camera.

Censorship of the electronic media is sporadically and whimsically imposed during times of crises for short periods of time, but people work around it. In some ways the tribal instincts of such a society go in its favour because they can still follow the old oral storytelling methods. Gossip and conspiracy theories taking precedence over facts is a looming danger. Every house, tea-shop, party acts as a qissa-khwaani bazaar.

Ali Salim, a cross-dresser, hosted the 'Begum Nawaazish show' on a private television channel by parodying a rich widow of an armyman. The programme was taken off the air. They say this is one more example of the government's clampdown, forgetting that President Musharraf had appeared on the show, as had several other celebrities.

At a party, an educationist is not excited about the cross-dressing. She says, 'It is insulting to women. People are accepting him only because the show has become popular, otherwise would he have the courage to talk about being gay? Did you read the reports about those two women who wanted to marry being harassed? This is the real society. Not Begum Nawaazish.'

Currently, Pakistani nationalism is playing to a western fantasy. It is recreating a mullahism that seems blacker when pitted against the garish colours of alien upheaval. The United States unleashed a Pakistani bomb in a bikini. The timing was perfect. Texas-based 22-year-old Mariyah Moten grabbed headlines as 'Pakistan's first Miss Bikini'. A small unknown contest was transformed into a political statement.

The cult of western paranoia about Islam had found one more voice. She had stated rather defensively, 'I have broken all barriers, and in the coming years there will be other Pakistani contestants who will carry this title. My intention was to project Pakistan in a very modern way.'

This was not about a leap from burqa to bare skin. It was about two stereotypes: of the woman forced to wear the veil and the other who fights it. Instead, she shrewdly chose to become the Muslim Barbie. While the extremists wish to put women behind burqas, women like her flaunt their flesh in their own version of extremism. As an individual choice it is valid, but to promote it as an extension of a society's level of modernity is tantamount to exploitation. Especially in a society where there are honour killings, where rape still requires male witnesses, where a woman's body is still not 'owned' by her.

She was being validated as the Other, the one who does not fly planes and crash into buildings. She was the model Muslim as opposed to the jihadi. It is not a role people like her are well-equipped to deal with.

She even began to don the mantle of a nationalist when she announced, '...my main aim is to project Pakistan to the world as a moderate place. I have succeeded in educating many girls who compete in these pageants about Pakistan, and cleared a lot of doubts people have about the country.'

Actress Meera thought she was taking her nation forward when she acted in a Hindi film. The trouble she got into was a similar fantasy. While hitting out at the mullahs, she was fanning the imaginary fires. 'They love me out there. And they're offended because I've kissed Ashmit Patel who is Hindu while I am a Muslim girl. They feel, ek Mussalman ladki ek Hindu ladke ko kaise kiss kar sakti hai (How can a Muslim girl kiss a Hindu boy)?'

A publicity-seeker was made the proponent of not only liberalism but of Indo-Pak unity. 'I have come here as a peace ambassador and there is a particular lobby in Pakistan that cannot digest this fact.'

Statements such as these sound farcical when we think of the several streams of consciousness and unconsciousness that constitute the Pakistani mindset. Its struggle with an artistic sensibility, the conscience — individual and political, the framework within which it works, all these cause it to extend as well as imprison the person and the thought process.

Many such people chisel the stone of an immoveable social construct. How can you see straw pillars as concrete?

Saadat Hassan Manto heard mostly sounds in his head. Yet it is his voice that has come to haunt every Pakistani and many South Asian writers. He did not take part in agitations, was not a member of any political party, was a waster, but with his sharp prose he sliced through dead consciences.

Manto could never explain his political ideology; he probably had none that could be overtly expressed. He spent his nascent years in Amritsar as a delinquent; his being a social miscast had nothing to do with bringing about change, but merely acting out his personal angst. Like many drug addicts, he took to lying. The lies flourished beyond a verbal sneaking away; he wrote them down as stories, stories that shone as truth because he was already questioning himself. He dithered between insecurity and arrogance. As he once said, 'As a human, I have several shortcomings. And I am always scared lest these give birth to hatred for me in others' hearts.'

In 1937, he moved to Bombay. Here he would meet the sort of people he liked to be with in his younger days. He observed the world of unreal stardom. It was easy to be feted and easier to be rejected. He experienced both. While his films did well, three of his short stories got him into trouble. He was tried under Section 292 of the Indian Penal Court for obscenity and exhibitionism.

He started working on *Ghalib*, the life of the 19th century poet. The film based on his script became a huge hit and won the first Indian National Award for cinematic brilliance. Manto was not there to experience the ecstasy. He had left

Dissent and Defence

for Pakistan, not because he believed in the new state but because a friend told him it would be safe. 'Who will know if I kill you some day?' asked music director Shyam. Instead of laughing it off, he packed his bags and left. This fear was strange for a man who wallowed in the idea of death and is known to have signed autographs with the words, 'Here lies Saadat Hassan Manto, buried under tons of mud and still wondering whether he is a greater storywriter or God?'

His delusions were representative of the individual crisis each one faced in Pakistan at the time. The country could have turned deviant as it got drunk on a false sense of complacency even as it battled with demons – the demons of cold flesh that Manto froze in his memorable work on the communal riots, *Thanda Gosht*.

His soul was turning to ice even as cheap alcohol burned his liver. The only way to cure him was to send him to a mental hospital; there were no de-addiction centres then. He watched the hallucinations around; they weren't too different from those in whose heads power played. He jabbed the pen on paper as mad men began to be shaped as characters imagining themselves to be people who changed political destinies. *Toba Tek Singh* was his catharsis and revenge.

Is the writer the real keeper of society's conscience? Can the artist's canvas draw lines beyond its boundaries? Would the peacenik be able to battle fiends that change with every new hell? Would the tapping of the dancer's feet sprout new buds in the soil? Are these the real Pakistanis?

Is suffering through shackles and travelling through darkness the most legitimate form of protest? Mine has been a fascinating exploration of people right up to the time when the Lal Masjid crisis erupted. In May 2007, a mosque, usually associated with devotion, became an arena for dissent against the Establishment. That is when Pakistanis had to refine their concept of nationalism to include the ordinary woman in the street wearing a slogan-smeared headband over the veil and kidnapping policemen.

However, even before the West could once again derisively point out at the ugly bearded patriot, I had seen the metamorphosis of an atheist into a fundamentalist.

9

Birth of a Nationalist Mullah

Feeling utterly humiliated, I walked away from his door, anger simmering within me. The veil that I so dreaded was becoming mine, an intellectual and emotional world of metaphorical darkness.

As a government servant, Saqlain was not supposed to speak with me – he said it was written in his contract that contact with Indians was prohibited. Yet, he had broken those barriers to be a fine host.

He was not a rich man. He drove a white Mehran, the Pakistani version of the small Suzuki. To save on escalating fuel prices, he operated it with a gas cylinder. Each time he wanted to start, he would have to give a small shake to the cylinder. He did this in a purposeful manner, like most other things. I could not imagine him making a wrong move.

One day as we were driving, he took a detour towards what seemed like an open expanse. He slowed down and pointed out something at a distance in the barren landscape that curved towards a hill. 'That is for you,' he said.

I was not expecting to be gifted a resort in Islamabad, so I kept quiet. 'That is where we make bombs. I don't think we will use them for anyone except Indians.'

I did not know much about his work but it clearly implied he saw me as the enemy. In the many conversations we had, he gave no overt indication of this.

However, on that particular afternoon I got to see a new man. He had invited me to his house, but on spotting his neighbour out in the courtyard when I rang the bell, he opened the door and asked, 'Who do you want?' I was horrified as he said aloud, 'You have got the wrong address.'

As I retraced my steps, I began to wonder. Here was someone who spoke about atheism, but could not get the conservative attitude out of his system. He insisted he was cosmopolitan but beneath the surface one found a borderline mullah. He, like many Pakistani men, wanted to 'return' to his religion.

On an earlier occasion I had presented him a book on Hinduism. Next day, after having spent a large part of the previous evening going through it, he spat out, 'What kind of religion is this? And you live among those people?'

When I was finally granted entry into that house for the first time, I was extremely thankful not merely for the hospitality but also the risk he took. As a friend of his told him, 'I would not have the courage to invite an Indian, that too a woman, to my house if I was in your job.'

That house became a prison. He had to leave on some urgent work, so I was locked in. Feeling a bit unwell, I asked for some medication. The instructions were clear: 'Please don't throw up, the sound will carry.' I sat there popping soothers.

It was a dreary house that seemed to have been inhabited as an act of kindness to its existence. The air smelled of disuse. The television was in mute mode. I was scared of moving from the sofa, so I began to survey the place from

Birth of a Nationalist Mullah

this vantage position. The cupboard was in the living room; a mattress was propped up against the wall of the bedroom, which was visible. Another room overlooking the corridor was shut; it had a window. On the sill, there was an electric blue eyeshadow, which Saqlain said was left behind by his sister-in-law when his brother's family had visited a few weeks ago. It was the only sign of life.

The feeling of imprisonment was giving me new insights. Did this feel like a prison to him too? He had told me earlier that the position he held at work reflected a stringent hierarchy. Not only did he have to rent a house as per the permitted allowance, it would also have to be in keeping with the standard of the grade to which he belonged. The allowance was never enough and he had to take a chunk from his salary to make up the difference. Was it worth it? He was not happy with his salary. He was not happy with many things. What kept him going was the conviction that his work was for the greater good of the nation. I did not know enough to understand what greater good could come out of this attitude.

After a while of rambling thoughts and trying to lip-read the news-reader, I picked up the courage to walk towards the heavily-curtained window. Through the dark green background and floral print, I spotted a small hole that was hidden in the pleats. This was freedom, the freedom to peep out. The street was deserted. In the largish house across, I saw a few bearded men bustling about. I was later informed that the Lashkar-e-Toiba probably ran one of its many small offices from here.

What if they discovered that hole, what if they had powerful binoculars? I had lost all fear for myself; I became concerned for Saqlain. I began to appreciate his predicament.

When he returned, he studied me with a mix of indulgence and uncertainty.

He was obsessed with India; in his mind it was a nation of kitsch. He imagined that the garish gods and goddesses were not merely about idolatry, but about everyday people. It disgusted him to watch from afar as his co-religionists not only lived with but even understood most of the things around them.

'This mere act excludes them from Islam, strips them of their identity. The other ways are tougher, which are sticking together and never yielding to their venomous propaganda about Islam and Muslim identity, hard work, fighting for rights within their constitution and seeking necessary changes. No constitution is a holy book; it can change in any direction. If Muslims have grievances, they can struggle for this.'

When I reassured him that there was always a ray of hope for the elite if not the rest among the minorities, his response was drastic: 'They will find some way, sooner or later it will happen. That brave guy from your city did something, it was a start.'

'Who?' I had asked.

'Mr Dawood (Ibrahim, the underworld don). Real reaction has to come from the affected majority. If they cannot manage, then someone else will...it is natural and it is history. Excuse me for saying this but India is a shameful country. All of a sudden people here in Pakistan have started thinking about it differently, including myself. We do have feelings for the Muslims in India.'

'Lip sympathy is easy.'

'Do you have a gun? If not, keep one.'

'Unnecessary paranoia is not required.'

'This is not paranoia, it's a simple way of making peace. There can never be peace between the armed and the unarmed; one should always be prepared. Just as we save money and put it in banks for the future, one should invest in everything.'

'Are you prepared?'

'Yes, always.'

'Which means you need to be prepared...you too are not free.'

'We never are, no one is, we must always prepare for the future.'

'I do not believe in a future based on fear.'

'It's not fear, it's a way of making fear evaporate. Think logically, use your head, read *The Art of War*, stop living in dreams, throw away this stupid philosophy of Mr Gandhi. Anyway, I really feel concerned. Just do what I say. Buy a gun. There will be more peaceful co-existence then.'

'I only co-exist with those I wish to, and I do not need a gun for them.'

'You cannot have control over your environment all the time.'

'No one can...floods, earthquakes, droughts, accidents happen all the time.'

'Yes and your friends can become enemies or they are already enemies in disguise. I think we are born to fight each other. To tell you the truth, hatred against Hindus here is ingrained. I remember when I was very young there was an old woman who used to work in my Nani's house. I suspected that she was a Hindu or had been a Hindu in the past. I refused to take anything from her. When she came to know about my feelings she tried her best to convince me. It took me some time to accept that she was Muslim and it was okay.'

He seemed steeped in the religious ethos, even though he claimed to be removed from it.

His recollections reflected that. As he recounted, 'I remember two white American convert Muslims, they were here during Ramadan and the weather was hot. I was with them at my friend's house. You know what they said at Maghrib (dusk prayers) while breaking their fast with a glass of water? They said it tasted much better than the best wine on earth.'

'Do you need a certificate from these goras (whites)? They come to India too and get excited about Indian customs and holy places.'

'But these were Muslims. They had converted to Islam long before travelling here.'

'It is a known fact that converts try hard to please.'

'No, no, they were educated businessmen and had no reason to impress us.'

'They wanted acceptance from the genuine Muslims. Had they never tasted water after fasting in America? So why was it suddenly so sweet and better than wine?'

'I think the point is that once in a while we should try to give up worldly comforts and prepare ourselves for the worst.'

'You sound like a mullah.'

'Do I? Just because I said a few things about fasting? I think you have a sort of urban disapproval of religious things. Tell me if I am wrong.'

'Not urban disapproval, but I believe there are kinds and kinds of perspectives and you cannot put them in one slot. I often feel as though you are trying to challenge them. . .or you want me as an Indian Muslim to fit into what you think is right, even though you are yourself confused about your Pakistani identity.'

Birth of a Nationalist Mullah

'I think some people do get carried away in their aloofness from their own. You may be surprised to know that I have criticised religion more than anybody else but never crossed the line, and honestly, most of my criticism was due to too much influence from the West and others. We must evolve in our own way, not by following others or under pressure from outside.'

'Your thoughts about religion are perhaps a result of the guilt you feel for having been critical at one point.'

'I think I was unjustified in my criticism. I wanted to be like the West, enjoy their freedom and everything. I was becoming a slave to western values.'

'Now you are a slave to other values, so you have not evolved at all because you have a mental block about seeing beyond what is stated and you definitely cannot think of anything outside the Pakistani and Muslim circumference.'

'When the economics of the Muslim world changes, everything will change. Maybe others will start thinking about how to make their religion and culture like that of Muslims.'

'Why this desperation to make everyone think and behave like Muslims?'

'My circumference always comes first. What I said was that when other things for the Muslim world may change then people from other faiths will envy us.'

'Do you envy the Christian world?'

'No.'

'See? It is better off economically, yet you don't envy it. Why, then, should people envy Islam? Your faith in your religion is quite shaky, which is why you cannot accept another viewpoint and feel the need for others to envy the religion.'

'My faith is as firm as a rock. I have no problem with other people of different faiths.'

'What about the Shia-Sunni-Ahmedi-Wahabi-Barelvi problems in Pakistan?'

'These will be handled. They are conflicts within, like fighting among brothers. When it comes to a fight with others we are all united.'

'Iraq war...Taliban...Chechnya...who was with whom?'

'Some I think are under too much pressure. Mullah Omar had none. He could have handed over Osama and become a billionaire.'

When the Gujarat riots broke out, I was in Malaysia. The first message I got enquiring about our well-being was from Saqlain. On my return to Mumbai, we spoke on the phone. He said he was so agitated about what had happened that he felt as though 'for four days dynamite had been placed on my body. Did you see those pictures of how Muslims were begging for their lives to be spared? You Indian Muslims have become cowards. Look at us. When the Twin Towers fell, even my mother who is not interested in politics felt that Allah takes care of shaitan and can use anyone as the medium.'

After coming back from Pakistan, we maintained courteous contact. With his comments on Gujarat, I felt he was trying to score a point. We transformed into two political animals.

'What about Daniel Pearl?' I asked.

'The poor guy was kidnapped and killed because some extremist group believed he was a spy. The reaction to his killing was largely that of sympathy. Some thought he was in fact an agent, others felt that it was justified because of what the other guys were doing in other countries...killings have been going on in Afghanistan and Palestine for so long. And the guy was on a mission to specifically investigate certain terrorist groups, so he got hit by them. His investigative job was the cause; he was after very dangerous people.'

He believed that the existence of dangerous people could be justified because everyone has a right to defend themselves. It is a closed society and he is aware of the pitfalls. 'Regarding the social problems in Pakistan, I am telling you the truth: they are insurmountable, beyond one's imagination. I think you underestimate the way things are here especially when someone is open about such things. If Salman Rushdie comes to Pakistan he will get immediately killed; it does not mean that I support his killing – like myself, many people would not want that to happen.'

He certainly felt strongly about it when Zulfiqar Ali Bhutto was hanged. 'I got very angry from inside when Bhutto was hanged and when that bastard (Zia) captured power. I was left-wing in my late school days until college. You will not believe me, I knew all these guys.'

His political views were clear. 'I have just a little more than a casual interest; actually there is no politics here anymore. I always thought that political repression has been the sole reason for our backwardness. Musharraf, a regular fellow, becomes chief of army and on seniority basis captures power. There are no institutions. People blame Benazir Bhutto but they forget that she was never in real power ever; it has been the army always. I am not calling her a saint, but believe me, these guys from the army and the civilians who have been associated with the establishment are corrupt beyond imagination. That Nawaz Sharif made most of his wealth by supporting military regimes and these guys from the establishment. The military has plundered this country.'

He hates the passivity. His old friends are still active in politics and he could get pulled into it. 'But only when I retire or resign. I work for a government department and it's a high security job that's why I am sometimes very worried because I am not supposed to be communicating with people, especially from your part of the world.'

Although he was not in a position to be privy to security details, he felt the rules were unambiguous and applied to everyone. I told him about human rights activist and lawyer Asma Jehangir who had stuck her neck out several times. 'I am an ordinary person. She can surely take many risks and sustain consequences, whereas I cannot. She also takes advantage of being a woman. I am sure if she was a man she could not have done these things so openly.'

'So, you cannot speak out?'

'I have been a non-religious person too but never cut off from my culture and people. I do not think all the values are rusted. Even if I try to do certain things, I have to be very powerful first; that is a struggle, a long one, not a stupid fight to become a martyr. But I will go out to fight a war if, say, my house or my country is attacked. If I had no commitment to my family, myself, friends or country I could have gone abroad, many people do that, it is very easy. I would have to suffer some pain but nothing comes easily. I have not left. I am still here and will remain here. At some point in time we all were boys and girls. What changed? Nothing, except that we developed biases, we started to think of ourselves as grown-ups supposed to behave and think in specific ways. I think nothing has changed except that our bodies have aged a little. Now I understand what you mean about my mental blocks. It is about trying to trace history. I have my cultural limitations and the place I belong to...I told you there was a lot of difference between Bombay and someone from here. I have a strong sense of identity in me; I know what I am and where I belong. There are things that matter to me most. I may enjoy my life without any label but it does not mean that I am not responsible.'

Three years later when I visited again, I thought about him. There had been no contact at all. We had drifted apart completely because he was often edgy, worried that his telephone might be tapped. Besides, there was also the realisation that we occupied different worlds. It would still have been nice to meet, though. I called him up. His response was cold. 'I am very busy. Hope you have a good trip.'

Nothing much had changed. The door remained closed.

10

Soliloquists in a Swarm

The singer adjusted her sequined chiffon saree, her face puffed with lard and layers of make-up. She waved her hand in the air to reach out to a besotted audience. Did she know what she was singing? The pain and the pining – could they be the masks she too was wearing?

> *Teri baatein hi sunaane aaye*
> *Dost bhi dil hi dukhaane aaye*
> *Phool khilte hain to hum sochte hai*
> *Tere aane ke zamaane aaye...*

Ahmed Faraz does not wrench your gut; he slowly reaches out inside you and you watch as a part of you leaves. He makes you an observer of your own foibles; he forces you to embrace anguish and the evanescent. It is quite likely that the singer would be among his admirers. High society in Pakistan courts rebels for their sheer curiosity value. If they rebel long enough, then they become antiques. Shelves make space for their revolutionary ideas to gather dust. A mutiny in sepia.

Soon after Partition, the new country decided that it needed new opponents. It found them in writers. They carried no weapons, but in their minds there was no room for quiet acceptance. They lost their privacy; prisons began to be filled with progressives. They were tortured, physically and emotionally. Intellectually they remained alert, every punch on their flesh gushing forth freshly-wounded words. As Faraz was to wryly comment on the chattels of the dictators, 'You are no soldiers, you professional assassins.'

His life and his poems can be interpreted in various ways, but there is no attempt to camouflage.

> *Tu khuda hai na mera ishq farishton jaisa*
> *Donon insaan hai to kyon itne hijaabon mein milein?*

> (You are no god nor my love for you angelic
> Both of us are human so why do we need to meet behind veils?)

'My conscience never forgave Cain,' he has said.

He might not be aware of it but he is indeed the conscience of Pakistan. He speaks about dead consciences and those striving to live, he speaks about consciences waiting to be woken up and consciences crying themselves to sleep.

I was to meet the greatest living Urdu poet. The National Book Foundation in Islamabad is a drab building that looked like any government-run office, which it was. He was the presiding Saab. I knocked on a wooden door. Behind a large desk sat a man in a brown shirt and spectacles with a brown frame. The uniformity and blandness of it all was disconcerting for a few seconds, until he said, 'I am Ahmed Faraz'. He smiled with his eyes and a crease deepened on his sunburnt cheeks. Suddenly the drab brown of his shirt spotted with sweat looked like earth wet with fresh monsoon showers.

He was clearly an attractive man made even more attractive by the fact that he accepted the confusions in his life. From turbulence to tranquillity, he had seen it all. This is why I had not expected this broad-shouldered founder of the Academy of Letters trapped behind a desk in an office where they served biscuits with tea and there were steel almirahs to push books into. Books that people were forced to read, not ones that they had lived through. Not the ones like he wrote, sometimes like feathery petals, often like crushed flowers squeezed to produce a scent so strong that it could awaken the dead.

My eyes were riveted by a painting on the wall on his right, at an angle where he could see it each time he glanced up a little. It was a woman's face. Despite the lurid colours, she leaped out of that frame with a look that was haughty and helpless at the same time. She could keep you away and yet ensnare you with a plea to be by her side. Was she the Pakistani identity framed in a room so alien to a man who wanted to breathe?

He was free then, but how free? What could being a Pakistani mean to such a man who had been imprisoned for saying what he felt like, for feeling, for thinking, for being? It was during the martial law imposed by Zia-ul-Haq that he wrote a poem, The Siege, about overthrowing the regime.

> *Main kat giroon ke salaamat rahoon yakeen hai mujhe*
> *Ke yeh hisaar-e-sitam koi giraye ga*
> *Tamaam um'r ki eeza naseebon ki kasam*
> *Mere kalam kar safar raigaan na jaaye ga*
>
> (Whether I live or die, I am sure
> Someone will break through the siege and demolish it
> In the name of the tortures I have gone through
> I assure the journey of my pen will not be in vain)

Words deep as a crevice, but the voice a mere echo resounding in the valley of the hopeless. What could they contribute?

'Isn't that how movements are formed?' he asked, aware that he was a symbol, like a framed painting with hurt eyes and a proud chin. He had read out that poem at a mushaira and was arrested.

He was thrown in jail, sentenced to solitary confinement. He was not permitted to speak to his family, his friends or even the guards. Then someone brought him books. The light from the 25-watt bulb cast eerie shadows; his eyesight became blurred. But he started writing again, staccato sentences like the sound of boots outside the prison bars. The world beyond these confines was perhaps even more shackled in putting on a brave face and making it look like those shackles were keeping them stable, preventing them from the burden of walking too far.

Faraz had his imagination, where imperfections could be malleable steel. Most creative people work best when they are alone, so wasn't the incarceration fruitful in a sense? He looked beyond the window into the nothingness of the sky before haltingly saying, 'Being alone is different from being in a situation of confinement that is forced upon you. When you are alone you have the choice to respond to the environment, to do things that are relevant.'

During this captivity, what did he experience most – humiliation, a feeling of repression or just restriction? 'I think it was the feeling of repression that affected me the most.' But he knew he was playing with fire and getting burned would be the consequence of his actions. 'I did. I knew what I was writing, but it had to be said; it was a form of protest. In all major revolutions in the world, intellectuals have formed an important backdrop.'

Activism through art is often like painting with water on glass. 'I don't like the term activism. Anything that you are active about and act upon is important. What I say may play a very minor role but I feel I have done my bit. I believe that the power of the pen will prevail over the power of the gun.'

Yet he was sympathetic to a military leader: 'Musharraf was an instrument and not the author of Kargil. He has not discarded the democratic spirit.'

His experience and observations have forced him to believe that democracy does not mean condoning the acts of democrats. When the dishonesty goes too far the army, he feels, fills the vacuum. There is an obvious contradiction here. For someone who was at the receiving end of a military regime, how could he say this? 'The difference between then and now is that Musharraf is more civilised. While Zia crushed even literary activities, this regime has not done so.'

He spoke too soon. The progressive Musharraf had to play politics. Under pressure from the leaders of the Muttahida Quami Movement who claim to have ownership of the Urdu language, Ahmed Faraz had to give up his post as chairman of the Book Foundation.

In the last couple of years he has been humiliated. His belongings have been thrown out on the street. In 2005 he was asked whether he wanted to quit or be sacked. He chose to be sacked. It made a point. He was giving them the chain to whip him with. Their hands got bloodied. The gashes on him would form more lines. He would be history's victim and recorder.

Can a creative person not be apolitical?

'Again, political-apolitical, romantic-unromantic are only terms. If you are a part of something you cannot remove yourself from it. I am a social animal.' And yet he chose to be a lonely reaper. 'I did not choose it; I just felt it was important to say certain things. I suppose I am over-sensitive. I cannot tolerate injustice; it makes me simmer with anger.'

This ire took him to England where for four years he lived with the uncertainties of his imagination. Pakistan was still that framed painting – lurid at the edges but beautifully etched at the core. He was not the sort to seek shelter, but he could have sought political asylum. He never did. 'There are emotional reasons for it. When you give up your passport, you give up your identity.' What does this national identity mean to him? 'It has to do with the concept of the homeland, one's people. I feel very strongly about these. I express the aspirations of the Pakistanis, therefore I represent not just myself but my entire country. My people have given me love because I speak their thoughts. They are a part of my cultural heritage.'

But culture can confine art – religious tyranny can completely destroy artistic expression. 'It is possible to protest against it.' That is a limited route – rebels often end up forming some sort of establishment themselves. 'But it has its relevance. Take fundamentalism. It does not have a popular base here, but there are a few who want to create a nuisance and propagate it. We have to speak out and find out what our role is.'

So how would he define himself in terms of Pakistani culture? 'I think it is best conveyed in a strong feeling for roots, a sense of belonging and expressing. I feel we do produce some of the finest poets. In India all are gone...here Faiz could make the sharpest political comment with the lightest touch. There are those who say that our culture will survive until the ghazal dies, and that is not likely to happen.'

What about the political turmoil – does it feed creativity? 'In many ways it does. You are trying to cope and respond to various stimuli and they challenge you.' But once out of the system after having purged oneself, doesn't numbness set in? 'No. Sometimes it is only an expression; often I cannot say more. For the ghazal '*Ranjish hi sahee*' I wrote only three verses and a year later I managed to write three more. I stopped when I felt that was all I could say.'

After a year when he returned to the poem, was the inspiration the same or were his feelings towards it the same? 'I think I was in a similar frame of mind when I went back to it. There are times when you take the eyes of someone and the lips of someone else to create a whole, and then the feeling recurs.'

Does this not dehumanise the inspiration? 'No. I am not saying that only those eyes are the ones that matter.' How did he feel when the 'same' emotions recurred for different people? 'I think it is a process. I am trying to fill in the gaps. One is always searching.' Does it have to be a real person, a real thing to shake him up, wake him up? 'Always. I cannot respond to inanimate objects.'

I turned once again to that life pinned to the wall, which was becoming an allegory for the artistic temperament of the country itself. Take that painting, I said, it is inanimate…would it be able to make him do anything? For the first time during our conversation, he looked at it as though he had been trying to hold himself back all along. Finally, he said in a voice that I now register as belonging to one who had just drunk of a goblet of wine and a bit of vinegar, 'That was my first love and she has haunted me for years…I might be doing something totally unconnected with her and she would appear in my thoughts.'

Was he obsessed with nostalgia and memories even if they hurt him? 'I don't think I am a masochist, but some things linger in your mind. Sometimes new people too give you the feeling that you have met them before, which makes you wonder about reincarnation.' But he did like to cling on to things. *'Aa phir se mujhe chhod ke jaane ke liye aa...dil hi dukhaane ke liye aa* (Return if only to leave me again...return to cause me sorrow)'...why? 'Sometimes one is just so captivated, like some thoughts that stay with you forever.'

How did he feel when he put so much emotion in what he wrote, and then it was out of his hands? 'There are many times when I am not happy with the way my words are emoted, about where the emphasis has been placed. But I too have rejected my own thoughts – my mind follows a system where some ideas are thrown out, others are filed away.' When he recreated these filed-away thoughts, did he find them better than what he had immediately expressed? 'In some ways.' Then, was he honest to begin with? 'I may not be a completely honest person, but I am honest to my work.'

There appeared to be some confusion here – he was an optimist looking for acceptance yet his work revealed a tortured soul. 'It is true. When I am with my friends I am laughing and joking and then there are my poems, which reveal a pain I genuinely feel. I sometimes wonder whether the other is a pose, but I don't think so because I am a spontaneous person.'

Sorrow is spontaneous too. 'It is. Such situations make me feel like a fish in water.'

Even if the water is murky?

'It is better than no water.'

His memory too is of water, constantly flowing. He says something about a canal or a stream. He remembers Patna, where he was born.

The first time I meet Khalid Ahmed, he is a hero to many. He has a doctorate in nuclear physics. He taught at one time, but his teaching too had a touch of the maverick. He moved to acting, direction and activism, and has often had to bear the brunt for being upfront.

His approach, however, is not brusque. He appears to be reticent with a wry sense of humour and extremely introspective. A new tele-serial in which he played an aging feudal criminal is being aired at the time. He is being showered with praise, and he looks decidedly uncomfortable, even irritated. Fame seems to have nuisance value. He talks about how we seek and sometimes never find what we are really looking for.

He is an escapist. His words seem to be battling with themselves in an internal monologue; sometimes he is too harsh on himself. He speaks in a voice like satin that is, every few minutes, being torn to shreds by soft hands. He listens to music on his laptop. There are pictures of him in Mumbai, sitting at the Prithvi café, playing the flute. Loneliness in his persona is like the reed of bamboo that creates music.

He has a new house in the same Clifton area. From the terrace you can see the neon lights try to wipe out the brilliance of the stars. We sit in the dark on a divan with bolsters.

Khalid is pained by the way Indian cinema portrays Pakistan. He is equally pained by the simplistic way in which people have to belong. He is in charge of the *Beyond Borders* concept in Pakistan, where stories on Partition will be filmed by directors from the two countries.

Why are we embedding ourselves in the past all the time? 'By the past, is it 60 years or thousands? It is not up to us to cut the past; if we cut one segment it will go away completely. If we acknowledge the thousands of years then the 60 years of confusion could be sorted out.'

Nihal has watched almost every Hindi film. He lands up at Bollywood awards functions that are increasingly being held overseas. The last one he went for got him an introduction with a debutante. He says he had a short fling with her.

We are sitting in a coffee shop. I am enjoying my bowl of soup; he is going through some papers. It is a curious meeting. He looks like any urban smart executive, married, with a month-old son. His eyes dart about. He is uncomfortable about being seen with a woman. It surprises me.

'You don't understand. This is Pakistan. If someone saw me, they would tell my wife.' He is afraid of arguments.

Does she not know about his aspiration of being a movie star, that too in Hindi films? 'She is not aware; she has no idea about the other life I lead. She thinks the trips I make are work trips. I really hope I can get a break. Bollywood is the place to be. Why do you think even our established actors want to make it there?'

For Nihal, there are no thousands of years or even 60 years of confusion. His goal is limited.

Khalid agrees, 'The whole of Pakistan watches Star TV and Indian films. The acceptance of it should be there rather than the insecurity syndrome where we feel we would be engulfed by India. We cannot stop cultures from spilling across borders. It helps creativity to show different streams of emotional thought.'

I recalled the sets of a tele-serial I had visited at the time. They were shooting in a bungalow. The upholstery was gaudy. A brass horse-head was on a table. The art director turned it at a rakish angle. 'These people don't understand aesthetics,' he grumbled.

In the make-up room, the heroine was dressed in a sky blue net dress with tinsel. Her face was being touched up over the heavy base. She thrust out her chest so as not to stoop beneath the burden of a large bosom stuffed with cotton. She was too young and certainly not wealthy enough to afford implants. 'She will grow,' an older actress said.

The lady playing her mother walked in. She was a complete contrast – poised in a string-of-pearls-choking-the-neck sort of way as she tried to maintain a face of studied camaraderie. 'This is just my hobby. I am actually a social worker.' She had done up her hair in the style of the 1960s' stars. She draped the end of her silk saree decorously across the front.

We went to the room where the shot was being taken. In the bedroom, a young woman had to either wake up from a nightmare or cause one, it was difficult to fathom given that she could not get her one-word 'dialogue' of 'Nahin (No)!' right.

The assistant director kept saying, 'Awaaz mein dum lao (bring some energy in your voice).' When she screamed, he would complain, 'Theek se utho (get up correctly).' More than her disastrous attempts, it was the colour scheme that screeched in loud tones. Yellows and reds, violets and greens clashed.

A television producer said that he had to add loud shades to the sets because people wanted what they see in Indian saas-bahu serials now.

According to Khalid, 'After America, India exports the greatest amount of junk culture. We do have our own junk culture of multinational corporations, wannabe TV channels on the path of Zee and Star Plus. Pop culture can run parallel but unfortunately it is increasing and swamping everything in its path. The trend is to submerge everything under this global phenomenon.'

What about submergence beneath the weight of one's own history? 'There are two aspects. One is the ground reality of different cultures and the interaction between them. Second is the preconceived identity the state has been trying to foist and in a lot of cases imposed by the government; it is a pan-Islamic identity that wishes to disregard other cultures.'

That seems to be changing. 'Not intrinsically. The second generation is influenced by state ideology and the imposition from the top causes uncertainty. The state itself is not clear. This ideology is constructed on a reactionary basis. Now that we have created a separate country, how do we make it look separate? There are glaring contradictions. If two sitarists were performing, how would you differentiate? The sari is seen as a Hindu dress yet women all over the subcontinent wear it; the salwaar is part of Hindu Punjab. There are no clear-cut divisions and this confusion prevents evolution.'

Khalid completely denies uniformity. 'The only real distinctiveness worth talking about is the strong Sufi tradition of Punjab and Sindh that gives uniqueness to Pakistani culture and poetry. If anything, they would be unique Pakistanis. Strangely, the two-nation theory sprouted in places where there were common elements.'

It was religion that gave it birth. 'Religion as an aspect of identity has been over-emphasised. And the liberal elite live with the sense of alienation regarding not sharing aspirations of the vast majority. A religion's cultural aspects are shared even by those who are not believers. It is conditioning. I would say one can remain a Muslim. The communists in the two countries, Sajjad Zaheer and Jyoti Basu, must surely have had different impulses. The problems arise when one is expected to pay attention to one way of thinking to the exclusion of all others.'

After Partition, culture in the Islamic Republic became the domain of Hindus; it was the stray having to subsist on chewed-up bones. When Hussain Shaheed Suhrawardy moved to Pakistan from Kolkata he was tagged as a 'mad dog let loose by India' by Liaquat Ali Khan.

For a brief period, around 1956, Suhrawardy renewed his old ties and invited people to rejuvenate artistic faith before it was trampled upon by dogmatic faith. They did have some government support at the time.

In the late 1960s, when Pakistan International Airlines was being consolidated to help tourism, it was decided that it should start a troupe. The PIA Arts Academy was formed. But after the 1971 Bangladesh war, since a lot of Bengalis were involved in the arts, another exodus took place. There was emptiness again. Before culture could be sculpted, the mould was broken.

Khalid cannot be part of one mould. 'I was born in Patna and lived there until my matriculation. Then we were in Dhaka before moving to Pakistan. I was an adult when I came here and could not share some things I had learned from elsewhere. But now certain aspects of my personality have evolved differently that I would not be able to associate with the environment from which I came. Historically, people have come from somewhere, whether the Aryans or the Rajputs. We cannot seem to celebrate such multiple identities.'

The alienation is not as complete as it is complex. The open-mindedness can get entrapped. 'We too live in a bubble, move within a set of people, mostly those who share our values. In India also people question the nationalism of those who do not belong to any particular religion, so they are alienated as well. I find Indian liberals far more nationalistic than us. Here we are more critical. A liberal interpretation identifies with the state.' In what manner? 'They go easy on the authorities, maybe because it is a state of consensus. India has a history of freedom but in the last two decades there is increasing intolerance. When I used to visit earlier there was greater awareness about Pakistan. Now there is less. With more money, people are living a closed life.'

Don't people have to make choices? 'I can carry all these – a Bihari identity, an Indian identity and a Pakistani identity. I don't have citizenship claims but no one can deny my Indianness. Yet, if I want to accept it, I am called a traitor in my country. It is a cross I am willing to bear.'

She was a cross between a mafia queen and pugnacious peacenik. Images of the godmother, holding court and dispensing justice, circled her demeanour. In the dark of the night, the house looked like a whitewashed monument; a maid opened the gate and shook my hand limply. Potted plants flanked the paved path. A couple of steps led to a patio where there was a swing and a few wrought iron chairs. A huge tree covered the area like a spider's web. Through it the sky appeared to be a shrouded fantasy.

At the entrance to the main house. old lanterns with bulbs hung from the doorway showing up a few cracks in the wall. When Sheema Kermani emerged she looked like a tale waiting to be told. She delayed it with tantalising craft. Suspense built up to add edginess to an already-sharp persona.

She was wearing a tie-and-dye blouse with a crimson saree, the loose end of which covered one bosom to register the fullness of the other. The hair was oiled and braided, much like a schoolgirl's, in stark contrast to a face that was a mix of intrigue and animation. The hazel eyes, a bit too large for the face, were heavily kohled but it was the mouth that fascinated me – the words seemed to be addressing an audience, the smile a favour being granted and the occasional frown expressed displeasure, with a hint of possible doom. She seemed to be constantly chewing on something. Just that mouth could cause hurt even as the eyes felt the pain, the pain of a woman who danced in a paean to unknown gods.

Her feet trapped in bells had freed her, their marks a testimony that she had broken many other chains. They hated her – the Establishment, contemporaries, liberals, conservatives. She relished that hatred, nourished it.

She mentioned a woman's seminar where she had raised her voice against Islamic fundamentalism. As she had stood up to make an impassioned plea to alter a single statement in a law that would change the whole context of how women were to be perceived, there was silence around, some defiant looks, a few averted eyes. Not one woman spoke up for her. On the way out a prominent activist told her, 'I agree with you.' Sheema retorted, 'Why did you keep quiet when it mattered?'

Her anger flickers even as she recollects. We went into the main hall, which had a floor-to-ceiling mirror on one wall; the other two had pictures of her in dance performances, theatre acts, television serials. Too many roles or too many masks? I was perplexed. What was she?

Was she the person who offered to drive me to the Chaukundi ruins saying, 'You must see it in the moonlight, it is beautiful'? Or was she the one who spoke in measured tones that appeared spontaneous because they had been uttered several times? In rare moments when she revealed the chinks, she would remember her armour, the steel melding her soul.

I did not have a stereotyped image of a Pakistani woman, but I am glad she was the first one I met.

She dances in a society where she is not permitted to, to the strains of Indian music in a form that was created as a celebration of Hindu gods. But for her Lord Krishna is not just a clay idol, but a vision of love. One could not see Sheema portraying the silently-burning Meera lost in a sublime trance; she is Radha, the flame that leaps out to tease and triumph. 'What you worship you can also love,' she muses.

Was this not illicit love in her country? 'I chose Odissi and Bharatanatyam. Immediately, they labelled it Hindu. If I interpret a Japanese form, then I imbue it with my style, so it becomes about me. And I am Pakistani.'

But the poses transported from temple walls on pliant flesh are indeed a part of an alien religious mythology. 'I don't see them as gods and goddesses. Radha and Krishna are not important to me personally, although the bhajans are about life. They can be Hindu only if you get literal.'

She has tried to go beyond the obvious. 'I use dance with ghazals and with English poetry. If we don't allow influences, then all culture will wither. But we only want Muslim culture here. We did not have a wide vision from the beginning. Those who came to build are called mohajirs, so what do you expect?'

In the word mohajir I could sense an emotional investment. 'My mother is from Hyderabad, she wore only sarees and identified with the rice-eating Madrasis rather than north Indians.'

What did she identify with, then? Her russet skin stands out amidst the alabaster bevy. Is she the keeper of her mother's memories or of customs that crave historical moorings? How would she define Pakistani culture?

She chooses to defy it. 'I don't think there is anything like Pakistani culture. You need generations for it to evolve. We do not possess a culture. The reason is that we have problems with roots. Pakistan has never defined what culture is. The Ministry of Culture allots nothing. There is no interest or understanding. Every government decides differently.'

Military rule had no place for it. When Zia-ul-Haq came to power, he banned all cultural activity, he barred women from dancing. No political party or military ruler has been able to completely reverse that.

For Sheema, this is as bad as amputation. 'They want to cut themselves off from Indian culture. They get scared of sending a sitar player, thinking that it would be associated with India. We have in this manner gifted away ancient culture. At the government level there has always been confusion. In the early days, there were people looking to see how it should evolve. Very soon they were put behind bars. Even thoughts were not allowed.'

What could a caged mind produce? 'Culture is the way people live. It is not folk dances and other art forms.'

So how do Pakistanis live? 'We try to align with Saudi Arabia because we want money. America is with us indirectly as they are supporting fundamentalism. We don't understand. Religions cannot define culture.'

But then a country like China, under a different kind of suppression, managed to retain a thriving culture. 'That is because China at least decides. Here we are in denial. We go looking for what Muslims performed. Someone says Mughals patronised Kathak, so Kathak is okay! Kathak is in fact completely based on the ras leela. These people are not bothered about such details.'

The ras leela in mythology was in fact a wooing by the gopis (milk maidens) of Lord Krishna. The dance played out at first to the sound of the flute and then drums and cymbals; at some point it reached the consummation of the soul. What could the Pakistani version of a ras leela be? 'If we look at it in a broader perspective, if it is expressive, then it is beauty and life. There is not a family today that will not get together and sing. There are circuses and fairs for the ordinary people. The elite don't go there.'

In some ways, she too is in denial. She is the elite who jumped the barricade. There are other ironies. She despises military rule, but her father was an army major. What she imbibed, however, was not knowledge about weapons, but the operas of Verdi. As the ivory-black keys tinkled beneath her fingers, her toes longed to pay obeisance to the floor. At 16, she started learning dance. She earned a degree in fine arts in London, and then studied in India with the doyennes of different dance styles.

What started as a vain exercise has now become her protest. 'If I would not do this, I would not be happy. I do not find contentment in material things. Had I been denied the bliss of dance, I would have gone mad or committed suicide. So this is an expression of frustration.'

The frustration fuelled creativity. A woman on stage is a threat, she feels. It could also be seen as objectification of another kind, could it not? As the woman contorts in agony and pining, her made-up face and bejewelled contours suddenly become a masquerade to be stripped off to reveal nakedness. Sheema believes that affirmation of the body is as important as conveying ideas. 'Here the woman is on her own, uncontrolled. Men do fear seduction and they may as a defence turn into aggressors.'

Freedom of thought impedes action. A No Objection Certificate is mandatory, scripts are censored. There are months when there are no performances. 'Every time I dance I have to say it is not a dance performance, it is a cultural performance. Officially I have to write on the card "Cultural performance by Sheema Kermani". If they come to know I am dancing, then legally I am committing a crime. If bad laws exist, you must voice disapproval.'

Why do these protests have to come only from women? What about men dancing? 'A man is acceptable because he does not have to worry about reputation and honour. Here moral rules apply only to women. A girl who learns dancing loses out in the marriage market. Men have more control over life and decisions.'

It is a constant battle. Hostility sneaks in. The challenge would be to express by withholding. She fights, but now it is not to prove any point. 'I stopped doing that. I have dropped out from the mainstream. In all these years you can't name five dancers of any consequence. I do what I want to do, so there is no confrontation. I have never fought to be accepted by the State because I disagree so violently with it. I hate what it stands for.'

It is not possible to completely alienate oneself from the political process, especially if you strive to bring about change. 'Ever since I became aware, my political commitment is part of my art. Even in my dance, where, how and what I choose to do reveals it. I would not agree to do a dancing role of a prostitute in a film or television serial.'

This statement came as a surprise. Although not wishing to debase the dance, one would have expected her to elevate the status of the prostitute. 'I am trying to give it respect by continuing to dance. In our society dance is anyway associated with prostitution. At a time when we could not perform, mujras were being allowed for the entertainment of ministers. Hypocrisy is rampant. Classical dance is banned but we allow mujras, a vulgarised form for male titillation.'

Being part of a liberal family helped. And it is this liberalism that she carries with her in her work among women and the peace initiatives she is part of. Instead of choosing exile, she diverts her energies in sensitising people to the politics of the country, to ideologies, to ways of thinking. That is her truth. To expose pretence.

She is certainly not among the best-liked people, even among the elite. I was often told she hardly represented the real woman of the country. There is a feeling that she is a mere drum-beater, a selfish prima donna and whatever she does through theatre is not a portrayal of reality but a sensational farce, to ridicule her surroundings in order to stand out. She has been indicted for obscenity in a society trying hard to maintain a forced dignity.

They accuse her of duplicity. If she gets death threats, is it because she is touching a raw nerve or because she is lying? No one has answers.

In 1980, when the conservatives cracked down on cultural activities, Sheema with a group of like-minded individuals set up Tehrik-e-Niswan. Realising that the state controlled the electronic media, she and her theatre group put forth radical ideas. They question stereotypes, they challenge laws, they ask questions. With the mobile theatre, they go into the small by-lanes. Their target is women who come out of their shells and slowly, as the drama unfolds, see their lives mirrored. Collective catharsis happens.

This is what keeps Sheema going. For, each day a problem finds its solution in scripted format. 'We take our plays to the low-income people; they don't have the time and money to come to us. We do get sponsors and we pay our staff and ourselves. The purpose is to provoke people to think, pose alternatives to life, to raise awareness. The response is amazing. Women want change. At the end of a performance, they come out feeling "enough is enough". Any revolutionary transformation in the State will be because of women. Women have protested since Zia's times against the blasphemy laws.'

And although it is said that only those who can afford the luxury of rebellion will associate with her, I met a woman whose daughter is learning dance at Sheema's school. Fazila is a maid. She came from Bahawalpur to Karachi. The city has given her the ability to be street-smart. She wants her children to learn classical dance. Does she know where it comes from, what it is about? 'Haan dekhtee tau hoon, achha lagta hai...aur aise waqt mein kuchh bhi seekh lo tau acchha hai. Hum tau bas shaadi kar liye the (I watch it, it looks nice, and these days it is good to learn something instead of just getting married, as I did).'

Sheema's belief that Pakistani women have moved on psychologically, unlike the men, is indeed true in many ways.

Is this success? 'I haven't achieved what I could because of the hurdles. Sometimes I feel I could have done more elsewhere. On the one hand I am controversial, and I don't mind it, and on the other I am looked on as a role model. A lot of people feel I should not have existed. It is sad but it does not defeat me. I cannot be bought with awards. People still look up to me. But when I wanted to rent a house initially, they felt I was going to run a brothel.'

She did not leave the country despite its flaws. 'Even today if I had an offer, I would not go. Now this conflict has become important. Now my achievement means much more, it is more meaningful as it has come despite opposition. Creating in such a situation becomes exciting and dynamic.'

Is it a feeling of belonging?

'Absolutely. My language, my clothes. My work would not be relevant in a cold environment. Anywhere else I would be more of an outsider, even the climate would be alien. Here only artificial forces are alien.'

Is there a pull of nationalism that she cannot voice? 'What is a nationalist?' she spits out.

Is it patriotism?

'I would not say so. I am not attached to Pakistan. I am attached to this area because I have lived here, it is an association of generations. Emotionally, I would not have been happy elsewhere.'

Food was brought out on a trolley, simple rustic dal, rice and spicy potatoes. Not only did she use her fingers to eat, she also scooped out the food from the bowl with her palm. There was something dichotomous, which was both charming and in a way an act. Would she be able to change life's trajectory? Where could she belong, isolated as she was from her very own?

I looked up at the sky. The blanket of sequinned stars unfurled like a scarf flying above her head. I left her alone. Her eyes flashed embers.

He sat still, his compact frame holding itself in as though movement would give him away. It was difficult to imagine that this man had been thrown in jail twice by General Zia's regime. It killed his output, not his hope.

That evening did not unravel much of Dr Enver Sajjad's mind. He needed chaos to convey the turmoil within. The chaos of an office where files piled up and staffers came into the room to ask, suggest. We were sitting in the chambers of the Geo TV office, where he headed the script department. It is not an alien medium. He wrote the first-ever commissioned play for TV in the subcontinent in 1964, three years after sitting for his MBBS exams.

Even as a practising doctor, he did not look at medical problems as isolated maladies. 'Once a patient came to me with severe depression. I gave him a lecture on ideas. He soon brought me down to earth. He said he had to pay his bills and the children's school fees and this was what had made him feel low. I had no answer. This makes me question existence today.'

Are there fears? 'I did not feel threatened. I had my medical practice, but you have to pay a price. As Marx said, revolution is always perpetual.'

Then who perpetuates it? If it is an ongoing process then every society is in a state of revolution. Isn't that what culture is about?

'Culture is not recognisable except for formal dress. Tribal chiefs exert influence in certain areas, so you cannot compare Karachi with the rest of Sindh. The major cultural division is urban versus rural. Urbanised culture is dominated by America. Unfortunately, culture descends from the top. It is all Americanised – the lingo, the colas, the fast food. The educated class would also like to speak in English. In villages too they use Lux soap, the labourers bring back wealth.'

Empowering of the poor even by such means can be beneficial. 'That is not how it works. A mazdoor cannot even pay an electricity bill, so they tell him, "Why can't you sell heroin and become rich?" There is foreign vested interest and the ruling class game. The local bourgeoisie want to establish their hegemony. It is a tough choice for the people. Can they be free even if they become independent?'

Dr Sajjad's writings, be they short stories or plays, are said to have redefined the language. The romanticised Urdu of boudoirs was not how his characters spoke. He tilled the soil of words. Perspiration spoke a different lingo. The poor who would have understood what he was saying had no time and those who did not understand were in charge of culture. He chose to stop writing.

There is revulsion in his voice as he recalls the time when he stopped. 'We don't have an education system; we have a class system, the elite versus the non-elite. The contradiction is there – we have piggy banks and soovar gaalis (pig-centred curse words). There used to be contemporary Urdu literature, but they wanted it out because they had no use for it. The only common factor here is religion. People take all of Allah's 99 names. One is *Al Adl*, the Just One, of whom they are scared. We had to face a dark age, worse than the western Dark Ages, when Zia came to power. For 11 years all development came to a standstill. Except for punishments and fights over interest, what Islam were they talking about? During Zia's regime I was invited for a conference. I returned the ticket because it was sponsored by the government. Who would want to represent such a government?'

Is Pakistan then about a religious identity? 'I believe that the last Christian died on the cross and the last Muslim in Karbala. Even Allah has said that religion is between me and you. God says it is my problem whether I forgive you or not. But here we seem to need forgiveness from our own.'

Then it is a half-baked Islam. 'Islam is a facade here. We are not Islamic, we are not a republic, and now after the 1971 war we are not even Pakistan, as it was. If I were Mujibur Rehman, I would have said that the country was created with 51 per cent of our votes, so we have the legitimate right to call ourselves Pakistan. Then it would have been fun...'

Pakistan does have a strong national identity, perhaps due to its insecurities. Dr Sajjad shakes his head. He is clearly agitated. 'Now tell me: if a region has come into being in this way, whose geography was forced, what kind of identity will it have? Zameen ne lahu nahin piya (the earth has not tasted blood)...this part of the country did not fight for its freedom. When a child is born in a time of hatred he sees history differently.'

Evolution is not static. Why does one need history to relate to the future? 'You don't understand. In Pakistan some of these people, instead of going into details, they ask about the validity of the creation of Pakistan. Most myths are created on misinterpretations. A serious student is confused, he asks what is wrong...there are all these big cars. The youth only values money. It sees corruption money.'

Pakistan has experienced democracy like punctuation marks in sentences. Has it made a difference to the mindset of the people? 'Democracy at the helm is a way of throwing dust and chillies in the eyes of the people. There are no inquisitive minds, they ask no questions. Power is everything. Democracy means tolerance and we tolerate fascists. We know why, but we cannot stop. We need permission for everything. The concept of freedom does not fit. What can a national identity be then?'

Isn't there any national pride?

'What is it? I am cynical. I don't know if this boiling pot can give a spirit for our people to be proud of. Our leaders blame others. Why can't they blame themselves? I do not think they believe in the destiny of their country. Their money is invested elsewhere. There is only a semblance of order. Laws are made for the ruling classes. Ideas have been snatched to make people idiots.'

Is the system itself cohesive? 'Of course not. The obscurantists do not believe in change. The poet Iqbal had said we have to revive history. It is the people who suffer. And Leftists are on their own trip. The NGOs are with the people, they see the light but they do not do much development work. They thrive on two issues, largely – madrassas and family planning. After they started getting involved, the population has doubled.'

Dr Sajjad was creating a bleak picture, his hands shook slightly as he lit matchstick after matchstick to light his cigarette. Was he saying there were no voices of rebellion? 'I get nightmares thinking that with all the vested interests around people are always "pro" something or the other. People do not read or contemplate. The anti-establishmentarians are genuinely interested in revolution. I feel Brecht is relevant as long as even one disadvantaged person is there.'

Squeezed in a small office space, commissioning people to write soaps that take them away from reality, the dilemma of this man was as hazy as the smoke that curled out from his tight lips. Like many intellectuals, he was superimposing a Brechtian dystopia on a state of nothingness. This was about Pakistani disadvantage, something he had experienced personally. How different was political imprisonment from the personal one? 'In the 11 years of Zia's regime I wasted my most productive years. They would come to jail to negotiate. Now I feel that if this global village commercial is not put an end to, everybody will be a slave.'

Who is the master? 'Conquest. It is driving cultures. Culture is the largest defence against the army.'

So even if there are restrictions on freedom of action, thoughts are unchained. 'It depends on how time tolerates freedom – the moment the ruling classes feel threatened, freedom is gone. Now even in libraries we have to be careful about not spoiling books.'

He, along with a group, had pushed for a Ministry of Culture; he was also the founder of the trade union for artistes. Here too there have been fissures. Some creative people felt that they had to take the fight to the streets. It clashed with Dr Sajjad's sensibilities. 'Sometimes blatant truth negates artistic merit. I wrote using symbols; even religious books are metaphors. Earlier metaphors were an artistic device, and then they became a way of working around restrictions.'

Was this a ruse used by all those who protested? 'No. The Progressives did not want to own me, they had a hierarchy. Someone once asked Mao about the revolution and he said, I am a man walking in the rain with a leaky umbrella. The writers had to rebel against the romanticism of the age. The progressives gave fatwas against other writers. They were expecting writers to leave their pens and pick up the sword. But there has to be a choice.'

How would he describe his artistic sensibility in relation to the country?

'For the last 20 years I have not written a word of fiction. From Zia to the present...I see no relevance. I am not a chronicler of history and the word has lost its meaning. I could not write pretty stories. But I must also say that if all is well and there is no conflict, then there are no stories.'

Why did he feel the need to constantly make a statement?

'Not in fiction, that has been introspective. Plays do put you in communion with others. So I resort to political theatre. They cannot understand some things I write. Pamphlets are the best. I am choosy about my audience and reader. If you blink you may miss what I have to say. You need training in knowledge so they cannot reject you. Otherwise it becomes for a privileged class and is self-contradictory.'

His too is the history of the closed room. He was one of the founder members of the Pakistan People's Party; he formed the breakaway PPP-ZAB (Zulfiqar Ali Bhutto) group in 1996 on grounds of ideological differences. In 2002 he was vice- chairman of the Quami Jamhoori Party; in the same year he contested as a Pakistan Muslim League (Junejo) candidate.

From this it is difficult to gauge his position. He had once said, 'I am not concerned with history itself but with history making'. To whom did it apply? 'I want to know why those who have the power, who are seeing history in the making are not doing anything. I do feel you can grab destiny from those who decide. It can be done.'

He taps his hands on the table forcefully. He says that among his contemporaries he is the most physically fit. He has the energy, the drive; he paints, he acts, he writes, he lectures, he is awake to every sound, be it the falling of a leaf or the shot from a gun. Or the cry of helpless insanity.

Enver Sajjad resurrected Manto's madman in *Cinderella*. The protagonist was looking forward to freedom, waiting to be driven away to the Prince's Paradise. The savage dog was lapping at her feet, the madman was stopping her. She turned to look at him.

'Don't go,' the madman repeated.

'I am going to the Prince's Paradise.'

'You will not be able to return.'

'How does that concern you? He is very handsome, he is a Prince.'

'Then listen to me. You must return before time stands still and the dying moment takes birth.'

She laughed.

'I'll wait for you,' he said.

Manto died waiting for nothing but a last drop of liquor. Dr Sajjad is now sitting at a friend's house holding his glass of drink like sleep holds dreams; he finishes the remainder in a gulp. 'I am asked, "Why are you so restless?" and I say, there is something within and I am trying to explore it.'

Although he had eyes and hair that revealed a desperate chaos, his demeanour was almost surreptitious. That was my first impression of Riaz Rafi. What was he hiding? He was sitting on his haunches at the doorway of the room where his guests were seated watching the conversation, rather than listening to it. That impression went on to reveal quite a bit about him. He was essentially an observer and the few times he was expected to participate, he panicked. Not out of fear but due to a distaste for the stratified norms around him.

Freedom for Rafi starts at his door. No embellishment, no craft, just a rough slab of wood that seems to have been freshly chopped. Along the wall of the stairway engraved panels beckon you to a different era. Niches become the keepers of heritage. Bruised windows hold mirrors, the plank of an old bed becomes a backrest for a seat. There are different sitting areas – one is a cosy place that can be divided by a screen. At the far end is the airiest portion of his house-cum-studio; it has asymmetrical benches, a large low table, lamps hidden behind plants, everything designed and created by him.

Rafi knows the value of nurturing. He was the youngest of five children. His mother died soon after he was born. Perhaps that made him acutely conscious of death and sustenance. He planned the first for himself when he was 23, but he shared his plans. Dramatised it. Naturally, his friends dissuaded him. He was for those few months seeing himself as an object. When he does not like something he has painted he effaces it, splashing it with a bucketful of colour. The physical erasure helps him wipe out its memory. 'For me a feeling is something I have never done before. I don't see this as destruction, but a new creation.'

The nurturing did not happen naturally. It first showed itself as a move to debunk it. He did not wish to be coddled. He did what no one around him did. He joined medical school and quit. He graduated in journalism, but words were not adequate to express himself. Art schools were expensive, so he used instinct and learned the rules well enough for him to join the Indus Art Gallery. 'I know the rules and then I take off.'

He keeps an open house. Sometimes, in the dead of night, there is a knock on the door. A person disturbed by the dissonance of his immediate environment comes here; it could be a celebrity. They pour out their woes. This is the time he paints or sculpts. Acrylic, wood, metal are ready to be shaped by him. Does the agony of others serve as inspiration? As in a sponge, does not the water he has soaked squish out sometimes? 'If it does, then I have internalised it unintentionally. Otherwise, art is like civil society...first, be a good person. You need basic values for that.'

Rafi at that time had no family, so he created one through his workshops. Since 1995, under the umbrella of Action Aid, he has been conducting art camps for children in the interiors of Thar, Gwadar and Baluchistan. For those few days, he becomes a parent. These are kids who have little exposure to the outside world. And these are the only times when he removes himself from his shell. He performs art. His hands move like a baton conducting an orchestra. He goads the young ones, 'Samjho yeh umeed hai...(Imagine this is hope)' and he whisks his brush above his head.

How does one draw hope? He takes what is there and works around it. 'Children are not conscious, they thrive in their innocence. You must create a hunger,' he says. For them to lose their innocence? 'No, to prepare them for what they could gain.' Through rudimentary pieces of paper and colours, he exorcises their demons. While they are trying out different strokes, he is opening their minds to a life outside their village. 'A child may not be able to stop his father from beating his mother but at least he will not beat his own wife. We try to use the environment and what is happening around to sensitise these children. Negative emotions should not be allowed to fester.'

He realised there was a lot of negativity when he saw a five-year-old draw a jeep with a dacoit carrying a gun. 'The child had been observing such scenes and this is what he expressed. This was life for him. Society influences us in subtle ways.'

Society is not static. 'Nothing is static. In rhythm there is hope. If I stop at a line while painting, I am a living corpse. I have faced resistance even while working with these children. They said I was not a Muslim because I wore pants. These things frustrate me. I used to pray, but stopped. If I have to be conscious of superficials, then it is not namaaz. If one has true involvement, then you are not conscious.'

In a society that at least ostensibly claims to be religious, do artists like him feel like pariahs, their disgrace frothing on their canvases? 'The Mullahs say we are haraam (impure), but God too is a creator.'

Isn't the problem not so much about the painting but the message that most nonconformists seek to convey? 'Even when a woman creates she can only say she has given birth; she cannot say whether the child will become a doctor, an engineer or an artist. That is left to the future and it is dynamic. Even if you read the Quran at different times in your life you will find new things. You cannot say the Quran is the last book; you have to move forward because there are many things not discovered yet. You cannot talk about qayamat (Judgement Day) because then life will be over. In the same way there cannot be complete satisfaction. If that happens then you cannot do better.'

Is there then a constant state of frustration to fuel the Muse? 'Not at all. It is possible to have complete enjoyment. It is like sex. Sex is meditation; animals also do it. To make a difference, enjoyment is the key. Even with art, something may look good, but you should feel good about it. I enjoy my boredom too.'

The room he works out of is the most inconspicuous. You are requested to remove your shoes. This is clearly his worship. There are canvases propped up against the wall, spread out on the floor, waiting for him to dip his fingers into the colours and carve them with his nails, poke, chisel, soil, smooth. He stopped using the brush and palette knife; he only paints with his fingers. The canvas is a lover. He wants to touch the body, not claim it. This too is his idea of freedom.

He starts painting at night till the early hours of dawn; music plays in the background, sometimes humming softly, occasionally piercing the air like a scream. His arms, his head, his whole body move to the symphony of sounds. Sometimes there are ayaats (verses) from the Quran, sometimes bhajans (Hindu hymns), sometimes western classical. When he lived in Gulshan-e-Iqbal, a predominantly middle-class area, people used to wonder what he was up to. The building society called a meeting to discuss his strange habits. 'I told them they had no right to look inside my window.'

Today he lives in the upscale Defence. His place is in the commercial area. There is a deathly stillness late in the evening when offices and shops close. They do not leave traces of themselves. Rafi's house has many traces. There are works by old masters. It shows his reverence for anything that is a part of his world. He does not say it, but all over his walls there are also paintings by young new artists; when people come to see his work, he shows them these too. 'I know about struggle. I did not ever imagine I would have a studio. It is intent. You run after what is not there, even after 95 per cent you want to compete. I don't want to reach 100 per cent in anything.'

Is that why he was afraid of marriage? 'Commitment to marriage is like a blank canvas; I would not like a woman telling me whom I should meet. There has to be the freedom to express in every area of one's life. I do not believe that being conventionally settled is all there is to life. I do have well-wishers who send their friends over, and I have to deal with them, but this is not a yateemkhana (orphanage).'

Despite the apparent instability and recklessness of his life, women find him attractive. He is sensitive. If his paintings project disruption and anger, his persona is quite the opposite. If he sees a home that can do with some embellishment, then he goes out shopping for the person. A woman he once knew who had rejected him, returned. 'Because my address changed from the footpath to here,' he says wryly. Yet, he does not judge her. 'We all have our needs.'

Mrs R is different. She is rich. She wooed him with flowers everyday. And would appear unannounced, wearing mogras in her hair. She would sit and watch him even as he went about his work – cooking, cleaning or hammering nails into new pieces of furniture he keeps making. Initially, he did not want to hurt her, but when she became too regular and her intentions clear, he had to resort to what in his mind was the violent move of avoiding her. She was intruding into his solitude. 'After working all night, early morning I go for a walk. Then, before going to sleep till noon, I spray the plants; it is like talking to them. How can I be lonely? I know exactly which leaf will peep out of the stem. When I see some of the visitors plucking at them so recklessly I start thinking that what has taken a week to grow can be destroyed in a second.'

Does the same apply to history? 'India, China, Egypt, Iran, these are ancient civilisations. It is tough to create history in just over half a century. I feel our roots are in India. Pakistan may have been formed as an Islamic republic but you cannot change the culture, the surs (musical notes) are the same. They belong to the subcontinent.'

This is the irony. Artists who are supposed to be individualistic ache to find belongingness within this cornucopia of uniformity. 'It is not about uniformity. History is recorded by artists, writers. If you want Sindhi culture then how can you have the Pakistani flag? Culture is a way of living, art, music. You cannot change cultures with borders, you cannot stop people from dressing as they do in a Thar village only because it is like Rajasthan. You cannot lock their hearts, their subconscious.'

Syed Sadequain, considered to be the greatest Pakistani painter ever, had once said, 'I am not an artist of the drawing room but of the dustbin.' His best-known works are the calligraphic impressions of verses from Ghalib and the Quran. Not many people living off dustbins would be schooled enough to comprehend the allegories. Does this then work as an artistic political statement? Rafi has himself used calligraphy extensively. He once superimposed the word 'Bismillah' on a canvas fully painted red. 'There were two things I was trying to say – that there is no breathing space even for God and also we talk of the Quran and then there is all this bloodshed in the name of a holy war.'

He, however, insists, 'My job is not politics.' After the Karachi blasts he did a series where he only drew female faces to show the fear, the wait. Would the fathers, sons, husbands return? 'A creative person is anyway sensitive and aware. Some will talk about "that" moment. For me when a feeling takes over it is a special moment. It is not deliberate in my case, so it cannot be a statement I am trying to make.'

An artist is often judged by his work. A painting even if it is a blob can reveal a person's thinking. 'My Nani used to say, look at a person's kitchen and bathroom to know who they are...there must be some logic in it. According to one hadith unless you have not slept, eaten or had any monetary exchange with a person you cannot judge a person, I do not take someone's word at face value; I study it first.'

He confronted an army officer once after the tribals were being decimated. 'I told him, "Earlier when someone in Wana died you used to say seven mujahideen (holy warriors) have died. Now you call these same people terrorists. Decide now. Isn't the army the biggest terrorist?" Who is judging these terms? In the Punjab Assembly they are planning to pass a law that there should be no vulgarity in art. Now, who is to decide?'

He had written a passionate letter against the hypocrisy of the Establishment. This isn't new for him. For someone who has maintained his job is not politics, he has been hounded by both the real as well as the moral police. When Moeen Qureshi became prime minister, he did a portrait and titled it, 'Who is he?' The question posed a danger, they said. Pamphlets were distributed with the words, '*Riaz Rafi Se Hoshiar* (Beware of Riaz Rafi).'

The glossies did not want to miss out on the opportunity to nail him. Dishevelled-looking anarchists make the others appear beautiful. They spread rumours about his relationship with Nighat Chowdhury, the well-known Kathak dancer. More than anything else, this bothered him. She was his guru, but now he calls her sakhi (friend), a charming term when seen in the context of its ancient Indian usage mainly by women addressing other women.

One evening we are sitting in his house. The Lata Mangeshkar song, 'Nainon mein badira chhaye, chamki thi bijuree haye (clouds gather in the eyes, lightning strikes)' is playing. Rafi gets up and strikes a mudra and then his hands twirl, his feet begin to move. He is not self-conscious about the effeminate posture. For him love for a woman means even becoming her.

Several years ago he had approached Nighat to learn the dance form. He was working on a series that was to be exhibited later as *Impressionistic Study of Women of Pleasure*. He wanted to get the nuances right, the language the body spoke as it entranced. He even spent time with prostitutes. 'Art is about life,' he believes.

And who is a good artist – one who lives well or paints well?

'Only history can decide who is a good artist. You cannot say he has a big house or car, so he is a great artist. I live in a rented house. But we have a situation where only because Jamal Naqsh cannot give you some time he is called big. We cannot even come to terms with what is the right history so how can we judge what is good or bad.'

Around that time there was an exhibition of Jamal Naqsh's works at the Mohatta Palace. This used to be the residence of Fatima Jinnah, the sister of the Quaid-e-Azam. Displayed were Naqsh's series of pigeons – grey, white, splattered with blood, feathers flying or curled beneath their own wings. There were also nudes. It seemed anachronistic. A heritage site that was an important landmark in Pakistan was exhibiting such works. They were not obscene but they celebrated the body.

If Pakistani society is supposedly not open then why is culture suppressed at all? 'The openness is not there because of a feudal attitude. Even bureaucrats stifle creativity in the public domain; they are the sons of these same sardars. These people are villains but lately they too have started pretending to have become "aware". It only means that what they want is a painting on the wall because they have money. They have not understood art. People have bars, they want nude pictures hanging somewhere near their liquor. For them a nude painting only means one thing – a naked body. They also display books in fancy shelves that they have not read or will never read. Cultured people are those who respect art and books.'

What about the living culture of a life beyond books and art? 'The enlightenment lies in hope. I go to the villages and interact with the children and their parents, and I know that now even when I am not there they will have respect for life and living. Only then can they qualify as good Pakistanis. It is sad but many do not know that Islam does not permit wife-beating.'

Once he was travelling in a train from Sukkar with a friend. They were discussing art. On the seat across there was a lady in a burqa with only her eyes visible; she was with her husband. After a few minutes of their conversation, he felt something on his feet. He looked down and saw that she had dropped a note asking for his telephone number.

Rafi was confused and even afraid. He became conscious of how trapped women are. 'The hadith says women should cover their head, should not wear anklets or perfume so that they do not attract men. But if there is something lacking in their partners why can they not break free? This woman must have been educated or interested in art because only when she heard the discussion I was having with my friend did she make the move. It is possible that not only her femininity but also her talent were being suppressed.'

Rafi is now married. He still paints at night. 'True communion is about giving each other space,' he says.

And where does the individual stand in all this? Who would be the ideal Pakistani? 'If I am a believer then nothing can affect my religion, my nationality, my humanity. I don't even know who I am, so how can I talk about an ideal Pakistani?'

11

Falcons in the Desert

Wood and leather could have given the room a macho sturdiness; instead they give it the look of an old English home of a nobleman returning from a hunt to sit and sip his Campari while listening to the strains of Tchaikovsky. Paintings, as subtle as the background, speak in beguiling tones. They don't look down from the walls with a hauteur they might well possess. There is a sketch in sepia tones of the poet Faiz. It is incomplete. Yet it has been displayed as though the owner wants to tell us that some things even in their nascent stages can make perspicacious statements.

We sit in what seems to be a special corner, two large chairs facing each other, a low table that holds a few antique pieces; the walls have alcoves with casually displayed porcelain. From the large French window overlooking the garden, alabaster busts of ancestors stare at you. This seems to be the only history the octogenarian columnist Ardeshir Cowasjee is willing to hold on to. Most Parsis follow the policy they do in every country – stay out of trouble. Cowasjee does not.

'This is a nation of uncultured people,' he says, as he asks his helper to change the floral decoration in the vase. 'I always like flowers of two colours.' It is the steadfastness in voicing an opinion other than the prevalent one that has made him into a permanent opponent. He speaks out against the powerful and yet can meet them. Admiration for him is interspersed with an element of cynicism. As one mediaperson told me, 'It is easy for a Cowasjee to get away with it. Who will question a rich Parsi?'

Every corner and expanse of his house spells of elitism. If not a religious minority, he would have been one due to his circumstances. How does it feel to be among the few? Does he experience a sense of alienation? 'No, why should I? There are only 2,000 of us Parsis, so what problem can we have?'

There is a pause. He looks outside. A gardener is picking out weeds. 'I pretend to have no problems. You have to learn to face them, instead of denying them. I dislike the fact that I am a perfectionist. If I see a picture slightly askew I want to straighten it.'

So wouldn't he want to see perfection around him?

'You can't have it.'

Does that mean that within the cocoon of his Bath Island residence, where propped up on the wall near the entrance is a picture of Picasso, a different-looking Picasso, much like Che Guevara in blue ink plastered on the walls of revolutionaries, stifling is passed off as comfort? He does not get agitated easily, although his manner can be brusque. 'I am not an insipid man. I may want to call you a damn fool. What is the use of education and heritage if I can't call you what I want?'

Despite his protests against the laws, including those of blasphemy, he feels, 'My life has been a waste.'

He refuses to call this pessimism. 'This is a realistic analysis. I have a right to feel the way I do.'

How does he reconcile the two – his sense of frustration and his not having moved out? It cannot possibly be the house. 'This is home. Where does a man stay?'

It is not as simple as that. What has kept him here? 'Responsibility. Family. The firm. My father and brother were partners in our shipping company. I was the eldest, the rear guard commander. Never thought about things being different. Even today I do not see myself as an intellectual. I remain a ship-owner's son. This is the only country with a 1,000 kilometre coastline and no private ship.'

A large model of their ship in a glass case looks like an imprisoned skeleton. Even the past has to be kept yoked. This is at the other side of the dining room where we have moved. On the wall behind the head of the table there are two portraits at the far ends. One is of his mother, gentility speaking through her eyes more than the string of pearls. 'Do you know she sat for this a day before she died?' he asks with evident pride. At that moment he is a son who has just lost a parent. His wife has an open smile. 'She was a better person than me.'

His son is in America and his daughter visits. 'I have chosen to live with three dogs, one cat, one cockatoo, all at peace.'

We sit down for lunch. Purple threads of onion peep through the rice. The fish curry is lightly spiced. He takes a spoonful of sugar and sprinkles it over the mound. I do the same, a Gujarati linkage has left a common legacy, however superficial. He thinks it is more, 'A motherland is a motherland. If I am asked where I was born I would say India. In 1929, this was India.'

And Pakistan – does he not feel any affinity? 'If I was India I would not even think of conquering this bhookha nanga (hungry, naked) community. They believe in what they will get in the afterlife. Has anyone told you frankly what they have managed to do in heaven? Yet they are capable of tying something on themselves and killing others. They don't bother to ask whether the other wants to become a shaheed (martyr) and go to heaven.'

He asked my driver, 'Namaaz ke liye kidhar gaya tha (Where did you go for prayers)?'

He mentioned a mosque a distance away.

'Idharse tumhara khuda ko awaaz nahin jaata kya (Can't your God hear your prayers from here)?'

Is it about different gods? What about the national mindset? 'I cannot understand this mindset, but first of all you have to find the Pakistani mind.'

Just across from where he sits to eat, there is a clock. It is at eye-level. That is the remarkable and unusual thing about it. 'People tell me, clocks are placed high on the wall. I don't understand it. I am sitting here and I want to see the time so why should I crane my neck for it? It should fit my needs.' It sounds like an apt analogy of how he sees himself in society. 'People take me more seriously than I am. Writing is an exercise. Others are not my responsibility. I am not a reformer. I cannot achieve the task of reforming anybody.'

How does change then come about? 'Do you want me to be unhappy by imposing thoughts? Everyone claims to have a conscience or speak the truth.' What about President Musharraf? 'I will say he is not a hypocrite. He has a one-point agenda. He has the capacity to take a 180-degree turn within 24 hours. In the Lal Masjid incident, he was making a point to America that he is indispensable while he is dispensable. The aggression is part of an insecurity complex.'

This seems like a chaise longue view which is completely different from his lucid and firm opinions. His eyes crease into a sardonic smile. 'I want an easy life. Do you have a problem? I would like to be called a gentleman, a normal person, go through life without harming people. I don't like trouble but I have been in it.'

There is a posse of security men outside his gate, at the entrance and inside his compound. A police van is positioned like a tanker. 'These cops come and tell me, 'Chaar charsi baahar so gaye (Four drug addicts are sleeping outside).' I tell them, 'Tumhara baap ka kya gaya (How does it bother you)?' There are other crises which no one is concerned about.'

For all his talk about a laidback existence, his conscience has not permitted silence. Zulfiqar Ali Bhutto, whose party he had joined, got him arrested. Why? 'He is dead. Who is going to tell me why I was in jail? When my father went to him he said he did not know what I had done. The simple fact is that Bhutto knew what I knew about him. He had the habit of harassing his friends. You know that line from the film *Casablanca:* "Round up the usual suspects." He did not realise he made a person of me. I saw helplessness all around me in the prisons.'

I mention the protest movements that were taking place everywhere in most cities at the time. 'They are all street fighters. They have a token hunger strike with full Pakistani breakfast and miss lunch. What does it achieve? I don't think Pakistan needs a democracy. It is made up of a bunch of unruly people. They need a benevolent dictator. Jinnah was one. They say he was a democrat. Ask whether he sought any mandate and the answer is no.'

Elections have been promised. Cowasjee, like many people, believes that the ISI decides who comes to power. It has a 'political cell' that ensures all polls are rigged for the benefit of the party in its favour; the public is incidental.

'The genesis of the cell was Mr Bhutto's idea. He created it in 1975 to suit his agenda. It turned out to be a bad move because he did not know when and how to stop it.'

He had created a monster.

It led to protests. Democracy was being opposed to pave the way for dictatorship, whose methods it had tried to use. 'No one has had the guts to curb the ISI till date.'

So, is the past the future of Pakistan? 'What future? In 20 years it will be gone. Look at Baluchistan. Internationally, nobody wants us. If you open taps, you get water, not oil. America does not need us. The forex reserves we have are less than one-third the endowment fund of Harvard University.'

How does the minority conscience in him react? 'We believe we have some responsibilities. My family and I give more than we take. What does a Parsi do? Build a hospital, a park, a school and die. As a rich man I feel everybody should not starve, everybody should be able to go to school.' And what does the Pakistani Parsi in him say? 'I won't die for Pakistan or for anybody, not even the man in the street. We don't need martyrs, but fighters.'

The Quaid-e-Azam University has an imposing arch at the centre of which is a block of concrete shaped like an open book. The motto states:

> *Padho apne rab ke naam se*
> *Jisne paida kiya*

(Read in the name of the God who created us).

The campus extends out towards arm-like lanes that take you to different departments. There is stillness as one enters the building that has the pallor of a ruin. It is an unhandsome pockmarked structure. A flight of stairs takes me to Pervez Hoodbhoy, head of the physics department. This has been his home for 35 years.

With a doctorate in nuclear physics from Massachusetts Institute of Technology, he has remained an outspoken critic of the nuclear movement, the army and the lack of scientific temperament. He is the author of *Islam and Science: Religious Orthodoxy and the Battle for Rationality*. Educating people to think scientifically is almost a daily battle. 'During the earthquake, they said it was God's will. They were saying it here in the physics department. I explained to them how earthquakes happen. This does not change perceptions. For Muslims the past is a big burden that ties us round our legs. It is a fictionalised, glorified past. Although it is true Muslims achieved a lot between the 9th and 13th centuries, they did not do it all by themselves. The budding of science was because of Islam as a culture and not a religion. Now the religion exists but the culture has gone. There is no open enquiry.'

Is culture open to enquiry? 'There is no Pakistani culture. It is a conglomerate of different ethnic and tribal identities. In 1947 the only commonality was that of religion but that proved insufficient to generate a feeling of being Pakistani. A schism came about between East Pakistan and West Pakistan. Today the common religion does not prevent intense feelings between Sindh and Punjab. Many ethnic Sindhis feel their greatest problem is not India but Punjab. Baluchistan is up against Punjab. The problem is as vexing as it used to be. There is an inward drawing. Ethnic and religious identities have become stronger not weaker, particularly as political options have diminished.'

To look for political options within an Islamic state is to search for a mirage. All political streams of thought must work within the circumference of a religious identity. Dr Hoodbhoy does not believe that is how it should be or was. 'In my university there used to be clashes between the Left and Islamic forces, debates over goals and vision. In Zia's time it was made into an Islamic state. All student organisations were banned. Even in a department of scientific knowledge like physics, the head would lead prayers. History was rewritten. Jinnah was made into a maulvi, so was Iqbal. But the idea didn't stick. Once religion comes in, ethnic groups find their own way. Today in this university there are only ethnic organisations. If there is a mundane problem like bad food there is no union. Instead they go to their ethnic group. Sometimes there is violence. Similarly, there are fissures between the Shias and Sunnis. Instead of a common identity there is more fractionation. Now as Pakistan matures it finds out that sowing that kind of seed was so destructive.'

He has had experience with such situations. His sensibilities as a person and a professional are revolted. 'It outrages you. Can you choose your environment? Since I became chairman of the physics department I started a film club hoping it would expand the horizons of the students. The first film we screened was *A Beautiful Mind*. Suddenly two bearded guys stood up, stormed out and switched off the lights.'

That moment when the auditorium was swathed in darkness came immediately after John Nash's wife was trying to seduce him. This, felt the new messiahs of human relationships, went against their culture. There were posters saying that the physics department had become a forum for vulgar display. They held a meeting and handed Hoodbhoy a petition signed by 80 students. He threw it back. 'I called a meeting, 200 students attended. I told them we had to see what was going on in the outside world. Some said, "We come here to learn physics, not watch films." But a few burqa-clad girls did say they watch TV so it is not against Islam.'

He has not shut down the film club. Is it to prove a point? 'If you are trying to prove something all the time, then what's the point? There are opportunities you work for to see if you will make a dent.'

When does one know that thought can be converted to action? 'It has been tough. One has to understand when to act and when to stop. Personal effectiveness and success depend on how one survives the lines. You can cross over and get hurt. Most people believe in what they learn by virtue of birth. But one challenges thought. One looks for opportunities to debate. We have that advantage.'

Is it an advantage to hammer at a wall? 'The resistance to modern ideas is there. Things have moved too fast; simply the shock of living in one world is too distressing for the human psyche. The fact is that science can lay open secrets of nature that were in the domain of God and religion and the realisation that medicine, not prayers, cure illnesses has upset the prevailing beliefs. In a world where we look for simple answers and hope that we are more than particles, there is a re-emergence of religion in every society as reassurance.'

This means that societies are feeling a certain emptiness? 'Islam has suffered debilitating failure in the last 700 years. There is no major Muslim scientist or philosopher. No achievements to show. The first centuries were good. There was science and development and art and culture. Muslim lands got colonised. Hopes started rising. There was a period of growth. In the mid-20th century there were secular governments. They started failing. Subversive elements started reworking borders. Palestinians were thrown out of their ancestral lands. That vacuum was taken over by fundamentalists. When all else fails you turn to God. Moderate Muslim societies turned to the extreme. During the US war in Afghanistan, they flew fighters from Morocco and Sudan. The effects on Pakistani society were devastating. It became a jihadist culture.'

Thirty years of military rule seem to have consolidated religious pugnacity. Dr Hoodbhoy has been a passionate opponent of nuclear assimilation. In 1996, two years before Pakistan conducted its nuclear tests, the Prithvi missile was launched by India. The Forum for Peace held a march in Islamabad. Some people infiltrated to disrupt it. Hoodbhoy was one of the speakers and he said that the country could not battle India at that stage. 'They misinterpreted my comments and declared that I had called the Pakistani army "rats". Politicians came into the picture and there was a demand for my removal.'

In June 2007, there were rallies against what was happening at the Lal Masjid. He was at one such demonstration. People were shouting slogans against the army, calling them killer dogs. 'Times have changed,' he says, an unexpressed question mark hanging over the statement.

The change is superficial. 'There is greater comprehension of what lies in different places. Urdu is understood by 95 per cent of the people because of the media. It is due to this that people knew about the earthquake and it resulted in an unprecedented response in 2005. Merely living in similar land has created a sense of familiarity.'

Does the whole of Pakistan represent this uniformity? 'First one rejects there is a Pakistani culture, but there is a commonality that comes from Islamic conservatism that can be traced back. One sees more emphasis on this with the passage of time. There is a deliberate attempt to "Saudi-ise" it as opposed to accepting a South Asian identity. You can see it in the way women dress in my department with burqas and hijaabs. In a public sector university it may not be voluntary. A deliberate attempt to change the culture has come from Islamists. The assertion of Muslim identity is reinforced. But the irony is no one watches Pakistani or Arab movies. They watch Hindi films, so we remain South Asian.'

What does Pakistan stand for, then? 'The idea of Pakistan is still vague. It does not have a democracy. It cannot say we are not India. It is groping to find a reason for its existence. A country should not need to find a reason for its existence.'

Ideologies do. 'Countries do not need ideologies. They are there. By historical accident, because of geographical reasons, people find it necessary to form a group. It is too far back to ask whether Pakistan should have existed.'

Section C
The Pakistani Question

12
Jinnah to Jihad

The autumn leaves were barely visible in the dark. I was on my way to the house of a Pakistani who had made it big in America. As a badge of affiliation to the good times, he had chosen to live amidst shrubbery that hid his mansion from the outside world. A winding lane in Palo Alto, California, took us to a gate that made the house seem ominous. The driveway was dark, except for a shaft of white light.

The host came out to greet us. He was a trim balding man with the demeanour of studied humility – a nervous smile and a shoulder that drooped to one side.

In the passageway, there was a life-size portrait of a woman who appeared to be caught in a time warp. She was dressed in the clothes of a past era, her beauty almost phantom-like. 'This is my wife,' said the man. The wife that no one knew about because she did not exist.

Is Pakistan an imagined nation? A few years after watching the film *Gandhi*, I was in search of the man Mountbatten called 'the evil genius' behind Partition, who was 'shown up for the bastard he was'. It began as professional curiosity, but soon I got sucked into not the concept of Pakistan but the idea that was Jinnah.

As often happens with perspective, I made new discoveries. Is it the Indian Muslim in me that rues the fact that the so-called 'akhand Bharat' (united India) that Veer Savarkar stood for allowed the Republic of India to become a pawn in the hands of the Hindutvawadis and their divisive ideology?

There has got to be something inherently wrong if we as Indians continue to blame every Hindu-Muslim discord on Partition. Communal riots predate it and, as recent events have proved, Jinnah's fears of Hindu domination have not been unfounded. The light did not strike him until 1938, at the age of 61.

When did the moment of truth occur? It was not until the elections of 1937. That was the time when Nehru declared that there was no such thing as a Hindu-Muslim or a minority question. It was after Gandhi had said, 'My faith in unity is bright as ever; only I see no daylight but impenetrable darkness and in such distress I cry out to God for light.'

It was perhaps at this point that Jinnah, who had a very hazy idea about God, decided to give him a try.

How Muslim was Jinnah? Minoo Masani, the veteran civil liberties man, had met him during his student days, often visiting his Mount Pleasant Road house with Yusuf Meherally. He distinctly remembered, 'Jinnah had no use for the Muslim League and he denounced its leaders as "those dadhiwallas" (bearded men).'

However, that did not stop him from attending Friday prayers dressed in a sherwani. During Ramzan, leaflets with a picture of Jinnah, sword in hand, were distributed. It gave the Muslims a threatening voice, warning the rest, 'Be ready... O Kafir!...your doom is not far...'

Jinnah to Jihad

A Columbus clone was being portrayed as a killer. But he was far too self-contained to be inflated grotesquely.

For a person who had 'never been a believer in mass movements', according to Maulana Azad, it was perhaps a seething response to Nehru's declaration: 'There are only two forces in India today, British imperialism and Indian nationalism as represented by the Congress'; Jinnah corrected him, 'No, there is a third party, the Mussalmans.' The results of the 1945 central legislative assembly elections proved Jinnah's hold on the masses. In Muslim constituencies the League got 86.6 per cent of the votes to the Congress' 91.3 per cent in non-Muslim areas.

A year later, on July 29, Jinnah said, 'Throughout the painful negotiations, the two parties with whom we bargained held a pistol at us; one with power and machine-guns behind it, and the other with non-cooperation and the threat to launch mass civil disobedience. The situation must be met. We also have a pistol.'

The tenth volume of The Transfer of Power, the detailed journals portraying the British view of the period, states, 'If Mr Jinnah thought himself betrayed he might derive great satisfaction by going down in history as a martyr for his cause, butchered by the British on the Congress altar.'

When Lord Mountbatten suggested that he could become the officiating governor-general of the new country, the offer was rejected. 'Do you realise what this will cost you?' he asked Jinnah, who replied, 'It may cost me several crores of rupees in assets.' Mountbatten continued the onslaught. 'It may well cost you the whole of your assets and the future of Pakistan.'

Pakistan was created with little money and even less goodwill, and as Jinnah wryly pointed out, 'Brother Gandhi has 3 votes, I (Brother Jinnah) have only one.'

In actual terms he had the price of 6 lakh lives and 14 million uprooted people on his head. 'As far as Pakistan is concerned we are putting up a tent. We can do no more,' said Mountbatten. Sardar Patel too saw it as blatantly: 'As for the Muslims they have their roots, their sacred places and their centres here. I do not know what they can possibly do in Pakistan. It will not be long before they return to us.'

The tragedy of the man is that while he had denounced Mahatma Gandhi for 'spiritualising Indian nationalist politics', it is Pakistan that has been burdened with a religiosity he had scant regard for.

Did the idealist get his utopia? If there is much anger against him in India, is it because of the man he was? It is perhaps more due to the idea he represented. The impression is that he put the germ of the lost land in the romantic's head and a niggling suspicion in the fundamentalist's, who felt cheated about an unrealised dream.

A major part of the problems we face with our neighbour is its instability. If this is the heritage he left behind, then was Jinnah in reality a failure?

The Partition is hawked from every street corner in both countries, either as second-hand literature or in the visage of the old and gnarled or the feudal form of homes fattened with the windfall of good timing.

'Do you think Partition was necessary?' asked Usma Rafiq. She had returned from London to her home in Islamabad. She was as different from many Pakistanis as I was.

'On hindsight it was the extension of democracy as chaos. Jinnah was giving a voice to the repressed needs of some. Therefore it cannot be belittled in any manner. The free expression for a free state is a part of the democratic, as much as it is of the demagogic, principle. But dictatorships need to constantly prove themselves.'

'Why are you always trying to emphasise the differences?'

'Because it is time we accepted that Pakistan is a different country; for us it is a nation that was formed with 'our' contribution.'

'Is that how most Indians perceive us?' she asked.

'This is the undercurrent. It is not always animus. It gives us the psychological advantage of being bigger in every way – more people, more land, and a larger heart.'

'I have been so out of touch with Pakistani politics, but on my return I find it weird. I had become so used to the idea of democracy.'

As an interested outsider, my main observation would be that Pakistan should not even strive for the western model of democracy. It was established for a section of the population that comprised a religious minority. In that its intention was clearly theocratic.

'You mean to say religious societies cannot be democratic?' Usma seemed concerned.

'Secularism and religion are not at odds with each other. If we call India a secular nation, then we have several religions screaming out from different directions. This does not denote secularism; this is multi-culturalism. A secular ideal is when people of different beliefs can live with those different beliefs under one roof without any one group being reminded that they are living under somebody else's roof.'

Usma returned to Pakistan because after 9/11 she could feel the change in the way people looked and talked with her.

'You know something,' I told her in a moment of introspection. 'Our 9/11 happened over a decade earlier after the fall of the Babri Masjid.'

'But you are not religious,' she said, astonished by the revelation.

'I know. Why then am I called a Pakistani jihadi?'

I was in Delhi when L.K. Advani visited Pakistan, stood clapping as Sindhi dancers performed, inaugurated the renovated Katasraj temple and sang the famous paean to Jinnah's secularism. The capital was abuzz with unnatural euphoria. Jinnah was everywhere.

I spent several hours in a library and the works of Kant, Goethe, Hitler, and Freud were edged out by volumes on Jinnah. The gaunt face on the covers of bulky books stared from behind glass panels.

From the shopkeeper at a Janpath stall to the steward at a restaurant to an intellectual, they asked me if I was a Pakistani. It made me look deeper: are we really one? Would I have got into a flap had I been mistaken for any other nationality? Are we evaluating ideologies, people or just the superficials?

I was completely taken by surprise when a lady at the India International Centre I had just met told me, 'You are so civilised. That is the reason I thought you were from there...'

How were Pakistani women more civilised? 'It is the way they talk, conduct themselves...the true feudals are there,' she said.

And she thought feudalism was a good thing. 'It lends character. Today, even in places like Lucknow, you do not see the tehzeeb.'

'You don't see it in most places. Besides, tehzeeb is not just behaviour and that too has little to do with geography and status.'

'But I certainly feel that Pakistanis have tried to retain some of that old-world attitude.'

She has never been to Pakistan.

Was this a quick-fix need to give credit only due to the opportunistic love for the neighbour, legitimised ironically by one who most Indians admit has been a symbol of bigotry? Wasn't it a curious paradox that secularism seen through the Advani prism made it mandatory to look for any Other, even if she was your own?

Rehaan Jameel had just got his 12 passports outside the Pakistani High Commission counter in Delhi where we waited to collect our copies. He was a Kashmiri. It was his sixth visit in the year. 'Kashmiris can go there easily,' he said.

There was a wedding in Rawalpindi, where his relatives lived. 'Some are in Azad Kashmir.'

'But you are from here?'

'Yes, yes.'

'Then why are you saying Azad Kashmir?'

'Really speaking, no one is *free*,' he pointedly emphasised the word. 'That is the reason most of my cousins moved away from those areas into the bigger cities.'

Haroon, his cousin, speaks to me on the phone. He was born in Mirpur. Mirpur is a slave of Pakistan or a cash cow. The wealthy, and most of them are, do not have any outlet where they can channelise their money. Even the Mangla Dam that produces power is a source of rich dividends for

Pakistan, not Mirpur. People like Haroon do not want to become a part of that country.

The pre-1947 status of Jammu and Kashmir is still desired, and this appears anachronistic when there are divisions taking place in other states in both countries. This would include the Northern Areas which were in fact pronounced as parts of 'Azad Jammu and Kashmir' and not Pakistan in the High Court, but such verdicts have never been respected.

Pakistan enjoys watching the dog and bone game it has started. Muzaffarabad is the capital of its part of Kashmir and is treated with the disdainful reverence one reserves for a ferocious animal on a leash. Give it direct bus services to Srinagar and deny it to the rest; the pot simmers.

Young trainees who crossed the border have learned how to fire, but have no guns. They don't have food or work. And they are under constant surveillance by the Pakistani authorities. Haroon says, 'Do you think for most of these people there is any understanding of jihad? Kashmiris have a tradition of Sufism, they are just trapped. We did not come here for political reasons but because one country occupied our land and those of my relatives who are on the other side have to deal with the consequences of this.'

Pakistani Kashmiris want to know how many of them are represented in diplomatic talks. They are pained because not only are they denied a political voice but they are silenced even as protesters. Haroon has known many activists who had to give up the fight. 'They used to say that at least in Srinagar the protestors can take out rallies and shout out slogans. The killings take place in Lal Chowk and soon work goes on as usual. Here even that is not permissible.'

Rehaan continues to live in the Valley.

'For now,' he emphasises. 'I am getting a job in the Gulf. I will have to leave. There is no work.'

'Why not try in some other Indian city? Going to an Arab country is so different, isn't it?'

'You think it is easy here? Our people do go to the bigger cities, but it is to sell what we make, so it is carpet weavers and such. Professionals are suspect. Even those guys are, but they don't have a choice.'

A 22-year-old labourer had confessed to throwing a bomb in Pulwama in Kashmir. His reward? Rs 1,000. It is the price for lives taken and for a life to survive until it is allowed to.

On an average, six people have been dying every day since the insurgency in 1989. We won't count those missing. The largest toll is of militants, then civilians and finally security forces.

Haroon admits, 'I used to do a lot of Pakistani propaganda with foreigners, telling them about the atrocities of the Indian army. There are eight lakh men deployed there. I had gone to Mirpur and other parts of Azad Kashmir and looked at the other side. Indians have put fences all around. This is not permissible in a disputed territory according to the Geneva Convention. The army earns a lot of money for Kashmir which is why it will not like the issue to be solved.'

The romanticisation of the role of the Indian army too is misleading. Five lakh troops have been deployed along the Line of Control. If the country is so protected that Rs 6 crore a day is spent on guarding the Siachen glacier, then why are an alleged 140 terrorist outfits operating inside India? How did they get here?

Today, the army in Jammu and Kashmir is told to 'go home'. It won't. Successive governments are known to earn millions in weapons deals while pretending to protect the country. 'Stop cross-border terrorism,' we tell Pakistan. Do terrorists seek the permission of the government before they start operations? How will we deal with local militants? Will the killings stop? Will the strength of the armed forces then be reduced? What excuse will we give to the people of Kashmir?

Yasin Malik, leader of the Jammu and Kashmir Liberation Front (JKLF) had stated candidly, 'All freedom movements are supported by outside forces.'

How does Kashmir qualify as a freedom movement? It started with Sheikh Abdullah in 1931. It is clear that it was not a part of the Indian struggle against the British. But then Nehru came in. A plebiscite was promised. Nothing happened. The Sher-e-Kashmir was happy being a 'lion' while Yuvraj Karan Singh took over as Regent in 1950. When hereditary rule was abolished two years later, he was sworn in as sadar-e-riyasat. In 1961, he was recognised as the Maharaja of the state by the Indian government.

Since then it has always been India versus Pakistan. As Malik rued, 'This is an imperialistic attitude, trying to solve a problem without involving the principal party involved...Kashmir is not an issue of borders but the future of people, their aspirations. We are not animals.'

They continue to be considered outsiders. During the Kargil conflict, we did not have the grace and faith to use locals to carry provisions for our soldiers, preferring outsiders, Nepalis. How can we lay claims over them, then?

Even a senior political leader like Farooq Abdullah was prompted to state, 'We are not enemies of the nation.'

A cry for self-determination has been coined a jihad. 'What

is this jihad people are talking about?' asks Rehaan. 'We are interested in freedom, not God.'

He invites me for the wedding. I think of the possibility of partaking of a Kashmiri wazwaan (a sumptuous meal served on special occasions). He stops me short, 'We are celebrating in Pakistan. It is different. For the real Kashmiri experience come to Srinagar.'

'In this atmosphere?'

'Which state is safe? Your city? Do you know that foreign tourists even manage to get army issued liquor from the barracks? Our soldiers get their alcohol rations on time and even do a bit of business with it.'

'What is the similarity between the Kashmiris on the two sides?'

'Both are unhappy.'

The banners in Pakistan stating, 'Dil hai Pakistan to dhadkan hai Kashmir' are hollow. How can a heart that is not a part of the body continue to beat? Its freedom is a dead organ in the political laboratory.

In the middle of 2007 when I was there, the 'danda chicks', a sarcastic reference to the Jamia Hafsa women wielding batons, had become the laughing stock or a symbol of rebellion, depending on which side of the veil you were on. By coming to the forefront, they strangely proved the dichotomy of power: any kind of women can exercise it and men can use them to push their agenda.

People were to explain these with various conspiracy theories, including one that said the ISI was a part of group that had congregated in the Lal Masjid, armed with the most powerful weapons.

The year exposed the chasm that exists within groups.

The Pakistani army is dealing with a delicate situation. With its top-heavy Punjabi cadre, there are ethnic dictates that prevail. Ijaz Akram, a senior bureaucrat, tells me, 'The Punjabi does not want to go to Waziristan. The Frontier Constabulary is made up of Pathans and they are reluctant to kill their own villagers who are fighting a jihad; they are not terrorists. The Taliban are not extremists.'

This statement appears out of place in the setting we are in. It is a Japanese restaurant and Ijaz Akram is dressed nattily in a suit. A silk handkerchief, a perfect triangle, peeps discreetly from his breast pocket. He has a most polished and gentle manner.

He looks out at the open expanse before us and says, 'Karachi has changed. There are power cuts and the city is no longer a thriving metropolis.'

His job comes with many perks, but that is not what keeps him going. His phone lines are tapped, but it has not been done secretly. People in his position are informed about it because of the nature of their work. He speaks to me sometimes from what he calls a 'VIP line'.

We have moved to the tea lounge of the Beach Luxury Hotel. It has a rather old-world clubby atmosphere with a high ceiling and paisley-print upholstery. He points in the direction of a room and says, 'That used to be a discotheque. In the '70s, we would jam here. There were several bands that played. And those little alleyways with the bushes were very convenient if we wanted to make out.' Further down is a bridge that leads to an anchored boat that serves dinner. The sea and palm fronds do not in any way convey the sheer divergence from the world outside.

In upscale areas like Defence and Clifton, people openly roll joints in restaurants. There are underground rave parties.

He says without a trace of embarrassment, 'I am an Islamist.' Seeing my look of surprise, he asks, 'I do not pray, I do not fast, I have never gone on Haj, I drink, so why do I call myself an Islamist? Because I believe in the teachings of Islam. If I admire the Prophet it is not because he is a prophet of the religion but because of his qualities as a man.'

This is an educated person whose demeanour reveals no trace of his religious moorings. The shift in dynamics is deeper than the 'Talibanisation of Pakistan'. Ijaz is clear, 'Lots of suicide bombings were taking place in the northern areas even before Lal Masjid. Nationalism itself is being diluted. Now there is no Pakistani Taliban and Afghan Taliban; they are the same. It cannot be wiped out; it is a movement. Liberal duplicity must accept that.'

The hypocrisy was evident in the way the two episodes of the Lal Masjid and the sacked chief justice, Iftikhar Chaudhary, were seen. Whenever the legal luminary, with the snake-like eyes of Zia-ul-Haq, would step out of his Mercedes Benz, there would be support rallies. He became the voice of sanity and freedom of expression. People were talking about cleaning up society.

The sort of drama surrounding the 'escape in a burqa' by chief cleric Maulana Mohammad Abdul Aziz underlined the complete disregard for the more important issue of why women participated in the movement.

Strangely, the women of the Jamia were striving to clean up what they believed to be a societal disease. Closing down of brothels is common. Most societies suffer from these double standards and the cleaning up can take different ideological colours. In Pakistan, because the shade is religious, the world is quick to wake up to 'backwardness'.

The maulvis come with their baggage of the Shariah. What is the excuse of almost 80 per cent of the population that wants the Shariah to dictate the laws of the land in some form?

By upgrading madrassas the government has only been following a policy of prudence. Scientific knowledge does not lead to a scientific temperament. The best bombs are not crude bombs. Pakistan has to live with its madrassas, unless it changes its Constitution to that of a secular republic.

The Taliban did not sprout in a vacuum. Militancy arises as much from the desire for a renaissance as any liberal thought and often has its basis in a humanitarian need. Liberals who want to battle the Establishment remove themselves from others who wish to fight it. They become spokespersons of the West. The US has been making Pakistan a scapegoat. Was it the doing of mullahs?

Crusading American policies have exacerbated the problems. However, the Pakistan predicament has essentially to do with prudence, unlike Afghanistan or Iraq or Iran. The mullahs of the Lal Masjid were fighting the Establishment within. Activists do it for different reasons. It is about ideology, more specifically the ideologies of disparate groups.

Pakistani fanaticism can most certainly not be seen as perfectly representative of Islamic fundamentalism, which has at its very basis an anti-colonial stance. It is still struggling with a quaint question: Would Jinnah approve?

While it would be an error to see the chaos as change, in its rather short life Pakistan has seen too many changes. The Red Mosque situation was only one of its hiccups.

In the same city, not too far from the mosque, Bertha Anderson's driver runs his hand over his luscious beard. He got married recently. He comes for duty only after 1 p.m. He is learning shorthand because his father-in-law insists that he should not remain a driver. This is most interesting. In a society where men, especially from a certain social strata, are supposed to treat their women with scant regard, here is someone who is certain that his daughter deserves better.

We are at Bertha's house. Whitewashed structures dot the leafy lane. She tells me how she got rid of the Pakistani curtains, the ones with aluminium channels. Yet, her rooms are full of the country she lives in now. Shawls are thrown over sofas, pewter jugs lie on low tables, the walls are covered with rugs from the north. The only concessions to her westernisation, besides her mode of dress, are a hat rack, paintings of Christ and the Virgin Mother.

From her terrace, she points in the direction of the road and says, 'There is this lady who supplies Ukrainian girls. Everyone knows about it.'

Was that woman spared by the Jamia people? 'There are so many. Do you know how easy it is to get girls, especially in Islamabad? At parties thrown by expats, Pakistani girls make every attempt to get in. You should see them, they are dead drunk smoking hash or having other drugs and before the party is over they are on the floor. They are temporary trophies for single men and they feel good becoming part of the UN Club.'

In most markets, I saw fewer women in burqa and hijaab than I have seen in Bradford or Bhendi Bazaar. But Lal Masjid had become the spark. President Musharraf is caught between his own army, opportunistic democrats, fundamentalists and various ethnic groups.

Pakistan is at war with itself.

❦

The face of protest was a peroxide blonde. Pictures of women with streaked hair and designer shades were being splashed in the newspapers. Where are their ordinary people?

Fouzia is a member of the left groups that have come together hoping to provide some sort of opposition. When I call her, she is recovering from wounds on her eye and forehead.

'You are seeing those pictures because ordinary people are afraid to come out and many serious activists are being arrested. Most of my friends were just bundled away in jeeps.'

Besides an emotional buffer, what purpose do these rallies serve? Would those black bands and slogans make a difference? Whom were they addressing?

'We go to the people, ordinary people. Our aim is to sensitise them – shopkeepers, hawkers, even women who stay at home in those cramped hovels. Sometimes we go in the streets when it is dark and paint the walls. We make banners all night, and distribute them. People are displaying them.'

The unfortunate fallout is that anyone flaunting such banners is arrested. Many of them are perhaps unlettered and do not even know what is written. They are not the ones who can later pen down their thoughts about conditions in prison cells.

'There have to be voices, some will be heard and in the forefront. The reason many of us try to stay behind is because we need to have some workers to continue. If all the educated among us go behind bars, then there will be no one left to fight.'

'Whom are you fighting?'

'By ourselves the Leftists cannot make a dent. We would

like to get together with others. There are people in the major political parties who are not as bad as their leaders.'

She was aware of the demonstration against the Emergency organised in Mumbai to show solidarity with the people of Pakistan.

'Did you go for it?' she asks.

'No. I don't think it is India's problem and am not sure it will make any difference except perhaps to make us look superior. Our private news channels are showing images of Islamabad streets and security vehicles and telling the viewers that the roads in that city are anyway deserted because it is mostly government offices and the diplomatic enclave. Isn't this misleading?'

'We are in such a state that we need as many supporters as we can manage to get.'

People like Fouzia are committed because they work among those who are disadvantaged, travel to the interiors.

On November 3, 2007, Pervez Musharraf imposed a state of emergency, the 13th time it has happened in the short history of the country.

This was done by suspending the Constitution of 1973, which was the creation of the democrat Zulfiqar Ali Bhutto. As prime minister, only four hours after the Constitution was promulgated and came into force, Bhutto had produced an order signed by the puppet President, Fazal Elahi Chaudhary. The prolonging of the state of Emergency and suspension of certain fundamental rights was to keep those opponents he had got arrested behind bars, where they remained until Zia took over.

According to Ardeshir Cowasjee, 'It has, throughout its life, been amended and tailored to suit the leaders of the day, and it has been an unlucky document that has brought the country no good, no stability, and has never ushered in progress or tolerance or peace.'

Musharraf, while complaining about the interference of the judiciary, decided to become lawmaker. He forced a legal ruling on the country. The National Reconciliation Ordinance withdrew all cases of corruption pending against politicians accused of looting the national treasury. The greatest beneficiary would have been Benazir Bhutto. But the law was on paper. It would work as carrot and stick.

No one seemed surprised that she agreed to his re-election. It was a convenient transaction.

On October 18, when Benazir returned, her cavalcade was to move towards Mohammed Ali Jinnah's mausoleum. Two lakh people had lined up to greet her. In South Asia, the concept of Mother Earth works wonders. She was a master when it came to political coquetry. She deftly marketed herself as the broadminded, non-jihadi face of Pakistan, when it was during her premiership that the ISI and the army encouraged the Taliban in Afghanistan. Her version of social democracy was embedded in the old-fashioned ideals of the dignity of other people's labour. She insisted on holding steadfastly to the dying socialist principles of her father. These principles were for the most part straw pillars meant for the masses; the Bhuttos remained committed to feudalism in their own lives. They had the luxury of encouraging coteries without seeming to court anyone.

They were comparing her with Fatima Jinnah, who had put up a brave fight against Field Marshal Ayub Khan, who too faked the civilian, discarded his uniform and rigged the elections. Interestingly he, like Musharraf, wrote his memoirs while in office. Unlike the Quaid-e-Azam's sister, Benazir was returning from a self-imposed exile of eight years. She had fled the country to live in Dubai and London mansions to escape corruption charges.

No one was in the mood to pose queries. And before they could think about it, a bomb blast killed 140 people. Benazir was unhurt. Those nameless corpses became evidence of the democratic mirage she stood for. No one seemed to realise that she was very much a part of the Islamic Republic of Pakistan and according to the Constitution would have to follow certain rules even if she was the first Muslim woman to become head of government.

Even before arriving, she had declared that it was not the Taliban she was worried about; the threat was from within. Yet, she had agreed to compromise with those within.

It is likely that her return and its resultant mayhem is what pushed the Emergency. All politicians, even militiamen, are insecure.

13

Requiem

As dusk was settling in, the last word she is said to have uttered was 'Allah'. No one is certain. On December 27, 2007, Benazir Bhutto was assassinated after addressing a rally in Rawalpindi. Her death was attributed to Musharraf, the ISI, terrorists, fundamentalists, the sunroof lever of her vehicle and even Punjab. As one mourner said, 'Punjab is responsible for this. We hate the Punjab. Benazir was safe wherever she went, but when she went to Punjab, she was martyred. The future of Pakistan is very dark.'

The present is bleak.

'It's a Kafkaesque nightmare,' he said. Ijaz, the bureaucrat, had mellowed. Benazir's death had caused more psychological damage than real. He did not talk much about the hypocritical liberals any more. 'My beliefs have not changed, my attitude has. It is bound to happen if you watch innocent people being killed. Karachi's streets have been on fire. They are looting and burning shops, cars...right now there is no elite except for the ruling class.'

Hasn't that always been the case? 'Never like this. We are not talking about tribal elements, this is civil society. A nation without a functioning judiciary.'

This has been Musharraf's worst error. Was it fear of the results of the elections? Had he not passed a law soon after his takeover forbidding a prime minister serving more than two terms to be constitutionally elected? Would that not have ruled out his major opposition – Benazir Bhutto, had she been alive, and Nawaz Sharif, both of whom served two terms?

'It has been no exit for Musharraf ever since he sent in the army to quash the rebellion in Lal Masjid.' At the time, I recall Ijaz saying that there could only be martial law or an Emergency because everything was going to be challenged in the Supreme Court. 'Musharraf will hold elections if his own party will win and this does not seem likely unless he has an alliance with Benazir. For that, he will have to give up his uniform. He may not do that because the army will have a problem.'

Now there was no uniform and no Benazir. Musharraf could contest as just another civilian. 'He being a civilian is hogwash. Removing his uniform does not make him less of an armyman; he has installed his man as chief of army staff. As for elections, I do not think we need them. This country cannot afford it. We need stability for at least two years and that is possible with a national government represented by all parties and a consensus prime minister.'

Is Pakistan ready to take this leap?

'I think so,' says Ijaz. 'This time the protests are at the ground level. Those who were removed from the nitty-gritty are now becoming participants. They may not be in the streets but there is a sense of helplessness and identification with the common man.'

He starts drinking early in the day. He has not been going to office. And there is the macabre mocking of his own situation. 'There is no fuel for our cars because 50 petrol pumps were torched. We have been without water for days. I am lucky. Chivas Regal is still available,' he laughs.

The laughter lacks humour. It rings hollow like the emptiness he is experiencing.

In a move reminiscent of the monarchies of old, before Bilawal could become a man, he has been forced into mama Benazir's shoes. He took on his mother's last name and was appointed heir apparent to the Pakistan People's Party throne.

Asif Ali Zardari transformed from corrupt criminal to keeper of a legacy at the graveyard. The delicious irony is that he says he will be the Sonia Gandhi of Pakistani politics and enact an advisory role. Sonia forced son Rahul into the fray to save her position and act as her front man and, although in his 30s now, he is still learning to walk the grassroots walk. However, Zardari may continue to work from the sidelines as he has done in the past to protect his position.

In Pakistan, it is very likely that Bilawal's absence will be seen as exile in Oxford. Pictures and stories about him on social networking sites indulging in un-Islamic activities are only adding to the aura and imbuing him with the decadence that is nursed in many hearts and realised by quite a few behind the hush-hush environs of large gates.

Senior politicians who have been talking about democracy have quietly taken this boy-man as their legitimate comrade in the fight for democracy. Vendetta has been an intrinsic part of the country's politics. 'My mother always said democracy is the best revenge.'

Once Bilawal realises the full import of the statement and of power, he will use it. His father may become his first victim. There is no denying that Zardari was in prison for 10 years and has stayed away from his children. Benazir brought them up; besides, there is the natural affinity of the son towards the mother and subliminal resentment towards what western gossip writers have referred to as her 'tiresome husband'.

Benazir Bhutto married a man with a reputation, which prompted the BBC to make a film called *The Princess and the Playboy*. Theirs was an unequal music. She had cribbed initially, 'When I first got elected, they said, "A woman has usurped a man's place! She should be killed, she should be assassinated, she has committed heresy!"'

Benazir decided to settle into arranged matrimony and baby-producing to give Pakistan the sort of woman who did regular things and had descendants to perpetuate the royal pure blood. She found a man way below her in status and calibre, whose debauchery stood in stark contrast to her rather sublime white dupatta-clad persona. She let him use her position, but the guy was downmarket and settled for the title of 'Mr 10 per cent'. She had found a spouse ready to play martyr. He began to relish the role and even said in an interview, 'Jesus Christ was crucified because they said he was a threat to Rome. We (the party and I) are being crucified ...because we are a threat to the establishment.'

The crucifixion will come in handy now. As a single father, he has to prop up a name not his own and keep the seat warm for his son, whom the media is portraying as a Prince Harry-who-will-be-Prince William clone.

He may have been away from Pakistani politics but the politics within the family would not have escaped his eyes.

He did not stay long enough to mourn with the rest of the country and his father. Had he decided to do so, he would have to campaign for the party and he does not know much about it or the country.

Other political parties decided to boycott the elections, but Zardari the predator realised this was the best time to cash in on his dead wife's memory. With no second rung leadership and only party spokespersons who essentially did the job of couriers while Benazir was away, the widower may not be able to whitewash his reputation but he has the field to himself.

Imran Khan shields his eyes against the sun with two fingers in a peace-like sign. In the photograph, he is sprawled by the poolside of a Mumbai socialite; thoughts of Pakistan do not appear to be on his mind.

Benazir has died; there is blood in the streets. He has left his country to party in a foreign city. 'India should back our democratic process,' he tells the media. He is giving soundbytes about democracy, a messiah in swimming trunks.

Jemima Khan, his ex-wife, has chosen to retain her married last name which, given her new role as expert on Pakistani politics, lends her some credibility. It is another matter that she is playing on petty peeves as commentator. It started with her famous swipe at Benazir Bhutto as the 'kleptocrat in a Hermes headscarf'; after the assassination she has decided whom she would like as the leader of the PPP. Her choice is Fatima Bhutto. 'It helps, in a lookist society, that she's also as beautiful as her aunt – a young Salma Hayek lookalike – and has similar tragic appeal: orphaned, like most Bhuttos, as a result of a political assassination.'

'Pity Pakistan,' she wrote and that seems to be her attitude.

Fatima Bhutto may mourn the death of her 'Wadi Bua' (older aunt) and genuinely believe in not capitalising on a famous last name. But she had earlier written a stinging critique on her: 'My father was Benazir's younger brother. To this day, her role in his assassination has never been adequately answered, although the tribunal convened after his death under the leadership of three respected judges concluded that it could not have taken place without approval from a "much higher" political authority.'

There is no strong opposition, except perhaps any that might be brewing within the army cadres. The nature of the anger over Benazir's killing is clearly parochial; the daughter of Sindh was murdered. No one is asking the inconvenient questions about how she was alienated from her own family and many members of the PPP.

The streak of vendetta that runs in the blood of the daughter of Mir Murtaza Bhutto could well be channelised.

Everyone is using vengeance.

Nawaz Sharif, Saudi Arabia's chosen man, and Pakistan's voice from Punjab, addressed the crowd, 'Benazir Bhutto was also my sister, and I will be with you to take revenge for her death. Don't feel alone. I am with you. We will take revenge on the rulers.'

Altaf Hussain, chief of the MQM, could use the occasion to capitalise on the mohajir constituency; many of them were targeted after the assassination. He also seems to have a good rapport with Musharraf, as he has with anyone in power. He believes that the president stood by his promises, let the exiled leaders return, took off his army uniform and announced elections. A pragmatist, he had said then about Bhutto and Sharif, 'It is common knowledge that both these leaders have returned to the country after hectic negotiations with the previous government as well as the president. They have come home with a certain deal.'

He knows a few things about deal-making, but his appeal is limited and reputation dubious.

Activists like Asma Jehangir too have become cynical and feel that the way forward is bloodshed. 'Who cares about elections?'

With a sharpness of mind that he manages to camouflage, Musharraf had said earlier, 'You go and meet human rights activists. Ninety percent of them may have never cast their votes. They sleep on the day of elections.'

On the day of the Emergency, Ms Jehangir was arrested. 'Because she was agitating and trying to disturb the peace.' He also called her 'quite an unbalanced character'.

When Indira Gandhi declared Emergency, the opposition was made up of strong leaders, many not even yapping for the scraps of power. The Janata Party was formed and won the elections. Morarji Desai became prime minister. It was India's first major attempt at breaking the dynastic stranglehold, but it did not last. Indira Gandhi returned as a stronger person.

Pervez Musharraf has the army fiefdom to uphold and hold on to. He has maintained that he is fighting terrorism and proved it by sending the Pakistan Army Special Services group into the Lal Masjid, killing hundreds. Militants are his 'vicious enemy'. This keeps America happy. It has been using Pakistan for its proxy wars and its leaders as convenient pawns against other nations. Musharraf is not as blatant as Ayub Khan. In his first cabinet address after banning all political parties, he had said, 'As far as you are concerned there is only one embassy that matters in this country: the American Embassy.'

A CIA report had stated, 'By the year 2015 Pakistan would be a failed state, ripe with civil war, bloodshed, interprovincial rivalries and a struggle for control of its nuclear weapons and complete Talibanisation.' President Pervez Musharraf has featured among a list of the world's 10 worst dictators.

In today's global scenario, democracies institutionalise dictatorial policies. Technically he is a dictator, but in Pakistan there are many dissenting voices today that are openly protesting.

There are interesting contradictions in the life and career of Musharraf. In a largely feudal set-up, he comes from a family of working parents. It is said that he was promoted in rank because he was not from the ruling Punjabi class and would pose no threat. But what Nawaz Sharif forgot is that not all soldiers are willing to suffer the humiliation of being asked to retreat. Post Kargil, Musharraf became an unlikely hero. Sharif's attempt to do away with him and prevent his plane from landing backfired. The armyman made contact with the Karachi garrison that took over the airport. Nawaz Sharif's house was barricaded by the military. Musharraf announced from the cockpit, 'Nobody can sack me.' Was it bravado? It seems like conviction, because the army and later the people were with him then. He promised to get back the looted monies. He promised equal rights for the minorities, the first leader since Jinnah to do so.

He admitted, 'Decision making is an individual process, and the more you are supposed to take decisions the more alone you feel.'

He is not as alone as he would like to believe. The knocks on the door have always been there. Everyone wants a piece of the pie. With the half-a-million strong army, this is not surprising. Many may not be able to relate to Musharraf's version of secularism, but he has not yet been tainted with corruption charges.

Israr Ahmed, the tourist guide in Lahore, had told me, 'He is good for the country, but not for democracy. He has fundamentalism under control. The world does not realise how complex Pakistani politics is. Indira Gandhi did a very good thing with the non-aligned movement, which is why Indian foreign policy is sound. India knew that there would be problems in Afghanistan because of the Taliban so it did not openly support it. Our fault is that not only did we align with the western bloc and become its puppet, but we also supported the Taliban regime, we were with them. We are simpletons. America, that has all the sophisticated equipment in the world, could not find WMDs and it wants us to go and look for Osama among 150 million people. Why should we look for him? He is not our problem. We were not involved in 9/11. Who knows, he must have shaved his beard and must be doing some farming in Kabul.'

He is angry with Pakistan's equation with America and insists that most of his countrymen are against any US-Pakistan relationship of convenience. 'America always tries to boss and this Musharraf thinks he should side with Bush. The US gave Turkey $25 billion; we get $10 million. And we did so much, and even this money we got after much begging.'

Yet Pakistan wants the US to be a part of a dialogue with India. 'India and Pakistan should sort out their own problems or it will be like the two cats who asked the monkey to cut the chapati in half and he deliberately made one half small, so the cats started quarrelling over the unequal bits. In the end the monkey got everything, the cats got nothing.'

It is interesting that the other time Indo-Pak relations were a little more than cordial was when General Zia-ul-Haq was at the helm. It raised the level of insecurity. Both sides were scoring political points.

Much later, it was the BJP government that tried to give momentum to the peace process, but with the proviso that it should have the upper hand. The Pokhran explosion was precisely a preamble to this. Our ruse is to use mistrust as a weapon.

India and Pakistan can talk peace, sign peace accords and even promise not to nuke each other, but they can never be at peace with each other. The moment the two governments start smoking the peace pipe, all their dreams will go up in smoke. When we were on the verge of signing some sort of agreement during the Agra Summit, political pressure from one group within the government stalled the effort, making President Musharraf leave at midnight.

Why continue with this charade? Getting a few more buses and a train to operate is not too tough a task. Cricket is about money and excitement. It was Imran Khan who made the most politically savvy statement in a television interview. He said that as captain he always wanted his team to play against India because it was a great way to test the mettle of his players. 'If they could play India, then they could play anyone.'

He understood the psychology of the people. We need to be at war with each other. Any kind of war.

Peace is a waste of time. We can make films and music together. The camels along the Rajasthan border discovered 'people-to-people' contact long ago when they began to go across the sandy dunes to mate.

On the eve of Independence Day, a group walks to the Wagah border with candles. If this is meant to herald peace, then the date is wrong. For, it was on that day that the two countries became two identities. Lyricist and film-maker Gulzar made the visit once and recounted, 'The road was long and straight. As evening fell, (Kuldip) Nayar sahib said, "If we drove straight on down this road, if no gate or wire came in our way, if no one asked us for visas or passports – then I could have taken a quick trip around Pakistan. Tell me, would I rob that country of something? Anyway, there are robbers everywhere – they scarcely have to travel overseas in order to rob." Then, after a spell of silence, he added: "After all, that too is my land. So much of me is still there, in that country."'

Cricket visas, shopkeepers refusing to charge money, taxi drivers giving free rides, and strangers inviting you home are humane gestures. Diplomatically, it works as a designer peace, meant for the emotional ramp. It means little. The embraces, the visits to temples, gurudwaras, churches, the Wagah border are premeditated and lack spontaneity.

This cannot be confused with political peace. It will not happen. If our scents, silks and sensibilities are similar, then why would one expend so much energy on a mirror?

Epilogue

There had been great resistance on my part to visiting the Wagah border. I hated the unsheathed anger and the charade of candlelit peace. What changed my mind was a chance encounter with a student. Danish was a lanky young man; he studied at the premier engineering institute. He had been watching me with the interest of someone trying to find a way of starting a conversation.

I was at a bookstore looking for something on Pakistani history. I saw him smirk. He had the scorn of youth, the need to express an opinion. 'You must be from India,' he said.

'Yes.'

'And you want to know about our history?'

'Yes, your history. Wouldn't you like to be known as a separate identity?'

'Definitely. Why are you here?'

'To meet relatives,' I lied. 'Wouldn't you like to come to India?'

'India is crossed out on my passport because I am an army son. . .only way I would be given a visa is if I have family in India, which I don't. I along with some friends had made plans to visit but then found out about the visa trouble as most of us were from army backgrounds. Anyway, I won't say I am a big fan of your country.'

'Is it the undercurrent of animosity?'

'I won't just call it undercurrents. My father fought in the wars of 1965 and 1971 and I have lost family and friends, who died in wars or border clashes. The thing is I too would have been in the army had it not been for my poor eyesight.'

Then, in a poignant recollection, he said, 'But I can say I stepped on Indian soil. At the Wagah border there is a point where only a white paint line divides India and Pakistan. I just crossed over and ran back!'

I called up the friend of a friend who had contacts. Mahwish did not know me, but agreed to take me to the border that same evening. She knew the soldiers, so we were ushered into a small open space behind the stadium-like seats. Unchilled bottles of Coke were brought in.

The Wagah 'Beating the Retreat' ceremony is absurd because it is done daily. Both the countries are marketing antagonism. The sun was on its way down. They got ready to open the gates. We were taken to the front row right next to the entrance or exit, however you wish to see it.

I looked at the crowds. Most of the locals were seated high up. Foreign tourists were being given detailed descriptions by their guides. Cameras were poised like guns. The soldiers marched in; the tallest and smartest ones are chosen. 'Allah-u-Akbar' rent the air. A huge Pakistani flag was waved.

The flag at the gate was lowered. I craned my neck to see the other side. The two duty officers shook hands. There was no warmth, but the crowds applauded. It is a formality. Like Kathakali dancers, the soldiers express anger and disdain with the orchestrated movement of arms and legs and the occasional twitch of the eye. The gate with its long spikes even when open looks menacing, as though it can pierce through the clouds like a rocket or a missile. Lata Mangeshkar songs played on the Indian side, songs that have more of an emotive value than a patriotic one. The music was loud, much too loud – the way they play it in poor people's weddings or festivals celebrated in the streets.

I was in a bit of a dilemma. My host was a Pakistani; she was applauding her soldiers. My country was a few metres away. I could see my people dressed in the colours of the field. I could spot children chewing what looked like wafers. It was an absurd sunrise and sunset exhibition of military might.

Mahwish kept clapping her hands and nudged me to watch what was before me. A soldier, apparently the most aggressive one, hoisted each knee up to his chest as he marched. He did that for the full length. It was supposed to be a neat display. I took one palm and crossed it over the other. They were clammy. I patted them together imagining I was acknowledging a good shot at a cricket match or expressing appreciation at the end of a ghazal concert. Something happened. I could not control myself. I burst into tears. Mahwish asked me why.

'It is not right,' I mumbled.

'What?'

I could not explain. Allah-u-Akbar and Lata Mangeshkar are both embedded deep in my consciousness. Both are part of my personal history. There were a few tourists from Spain on my right. One of the women asked me, 'Do you have relatives there?'

I uncovered my head and threw my arm in the direction of the gate that had now been closed. 'That,' I told her, 'is my home. I am a tourist here, like you are.'

On the way out, Mahwish recounted the incident of my breakdown to a friend who had joined us. He said he understood. '*Yeh faaslon ki kya zaroorat hai* (Where is the need for such distances)?'

For me it wasn't the distance but the proximity that was disturbing.

Many are surprised that I am not a big proponent of peace initiatives. Is it insecurity?

What has changed? I am still seen as a traitor if I don't wear a badge of nationalism, if I do not consider Pakistan my enemy or if I critically appraise my own country.

I have something more to taint me now. A passport with Pakistani visas.

The first time I filled the form in the column that asked 'Purpose of visit', I scrawled 'Tourism'. I did not know that the two countries do not issue tourist visas to each other's citizens. So I wrote out names of people, addresses I would never visit.

The anxiety I felt on each trip made me less cautious and more vulnerable. I opened myself to experiences. Shujaat and I had only one thing in common: Frank Sinatra's *Strangers in the Night*. More than anything else, I am surprised to think that we saw each other as exotic creatures. Neighbours need not have identical houses.

It has been a while now. Frenzied notes had slashed through several pages. I did not have the will or perhaps even the courage to put them down into a structured whole. I wrote no travelogues.

Even as I completed this manuscript, I realised the journey has remained incomplete. Four trips in six years, meeting several people, walking through lanes I continued to get lost in but that seemed vaguely familiar – wasn't there more I should have written?

Today, a lot of it seems like fiction. It isn't. Some names have been changed, some places blurred. But I have bared myself.

I had returned to that place on the last day of the last trip. I sat at a table swathed in darkness. It gave me a view of the other table where sunlight streamed in. I replayed every minute detail, every emotion I experienced over the words, 'You need to be deported.'

Why did I go to Pakistan? I have to be honest with myself: to understand the hurt. That first time I had been too numb, not felt its full gust. That day as I sat a little away, I could see myself, the hair a bit dishevelled, and my eyes – eyes that had been pierced into and been rewarded with disdain.

Not every encounter was like that. But we all carry memories – countries do, people do. Dramatic moments reveal life's truths. What was my truth? Indian? Muslim? Woman?

Someone asked, 'What are you carrying back with you?'

Images of another sky.

HarperCollins Readers' Club

Become a Member today and get regular updates on new titles, contests, book readings, author meets and book launches.

Join the Readers' Club today!

You can share your reviews and build a literary network of your own.

Register at www.harpercollins.co.in